Sexual Crime

Series Editors
Belinda Winder
Nottingham Trent University
Nottingham, UK

Rebecca Lievesley
Nottingham Trent University
Nottingham, UK

Helen Elliott
Bishop Grosseteste University
Lincoln, UK

Kerensa Hocken
HMP Whatton
HMPPS
Nottingham, UK

Nicholas Blagden
Nottingham Trent University
Nottingham, UK

Phil Banyard
Nottingham Trent University
Nottingham, UK

Sexual Crime is an edited book series devised by a team at SOCAMRU led by Professor Belinda Winder in the Psychology Division at Nottingham Trent University.

It offers original contributions to specific avenues of research within the field of sexual crime with each volume drawing together a review of the literature from across disciplines, including cutting edge research and practice, original material from services and offenders themselves as well as future directions for research and practice.

These volumes will be highly relevant to clinical and forensic psychologists and therapists, offender managers and supervisors, social workers and those working in the field of rehabilitation. They will be a great source of insight for academics, researchers and students in these disciplines as well as criminologists and policy makers.

More information about this series at
http://www.palgrave.com/gp/series/15477

Rebecca Lievesley • Kerensa Hocken
Helen Elliott • Belinda Winder
Nicholas Blagden • Phil Banyard
Editors

Sexual Crime and Prevention

Editors
Rebecca Lievesley
Nottingham Trent University
Nottingham, UK

Helen Elliott
Bishop Grosseteste University
Lincoln, UK

Nicholas Blagden
Nottingham Trent University
Nottingham, UK

Kerensa Hocken
HMP Whatton
HMPPS
Nottingham, UK

Belinda Winder
Nottingham Trent University
Nottingham, UK

Phil Banyard
Nottingham Trent University
Nottingham, UK

Sexual Crime
ISBN 978-3-319-98242-7   ISBN 978-3-319-98243-4 (eBook)
https://doi.org/10.1007/978-3-319-98243-4

Library of Congress Control Number: 2018958919

© The Editor(s) (if applicable) and The Author(s), under exclusive license to Springer International Publishing AG, part of Springer Nature 2018
This work is subject to copyright. All rights are solely and exclusively licensed by the Publisher, whether the whole or part of the material is concerned, specifically the rights of translation, reprinting, reuse of illustrations, recitation, broadcasting, reproduction on microfilms or in any other physical way, and transmission or information storage and retrieval, electronic adaptation, computer software, or by similar or dissimilar methodology now known or hereafter developed.
The use of general descriptive names, registered names, trademarks, service marks, etc. in this publication does not imply, even in the absence of a specific statement, that such names are exempt from the relevant protective laws and regulations and therefore free for general use.
The publisher, the authors and the editors are safe to assume that the advice and information in this book are believed to be true and accurate at the date of publication. Neither the publisher nor the authors or the editors give a warranty, express or implied, with respect to the material contained herein or for any errors or omissions that may have been made. The publisher remains neutral with regard to jurisdictional claims in published maps and institutional affiliations.

Cover illustration: ivanastar/gettyimages
Cover Design: Fatima Jamadar PLS

This Palgrave Macmillan imprint is published by the registered company Springer Nature Switzerland AG
The registered company address is: Gewerbestrasse 11, 6330 Cham, Switzerland

Foreword

I am delighted and excited to introduce this important and much needed book about the prevention of sexual crime. This particular area of work has been a consistent feature of much of my professional life, and this text provides a welcome contribution to the development of knowledge on the subject using evidence from around the world.

It is vital that we continue to provide help and support to victims of sexual crime, but to prevent further victims we should use the knowledge and experience we have gained working with people who have abused others, to develop prevention strategies, policies, and programmes to help deter future crimes. According to the National Crime Agency, there are large numbers of people accessing child sexual abuse images online, and according to international studies there is a significant proportion of the population who have a sexual interest in children and young people. Understandably, both these issues are concerning for law enforcement and child protection agencies.

For much of the last 30 years, the body of knowledge has grown and continues to grow. We continue to develop our understanding about why people commit sexual offences, and what needs to be done to help them not to re-offend in the future. As part of my work as the governor of a specialist treatment site for people with sexual convictions, I have had many conversations with people who told me how they had tried to seek help when they were frightened and worried about their sexual thoughts and behaviour before they committed an offence. Yet they found that nothing was readily available. I also know from my work the impact that sexual crime has on the family members of people who are convicted of sexual offences, and it is thus vital that support and help are offered to people before they offend. If we are to prevent future victims and protect family members and friends from the burden of the sexual conviction of a loved one, we must take this issue seriously.

I hope that this book will help to develop strategy and thinking on the subject. Its eight chapters cover both the history and theory of the prevention of sexual offending and some interesting insights into current practice and future plans in this area of work. The first section considers the theoretical underpinnings and history of prevention work. Chapter 1 provides an introduction to the explanations and definitions of sexual crime and theoretical underpinnings of prevention. Chapter 2 provides an overview of prevention initiatives to date from across the globe. The middle of the book then turns to the practical solutions to the prevention challenge and explores some current prevention projects in England and Wales. Chapter 3 introduces the work of the Lucy Faithfull Foundation, Chap. 4 examines the work of the Safer Living Foundation and their innovative project in preventing sexually harmful behaviour, and Chap. 5 explores the prevention project operating in the NHS in Merseyside. The final part of the book explores additional aspects and issues in the prevention debate. Chapter 6 considers prevention from a service user perspective. It contains powerful insight from someone who has first-hand experiences of the challenges faced by someone with troublesome sexual thoughts and his perspective on the importance of prevention. Chapter 7 discusses the media and societal responses to people who commit sexual offences, and the idea that paedophilia is a sexual orientation, and the implications of this. Finally, Chap. 8 considers the future directions and barriers to effective prevention strategies and practice.

It is vital that we think about new and imaginative solutions to this troubling problem, and this book offers a useful and thought-provoking basis upon which to build.

HMP Whatton
Whatton, UK
Safer Living Foundation
Whatton, UK

Lynn Saunders

Preface

This Series: Sexual Crime

This book series will offer original contributions to current books available on this fast-growing area of high public interest. Each volume will comprehensively engage with current literature, and make efforts to access unpublished literature and data by key authors in the field. The series will also, by the end of each volume, suggest potential new directions for researchers and practitioners.

These volumes are relevant not just to psychologists, criminologists, social workers, and final year undergraduate, postgraduate, and doctoral students in all these areas, but to practitioners and the general public with an interest in learning more about the topic. The aim is to create books that are readable, yet firmly anchored in a sound evidence base from both researchers and practitioners. The volumes will therefore include a robust synthesis of the literature, consideration of the theories relevant to each topic, a focus on projects that are relevant to the topic, with a summary of the research and evaluation of these, chapters focusing on the service user voice, and a final summary chapter, highlighting future possibilities and directions (as suggested by others in the field or by the authors themselves).

This Volume: Sexual Crime and Prevention

The volume begins with an exploration of the theoretical underpinnings of sexual crime prevention, as well as the history and development of prevention work over the years, providing an overview of prevention initiatives around the world. The text then moves into a 'spotlight' section, looking in depth at three organisations that are delivering prevention work in the United Kingdom. Lastly, the service user experience, impact of the media, and attitudes and consideration of future directions for prevention work are explored.

Future Texts

This series is ongoing, with planned future volumes including experience of imprisonment, spirituality, intellectual functioning and problematic sexual arousal.

Nottingham, UK	Rebecca Lievesley
	Kerensa Hocken
Lincoln, UK	Helen Elliott
Nottingham, UK	Belinda Winder
	Nicholas Blagden
	Phil Banyard

Contents

1. Theories of Sexual Crime Prevention 1
   Stuart Allardyce

2. Prevention in Action: Exploring Prevention Initiatives and Current Practices 27
   Candice Christiansen and Meg Martinez-Dettamanti

3. The Lucy Faithfull Foundation: Twenty-Five Years of Child Protection and Preventing Child Sexual Abuse 57
   Alexandra Bailey, Tom Squire, and Lisa Thornhill

4. Safer Living Foundation: The Aurora Project 83
   Kerensa Hocken

5. Mersey Forensic Psychology Prevention Service: Pilot Project 111
   Lorraine Perry, Simon Duff, and Lisa Wright

6. The Need for Prevention: A Service-User's Perspective 133
   Peter Binks

7 **Social and Professional Attitudes in the Prevention of Sexual Abuse** 157
   Craig A. Harper

8 **Future Directions: Moving Forward with Sexual Crime Prevention** 181
   Rebecca Lievesley, Helen Elliott, and Kerensa Hocken

Glossary 201

Index 205

Notes on Contributors

Stuart Allardyce is a qualified social worker who has specialised as a practitioner and manager in working with sexual offenders as well as children affected by abuse for more than 15 years. He is national manager of the child protection charity Stop it Now! Scotland and manager of the Eradicating Child Sexual Abuse project (EVSA). Additionally, he is chair of the National Organisation for the Treatment of Abusers (NOTA) Scotland, and chair of the NOTA UK and Republic of Ireland Policy and Practice Committee. He is an associate at the Centre for Youth and Criminal Justice at Strathclyde University and a member of the Scottish Government's Expert Working Group on preventing sexual offending amongst adolescents. He is co-author of 'Working with Children and Young People who Have Displayed Harmful Sexual Behaviour' (2018).

Alexandra Bailey has worked for the Lucy Faithfull Foundation (UK) since 2005, and is a Registered Forensic Psychologist and Practitioner for the Foundation. Bailey is involved in the assessment and intervention of adult males who have committed/alleged to have committed sexual offences against children and those who are non-abusing partners, and has a central involvement in the Foundation's work with women who have committed sexual offences. Bailey has additionally worked with adult males and females with mental disorders within secure forensic mental health services.

Peter Binks is a middle-aged man born and resident in the UK. He is writing as a service user. Prior to conviction, he studied to degree level and worked continuously in IT. He is married but ceased to live with his partner at the time of his arrest and remains separated but on friendly terms and not divorced. He has no children. Binks believes that if prevention had been available he would have grasped it with both hands and benefited from it to the additional benefit of his victims. Binks deeply regrets the distress his actions caused.

Candice Christiansen LCMHC, CSAT-S, is a trailblazer. She is the founder of several programmes, including her outpatient treatment centre Namasté Center for Healing that specialises in treating a range of sexual issues from infidelity, to sex and porn addiction, to general intimacy issues and trauma. Christiansen's global programme, The Prevention Project™, specialises in the treatment of risky and problematic sexual behaviours, specifically non-contact sexual offences. The Prevention Project™ also provides mental wellness support to adults with minor attractions who have not committed any contact offence, with the goal of increasing their quality of life. Her podcast The Prevention Podcast™ went viral in its first week of launching in January 2018 and has reached over 50 countries. Christiansen is an influential global change agent whose expertise in assessing and treating individuals on the autism spectrum and those with brain injuries has gained international attention and accolades by the leading experts and advocates in the US criminal justice system.

Simon Duff is a chartered and registered forensic psychologist, working both at the University of Nottingham's Doctorate in Forensic Psychology and the NHS' Mersey Forensic Psychology Service in Liverpool. Duff's research interests cover a range of areas, strongly linked with his clinical work, and include fetishism, sexual offending and stalking. He recently co-authored a book with Professor James McGuire of the University of Liverpool, *Forensic Psychology: Routes Through the System* (2018).

Helen Elliott is a lecturer in Counselling at Bishop Grosseteste University (UK). She has a background in forensic psychology with a focus on offender rehabilitation and therapeutic change and is a trainee integrative psychotherapist. Elliott is also co-founder of the Safer Living Foundation—a charity set up to run rehabilitative initiatives.

Craig A. Harper is a lecturer in Human Psychology at Nottingham Trent University (UK). His research interests lie in the psychological processes that underpin decision-making in relation to controversial social and political topics. Most of his research has been focused on how people form and express attitudes towards people with sexual convictions, with the aim being to promote progressive and evidence-based policies to prevent and reduce sexual victimisation. Away from forensically-based research, he is a member of the Heterodox

Academy, which is an organisation seeking to promote viewpoint diversity and reduce political polarisation in higher education.

Kerensa Hocken is a registered forensic psychologist. She is an award-winning expert in the field of sexual offending, and has a special interest in people with intellectual disabilities who commit sexual offences. Hocken is employed by Her Majesty's Prison and Probation Service where she has oversight for the assessment and treatment of people in prison for sexual offending in the Midlands region. Hocken is a co-founder, trustee and the clinical lead for the Safer Living Foundation.

Rebecca Lievesley is a lecturer in Psychology and member of the Sexual Offences, Crime and Misconduct Research Unit at Nottingham Trent University. She has worked and researched within the Criminal Justice System for many years, working closely with a number of prisons, the National Offender Management Service and Ministry of Justice on research and evaluation projects. She is also a co-founder and trustee of the Safer Living Foundation.

Meg Martinez-Dettamanti is an Licensed Associate Clinical Mental Health Counselor (LACMHC), an Certified Sex Addiction Therapist (CSAT)-Candidate and the Assistant Clinical Director of Namasté Center for Healing and The Prevention Project™. Martinez-Dettamanti has worked closely with Candice Christiansen for years in regard to programme and curriculum development for those in recovery as well as those engaged in problematic sexual behaviour and, further still, those with minor attractions who have committed to not offending and are seeking support. She is well versed in the legal system and child welfare. Through her past work with youth who had sexually offended and then for the Division of Child and Family Services working to overcome addiction, strengthen families and provide safety and stability to children, Martinez-Dettamanti has learned the importance of 'prevention' as a healthy intervention. She oversees the outpatient and intensive programmes at Namasté Center for Healing and The Prevention Project™, is the lead facilitator of the project's several psycho-educational support groups, and is active in the global community advocating for the well-being of minor-attracted individuals.

Lorraine Perry is a clinical psychologist leading the Prevention Service at Mersey Forensic Psychology Service in Liverpool, which is part of Mersey Care NHS Foundation Trust. Perry has experience of both inpatient and community forensic psychology work, having previously worked in a medium secure mental health hospital. Her interests are working psychologically to help reduce risk of offending or re-offending, particularly with sex offenders.

Tom Squire is Clinical Manager at the Lucy Faithful Foundation. He has worked for the Lucy Faithfull Foundation since 2007 and has a background in the Probation Service. Squire undertakes specialist risk assessments for a range of agencies, and provides training, advice and consultancy to other professionals. He provides clinical oversight of the Stop it Now! Helpline, a freephone, confidential helpline for adults concerned about either their own or another person's sexual thoughts, feelings and/or behaviour towards children. More recently, Squire has contributed to the development of the Foundation's online 'self-help' resources.

Lisa Thornhill is Senior Practitioner for Children and Young People at the Lucy Faithful Foundation. She has worked for the Lucy Faithfull Foundation since 2012 and has specialised in sexual abuse since 2005. Thornhill works with families affected by sexual abuse, including adult perpetrators, protective carers and young people who exhibit harmful sexual behaviour. She undertakes assessments for family courts and delivers intervention programmes. She also provides training and consultation for professionals. Thornhill is a professional doctorate student at Bedfordshire University.

Lisa Wright is a clinical psychologist working for Mersey Care NHS Foundation Trust. Wright has worked in secure hospitals, prisons and in the community and specialises in working with personality disorder, psychosis, trauma and various offending behaviours, using a range of therapeutic approaches. She manages a community psychology service which provides therapy aimed at reducing risk of sexual and violent offending/re-offending. Schema Therapy and Eye Movement Desensitization and Reprocessing (EMDR) are core components of the service, and Wright has gradually incorporated various aspects of these approaches into the intervention programmes.

List of Figures

Fig. 3.1 Number of calls to the Stop it Now! Helpline from 2002 to 2016   63
Fig. 3.2 LFF initiatives within the prevention framework   78

List of Tables

Table 3.1	Statistics from the Get Help website in comparison to the CROGA website	76
Table 4.1	The six core processes of psychological inflexibility and psychological flexibility	99

1

Theories of Sexual Crime Prevention

Stuart Allardyce

Introduction

Sexual crime is increasingly recognised by practitioners and policy makers internationally as a significant global public health issue. The World Health Organisation (WHO) estimates that one in three women worldwide experience either physical and/or sexual intimate partner violence or non-partner sexual violence in their lifetime (World Health Organisation, 2013). Many first experiences of sexual violence occur in childhood, with around 19% of girls and 8% of boys worldwide experiencing contact sexual abuse by the age of 18 (Pereda, Guilera, Forns, & Gómez-Benito, 2009). The scale of the problem is vast: 1.8 million children worldwide are estimated to be sexually exploited every year (International Labour Organisation, 2015).

S. Allardyce (✉)
Stop It Now! Scotland, Edinburgh, UK

Lucy Faithfull Foundation, Epsom, UK
e-mail: StuartAllardyce@stopitnow.org.uk

© The Author(s) 2018
R. Lievesley et al. (eds.), *Sexual Crime and Prevention*, Sexual Crime,
https://doi.org/10.1007/978-3-319-98243-4_1

The issue of sexual violence experienced by both children and adults is as pressing now as it has ever been, with reported sexual crime in the United Kingdom at an all-time high and all national jurisdictions across the United Kingdom having ongoing or recently concluded public inquiries into historical abuse. Furthermore, the widespread use of the social media hashtags #TimesUp and #MeToo since late 2017 foregrounded, with a new-found urgency, questions about the prevalence of sexual violence and harassment and their relationship to gender inequalities within society. The cultural commentator Rebecca Solnit described this moment in the following way:

> You could say a dam broke, and a wall of women's stories came spilling forth – which has happened before, but never the way that this round has. This time around, women didn't just tell the stories of being attacked and abused; they named names, and abusers and attackers lost jobs and reputations and businesses and careers. They named names, and it mattered; people listened; their testimony had consequence. (Solnit, 2018)

How we respond to sexual violence in its many forms is therefore increasingly becoming one of the key cultural questions in contemporary society. Central to this question is the recognition by those who have been affected by sexual abuse and violence that the approaches to tackling sexual crime offered by legal and statutory authorities often provide inadequate responses to a social issue of this nature, complexity and scale.

There is little controversy over the significant physical and psychological harm that sexual crimes can cause through the violation of personal physical and emotional boundaries. Although impact varies from individual to individual and can relate to factors such as age of onset, frequency, severity, and relationship with perpetrator, a range of studies show that sexual abuse in both childhood and adulthood is statistically associated with compromised mental and physical health outcomes that can be experienced across the life course (Irish, Kobayashi, & Delahanty, 2009; Sawyerr & Bagley, 2017). Sexual abuse in childhood in particular has been linked to a range of issues, including depression, anxiety, dissociation, low self-esteem, hyper-sexuality (Davidson & Omar, 2014), and complex post-traumatic stress disorder (Kisiel et al., 2014). Victims of sexual crime are statistically likely to have experienced other forms of maltreatment in their life, and some of these incidents may pre-date the experience of sexual crime. Accordingly, it is often polyvictimisation—the accumulative impact of a range of adverse experiences—that leads to poor outcomes in later life rather than being a victim of sexual crime in and of itself (Felitti & Anda, 2010; Finkelhor, Ormrod, & Turner, 2007). However, treating the experience of sexual abuse as a maltreatment on a par with other adverse child experiences obscures some of the particular sequelae characteristic of sexual violence: subsequent sexual re-victimisation, for instance, particularly in later adolescence and young adulthood, may be a negative outcome characteristic of sexual abuse that distinguishes it from other harmful experiences in childhood (Papalia et al., 2017).

There are significant economic savings to be made through the prevention of sexual crime. Considerable costs are accrued by law enforcement agencies in detecting sexual crime, by legal processes in prosecuting those who commit sexual crimes and by social work and other correctional agencies related to the punishment of offenders and the protection of the public from further harm. There are also significant costs relating to medical expenditure and the provision of appropriate therapeutic and mental health care for many traumatised by their experiences of sexual crime. Some studies have tried to quantify these substantial economic costs: the National Society for the Protection of the Child (NSPCC) estimated that the cost of childhood sexual abuse in the United Kingdom in 2012, once figures for the costs of health care and loss of earnings for adult survivors of abuse were added to costs of policing and prosecution, came to £3.2 billion (Saied-Tessier, 2014).

The prevention of sexual crime is particularly important because the majority of cases of sexual violence are never known to statutory service. Estimates suggest that only one in eight children experiencing abuse is known to the police or social services, with only a fraction of reported cases leading to the conviction of a perpetrator (Office of the Children's Commissioner, 2015). This is congruent with media coverage in 2017/2018 of allegations concerning the sexual misconduct of celebrities both in the United Kingdom and the United States which highlighted that many who experience sexual violence in adulthood also do not report crimes against them until years after the event—if at all. The relationship with the perpetrator, feelings of shame and guilt, confusion, and perpetrator tactics (including their fears and anxieties being manipulated by the perpetrator) are all factors that contribute to the significant shortfall between reported sexual crime and actual prevalence (Allnock & Miller, 2013). If our social response to this issue does not extend beyond legal and statutory interventions that are only triggered after sexual crimes have been reported, our responses will only ever relate to a minority of those who actually offend.

All of these arguments suggest that we urgently need to address the root causes of sexual crime and refocus efforts on prevention. This chapter will look at how we define what sexual crime is before examining what we know empirically about the nature and dynamics of the heterogeneity of situations involving sexual crimes. It includes an appraisal of some of the theoretical concepts that have been used to inform sexual crime prevention activities over the last 40 years and concludes by considering issues relating to how theory links to the practice of prevention.

Understanding Sexual Crime

Sexual crime has been defined as 'a crime involving sexual assault or having a sexual motive' (Oxford English Dictionary, 2007, p. 2777). However, there is no global standard about what constitutes a sexual crime and considerable regional variation: many sexual activities that are criminalised in one jurisdiction are not necessarily criminalised in another. The legal age of sexual consent for heterosexual activity varies between countries, for instance, while same sex relationships are criminalised in some jurisdictions such as parts of Africa, South East Asia, and the Caribbean. Furthermore, sexual motive is not always apparent in all sexual crimes, and not always relevant to whether someone is prosecuted. For example, a person who views child sexual exploitation material out of curiosity or because they are trying to make sense of their own experience of victimisation in childhood may be prosecuted in UK courts as having committed a sexual crime, even though motivation of a sexual nature is absent.

The term 'sexual crime' is therefore problematic, and the concept of a 'continuum of sexual violence' has been proposed in recognition of the fact that the experience of sexual harm cannot be contained within legal parameters that define sexual offences (Kelly, 1988). The term 'sexual violence' has in turn been defined in WHO's 2002 World Report on Violence and Health as:

> any sexual act, attempt to obtain a sexual act, unwanted sexual comments or advances, or acts to traffic, or otherwise directed, against a person's sexuality using coercion, by any person regardless of their relationship to the victim, in any setting, including but not limited to home and work… coercion … (can include) a whole spectrum of degrees of force. Apart from physical force, it may involve psychological intimidation, blackmail or other threats. (Krug, Mercy, Dahlberg, & Zwi, 2002 p. 149)

The report goes on to describe a range of acts that would be covered by this definition, including rape within marriage or dating relations, unwanted sexual advances or sexual harassment (including demanding sex in return for favours), sexual abuse of children and vulnerable adults, violent acts against the sexual integrity of individuals (including female genital mutilation), and systematic rape during armed conflict (p. 149).

The ECPAT 'Luxembourg Guidelines' on terminology relating to the protection of children from sexual abuse and exploitation states that the term 'sexual violence' has been used mainly with reference to adults, 'often in relation to gender-based violence… and… often associated with rape' (p. 12). The term 'sexual violence' is increasingly used in international policy contexts with reference to children who have experienced sexual crimes. However, there remains a tension when applying this term to the abuse of children, and in many domestic legal systems, the use of violence can represent an aggravating factor in a sexual crime against a child (Greijer & Doek, 2016). The terms sexual abuse and exploitation are, therefore, preferred terms in many jurisdictions for describing sexual crimes involving a child victim, and these terms are referenced in several international protocols such as Article 34 of the United Nations Convention on the Rights of the Child (UNICEF, 1989).

Sexual crimes therefore cover a wide range of different behaviours perpetrated by a variety of kinds of individuals towards a range of different types of victim in a diversity of contexts. The heterogeneity of situations that can be labelled as sexual crimes means that caution is necessary when examining what empirical research has to tell us about sexual crime. Nonetheless, there are some clear messages from research that have significant implications for prevention efforts. Understanding the 'who', 'what', 'where', and 'when' of sexual crime is necessary if prevention efforts are to be targeted in effective and evidence-based ways.

Both boys and girls and adult males and females can be victimised, as can people who define themselves in other terms, for example, transgender individuals. Girls are generally twice as likely to be victimised as boys, just as adult females are more likely to experience sexual crime than adult males (Burrowes & Horvath, 2013; Pereda et al., 2009; Stoltenborgh, Ijzendoom, Euser, & Bakermans-Kraneburg, 2011). Although any child can be at risk of sexual abuse, some groups may be at elevated risk. Studies of children with disabilities suggest that they are twice as likely to be sexually abused as children without disabilities (Jones et al., 2012). Other factors that elevate risk for children can be familial (e.g. living with conflict and separation; insecure attachment styles or experiencing other forms of maltreatment), social (e.g. peer rejection; or association with peers who are not pro-social), or relate to organisational factors (e.g. poor safeguarding processes within an institution) (Smallbone, Marshall, & Wortley, 2008).

Sexual crimes generally occur in a context of secrecy and in physical spaces where there is low chance of the perpetrator being observed by witnesses. Around 80% of sexual crimes against children take place in domestic contexts, usually in the victim or abuser's home (Wortley & Smallbone, 2006). Abuse can also take place in organisational settings (schools, hospitals, residential units, etc.) and—more rarely—in public settings (swimming pools, shopping malls, public parks, etc.) (Smallbone et al., 2008). Although random selection of victims can occur, victim and perpetrator are more commonly known to each other in most sexual crimes involving both adult and child victims (Finkelhor, 1994).

Over the last 20 years online sexual crime, including the grooming of children for offline or—more commonly—online abuse (see Shannon,

2008) and the viewing of child sexual exploitation material, has become a significant issue for law enforcement. It is likely that detected crime is only the tip of the iceberg with online crime as it is with offline crime: Dombert et al. (2016) in a German study of a non-clinical sample of 8718 men found that 2.2% stated that they had viewed sexual images of children while a study of 1978 Swedish young adult males found 4.4% had viewed such images (Seto et al., 2015). These figures are considerably higher than those charged with online sexual crimes each year.

The vast majority of perpetrators of sexual crimes against both adults and children are male: 2.2% of sexual offences reported to police are committed by females, with victimisation studies suggesting that females account for 11.6% of sexual crime (Cortoni, Babchishin, & Rat, 2017). In terms of age profile of perpetrators, 20–25% of all sexual offences reported to police involve a young person under the age of 18 as the identified perpetrator; the mean age of onset in cases where children are involved in the commission of the crime is 13/14 (Finkelhor, Ormrod, & Chaffin, 2009).

Furthermore, 75–80% of convicted adult sex offenders have no known sexual offending history (Smallbone & Wortley, 2000). Once convicted, official sexual recidivism rates are generally low: Hanson and Bussiere (1998) found a sexual recidivism rate of 13% over four to five years in a meta-analysis of 23,393 adult sex offenders, with figures being even lower for adolescents who commit sexual crimes (Caldwell, 2016). Only around 5–10% of convicted offenders become highly persistent, with recidivism associated with factors such as abuse of male children, non-familial abuse, anti-sociality/psychopathy, sexual deviance, and general criminality (Hanson & Morton-Bourgon, 2005). Re-offending rates are still low even when under-reporting is accounted for. This finding may seem counter-intuitive as media coverage of sexual crime typically focuses on high-profile—but relatively rare—serious cases. These tragic situations usually involve serial offenders and the sexual murder of victims, the predations of celebrities, or offending in institutional settings. These depictions obscure the picture that emerges from empirical research (McCartan, 2010); although those who take considerable efforts to abuse children do exist, it is likely that the majority of sexual crimes involving children as victims are much more opportunistic or situational in nature (Smallbone et al., 2008).

This heterogeneity creates a key challenge for those developing initiatives involving prevention of sexual crime. Consider the following situations:

- A 35-year-old male who has physically assaulted his wife on several occasions and anally rapes her in the course of a physical attack;
- A 22-year-old female teacher who becomes preoccupied with a 15-year-old male student and kisses him when alone together after a class;
- A 70-year-old retired male who is charged with viewing child sexual abuse material online;
- A 40-year-old male prisoner who threatens a 20-year-old male inmate in custody with a knife and forces the inmate to fellate him;
- A 13-year-old male who digitally penetrates his 5-year-old step-sister while she is sleeping.

All of these situations would constitute sexual crimes in most jurisdictions. All are very different in nature and context, with contrasting causal factors that will have led to the emergence of the behaviour. Accordingly, different measures will be necessary to prevent each of these sexual crimes occurring in the first place. Although there may be commonalities in how we prevent sexual crime, many of the specifics of prevention programmes will need to be tailored to particular contexts and victim and perpetrator types.

The History of Sexual Crime Prevention

Our contemporary understanding of the prevention of sexual crimes against both adults and children can be traced back to the 1970s. In the early part of this decade, grass-roots movements led by survivors of sexual violence, feminist activists, and survivor advocates campaigned to raise public awareness of male sexual violence, arguing that it was both commonplace and not pathological in nature, but rather linked to patriarchal power structures within society. This 'anti-rape' movement paralleled work being done to raise public awareness around domestic abuse at this time (Bourke, 2015). Rape crises centres started to emerge in both North America and the United Kingdom, often established by activists rather than professionals. Volunteers accompanied rape victims to hospitals, activists were involved with public-speaking events to destigmatise the role of being a victim of sexual violence, and pressure was placed on law enforcement agencies and courts to respond to this issue as a serious form of crime. If many forms of sexual violence were criminalised before the 1970s, the significance sexual crimes now have in most contemporary legal systems results from the campaigning efforts of committed groups and individuals at this time, who were in turn responding to the lived experiences of those who had survived harm.

As part of this paradigm shift in the 1970s, child sexual abuse also started to be conceptualised as a social concern. Prior to then, child sexual abuse was considered to be relatively rare, was commonly referred to as 'incest' in clinical and forensic literatures, and was often considered to be caused by 'seductive children' who provoked sexual contact with adults (Rush, 1980). In the context of awareness raising around the subject of rape, activists in the 1970s began to discuss child sexual abuse as a political issue. Additionally, rape crises centres found they received calls from adult survivors of childhood sexual abuse and accordingly had to develop ways of responding to this issue. Services focusing on the therapeutic needs of both children who had been sexually abused and adults who had been sexually abused in childhood started to emerge, as did pressure on statutory services to develop systems and processes to protect children more effectively, to investigate crimes more rigorously and prosecute offenders more robustly.

Very early approaches to the prevention of sexual crime foregrounded its status as a gendered form of violence. Self-defence classes were a mainstay of programmes designed to prevent sexual crimes involving adult women as victims. Whittier (2009) in a history of early activism concerning child sexual abuse notes that recognition of risk towards children meant that such classes were made available to children. For instance, the Feminist Karate Union of Seattle offered 'self defence classes to all women over seven years of age' in the late 1970s and some self-defence classes offered special classes for girls (p. 26).

In 1985, Finkelhor and Araji edited the influential textbook 'A Sourcebook on Child Sexual Abuse' which gathered together findings from emerging research on prevalence, risk factors, impact and what was known about abusers at that time. The authors noted:

> Sexual abuse prevention is a new field. Programmes having prevention as their primary objective did not appear until the late 1970s, several years after programs had been established to identify and treat sexual abuse victims… it was not until 1980 that any federal funds… became available for prevention work… For the most part, prevention programs originated from the grass roots without government sponsorship. Most grew out of the volunteer efforts of rape crises counsellors, were sponsored by local social service agencies or police departments, or originated simply, from the efforts of concerned educators or parents. By 1983, however, prevention programs were among the fastest growing components of the movement to deal with child sexual abuse. (Finkelhor & Araji, 1986, pp. 224–225)

Many of the prevention interventions described by Finkelhor at this time focused on educating children about child sexual abuse. Books and resources for children such as 'No More Secrets' described what sexual abuse was and highlighted that children could take particular actions such as telling a trusting adult if someone tried to abuse them. Other prevention resources at this time focused on raising awareness of parents and helping them discuss risk with their children. Programmes engaging adults on the subject of prevention assumed that parents were protective and not abusers or having the potential to abuse, although Finklehor noted that they may provide a deterrent effect as they reinforce the norm that such behaviour is exploitative and damaging to the development of the child. Only in the 1990s and 2000s did prevention programmes such as Stop It Now! in the United States, United Kingdom and parts of Europe as well as Dunkelfeld in Germany start to emerge, focusing on deterring individuals who present a risk to children or providing early interventions for individuals who have troubling sexual thoughts or who have committed sexual crimes.

Contemporary Theories of Sexual Crime Prevention

Sexual crime is clearly a criminal justice matter, but since the 1980s it has increasingly also been seen as a preventable public health issue. Public health approaches usually involve strategies such as the use of vaccines and immunisation, sanitation of drinking water as well as the dissemination of health information to the general public to improve health outcomes across the population. Some proponents of public health models have argued that similar approaches targeted at raising public awareness of the impact of sexual violence and the practical steps adults can take to protect children could significantly reduce incidence rates of child sexual abuse in society (Brown, O'Donnell, & Erooga, 2011).

Public health interventions can be primary (or universal), secondary (or selected), and tertiary (or indicated) in nature. Although there is no universal agreement about how these terms are defined, primary prevention strategies are generally targeted at a community or whole population, secondary prevention strategies focus on at risk groups or on situations where problems are starting to emerge and tertiary prevention strategies are interventions designed at reducing harm and preventing the re-emergence of an issue after it had been identified.

When these terms are applied to crime, interventions may be directed to preventing crimes before they would otherwise first occur (primary or secondary prevention); as well as after its occurrence, to prevent further offending and victimisation (tertiary prevention) (Smallbone et al., 2008). Primary prevention interventions would therefore include initiatives such as schools-based child sexual abuse prevention programmes rolled out universally to all children. Targeted secondary prevention might include initiatives such as those helping individuals with sexual thoughts and feelings towards children manage their behaviour effectively.

The majority of interventions targeting sexual crime prevention in the United Kingdom and North America are tertiary in nature. Police, courts, and correctional staff in custody and community settings all have vital roles to play in the prosecution, conviction, and rehabilitation of those who have committed sexual offences. Since the 1990s sex-offender registers have been introduced in Anglophone jurisdictions such as the United States and the United Kingdom, supplemented in some areas by community notification processes, residence restriction requirements, preventative orders, and multi-agency public protection arrangements. Vetting and disclosure arrangements are in place in many countries to ensure that those who are perceived as presenting a risk to children and vulnerable adults have reduced opportunities to access potential victims. All of these measures contribute to prevention, but they apply only to those who are known to have previously committed sexual offences.

There has been some general research into whether criminal justice interventions go beyond tertiary prevention and also have an impact on primary or secondary prevention. Such findings have not been specific to the question of sexual crime and have tended to look at property crime and violence, although they may have some transferability to the field of sexual crime prevention (Smallbone et al., 2008). There is some evidence that intelligence led targeting of police patrols in particular crime 'hot spots' at particular times has a deterrent effect (Sherman & Eck, 2002). This may have relevance for both the prevention of child sexual exploitation where vulnerable young people may be groomed in public settings where youths gather (such as transport hubs, shopping malls, and 24-hour fast food restaurants) and the targeting of particular Internet sites by law enforcement and the visibility of policing online. Conversely, there is little evidence that increasing sanctions for crimes has a deterrent effect with non-sexual crime (Doob & Webster, 2003; Gendreau et al., 1993), and it is questionable whether escalating sentences for sexual crime would contribute markedly to prevention.

Public health approaches tend to be ecologically orientated and focus on defining the problem, establishing and tracking prevalence, identifying risk and protective factors statistically associated with aetiology, and the development and testing of relevant interventions. Although they have value in helping practitioners and policy makers think more broadly about what we mean by prevention, there are other ways of conceptualising approaches to sexual crime prevention. For instance, Tonry and Farrington (1995) contrast criminal justice intervention with three other categories of crime prevention interventions: developmental crime prevention, situational crime prevention, and community prevention. This provides a useful way of making sense of contemporary sexual crime prevention approaches, many of which straddle the categories of primary, secondary, and tertiary prevention.

Developmental Crime Prevention draws on risk and protective factors that tend to be associated with individual criminality or likelihood of victimisation across the life course. Although not targeted at the prevention of sexual abuse specifically, general maltreatment prevention programmes, particularly those focusing on the development of protective attachment bonds between children and carers, may reduce vulnerability of individuals becoming victims of sexual crime in childhood or beyond. Impact of such programmes on prevention of sexual crime has been under-researched to date.

School-based sexual abuse prevention programmes and personal safety programmes can also be considered to be developmental approaches as they are premised on the idea that the children's lack of knowledge about sexual abuse is a key factor contributing to their victimisation. Such programmes have been widespread in some jurisdictions, with Finkelhor and Dziuba-Leatherman (1995) estimating that 2/3 of children in the United States were exposed to these programmes at some point between age 5 and 12 in the 1990s. There is good evidence that such programmes increase knowledge of protective strategies amongst children, although findings about whether they genuinely result in reductions in child sexual abuse have so far been elusive (Walsh, Zwi, Woolfenden, & Shlonsky, 2015). Common critiques are that they place the burden of the prevention on the child and are premised on the notion of 'stranger danger' despite most incidents involving the sexual abuse of children taking place within a domestic context with a known adult or adolescent as perpetrator. Programmes educating parents about how they can support healthy sexual development in childhood, targeted work with those who have already been abused to prevent further victimisation, and the integration of messages about consent and healthy sexuality within a wider educational framework are other forms of developmental prevention that have a grounding in the literature about why sexual crime occurs in the first place (Allardyce, Wylie, Ritchie, Sharpe, & Barron, 2016).

Another aspect of developmental prevention relates to disruption of the cultural transmission of harmful masculine norms and how those norms link to the commission of sexual crimes. As a recent report put it:

> Harmful gender norms that associate "manhood" with heterosexual prowess and access to/control over women's and girls' and boys' bodies contribute to male perpetration of sexual exploitation … Children are targeted for and vulnerable to sexual exploitation precisely because they have less power, with girls at the bottom of the gender-based hierarchy… Qualitative data

on the demand side of child sexual exploitation point to the deep influence of masculine norms of power, control, and sexual conquest. (Heilman, 2018, p. 42)

Examples of operationalising these ideas about 'toxic masculinity' in a prevention framework would include the international work of White Ribbon Campaign and Promundo, as well as the educational programmes for men and boys provided by the Coalition Against Trafficking in Women (CATW) outlining the harmful consequences of commercial sexual exploitation of women and children within the context of a gendered analysis (Heilman, 2018).

Although developmental approaches to sexual crime involving adults as victims are rare, recommendations about prevention of intimate partner violence—and sexual violence in this context—generally identify risk and protective factors and focus on how they are reduced. Jewkes (2002) in a review of the literature argues that primary preventive interventions should focus on improving the status of women and reducing norms of violence, poverty, and alcohol consumption. Similarly, a WHO report from 2007 outlined the contributions to prevention in this area that can be made by early childhood and family-based approaches to reducing risk of maltreatment (which can be a factor for perpetrators and victims in adulthood), positive messaging in school environments (including targeted work with boys), interventions to reduce alcohol and substance misuse, and public information and awareness campaigns (Harvey, Garcia-Moreno, & Butchart, 2007).

Situational Crime Prevention is concerned with the environmental factors that facilitate offending (Smallbone et al., 2008). It is premised on the idea that for a crime to take place, a victim, an offender, and a suitable location or setting need to be present. Just as not all individuals are equally disposed to act in sexually violent ways, and not all individuals are equally at risk of being victimised, not all settings are equally likely to be scenes of sexual crimes. Thinking about sexual violence as an incident occurring in a specific time and place involving more than one participant encourages a shift from viewing criminality as inherent to an individual with certain dispositional traits to seeing risk of abuse as involving an interplay between self and environment. Accordingly, particular environmental adaptations in certain settings may contribute to reduction in risk. Such approaches are now being operationalised, particularly with reference to prevention of abuse in organisational settings (e.g. Firmin, 2018; Higgins, Kaufman, & Erooga, 2016; Rayment-McHugh, Adams, Wortley, & Tilley, 2015).

The prevention of abuse, and the changing of the decision-making of potential offenders, generally includes increasing risk of discovery, increasing effort necessary to commit the crime, removing excuses/reducing permissibility, and controlling prompts (Smallbone et al., 2008). Situational crime prevention is not exclusively concerned with the risk and behaviour of potential or actual offenders; it also recognises the roles of other parties, for example, 'guardians' and 'place managers'. It therefore has affinities with bystander theories that increasingly underpin many primary and secondary sexual crime prevention interventions. Bystander programmes target friends, families, peers, co-workers, and members of the general public rather than potential perpetrators or victims and encourage them to consider challenging at-risk behaviours or attitudes that may be precursors to sexual violence, or to intervene or reach out for help if they see evidence that a crime is occurring or about to occur (Tabachnick, 2008). There is promising qualitative data in relation to 'whole school' interventions such as Mentors for Violence Prevention, Green Dot, and Bringing in the Bystander, which enhance school and college students' abilities to become active bystanders in the prevention of bullying, sexual harassment, and teen dating abuse (Coker et al., 2011; Katz, Heisterkamp, & Fleming, 2011; Moynihan, Banyard, Arnold, Eckstein, & Stapleton, 2011).

Community prevention describes an eclectic range of methods focusing on specific crime problems in particular communities. The prevention of sexual violence on university campuses would be an example of an approach focusing on a specific community. Over one-third of UK female students have experienced unwelcome sexual advances (McCarry, 2017). Emerging prevention efforts focusing on the campus community are typically ecologically orientated and multi-dimensional, often drawing on tools such as the 'spectrum of prevention' that suggests effective preventative strategies need to strengthen individual knowledge and skills, promote community education, educate providers, foster coalitions and networks, and change organisational practices (Davis, Parks, & Cohen, 2006). This ecological orientation can be seen in resources such as the Equally Safe in Higher Education Toolkit (Donaldson, McCarry, & McGoldrick, 2018).

Community prevention programmes need to target multiple risk and protective factors and incorporate strategies across the social ecology. Tilley et al. (2014) illustrate this principle when describing work with a community in Queensland, Australia, in which sexual violence among young people was prevalent, particularly within the indigenous population. Reports of group rapes, girls drawn into under-age sex through peer associations, girls trading sex for money on the streets, and the rape of girls while intoxicated were common. In one area, rates of reported sexual offences were almost 7 times greater than the state average, and rates of sexually transmitted infections 56 times greater. These problems were compounded by a local context, in which many places were considered by locals to be unsafe (particularly at night), where there was a high frequency of missing school, low levels of family supervision, and a deep reluctance on the part of community members to intervene directly in problem behaviour or to contact the police with concerns.

An intervention strategy was delivered across various domains: public spaces, domestic spaces, and in school and youth group spaces. The targeting of public spaces by 15-minute 'pulse patrols' staged at 'hot times' on 'hot days' of the week occurred, with training provided to police in order to improve engagement with young people. Extra lighting and CCTV supplemented this, and night patrols were undertaken by community members, who were better placed than police to enter into informal conversations and information-sharing about available services. Creating safer domestic spaces was achieved through professionals working closely with communities, sharing information about the problem through community forums, and undertaking developmental work with parents focusing on parenting skills tailored to suit different community contexts and cultural backgrounds. Finally, a sex, ethics, and guardianship programme for young people was developed to address attitudes that supported sexual violence towards girls and to improve their ability to interrupt risky situations. All of this was achieved by a holistic and ecological conceptualisation of the problem and close consultation with affected communities.

This layered approach to complex social problems involving child sexual abuse, integrating primary, secondary, and tertiary interventions, is being further developed internationally by the Lucy Faithfull Foundation's Eradicating Child Sexual Abuse project (ECSA) (https://ecsa.lucyfaithfull.org/).

Theories of Sexual Offending and Prevention

Tilley and Sidebottom (2017) argue that theories of crime prevention should ideally:

- Specify plausible casual mechanisms that can be applied in policy, practice or in programmes;
- Those causal mechanisms must speak to one or more of conditions responsible for the genesis of crime;
- The conditions (or context) for the activation or deactivation of relevant causal mechanisms must be articulated; and
- The conjectured mechanisms/contexts/outcome configurations need to be testable, by which we mean they are open to refutation. (p. 5)

This would suggest that prevention of sexual crime needs to be embedded in a sound understanding of why sexual violence occurs in the first place. In addition to the 'who', 'what', 'where', and 'when' of sexual crime, we also need to understand the 'why'.

Early work in the 1980s and 1990s on the causes of sexual violence in adulthood generally accepted that there were common causal factors explaining sexually violent behaviours, with early theories focused on specific psychological deficits that were purported to hold the key to understanding the roots of sexual aggression, for example, sexual deviancy (McGuire, Carlisle, & Young, 1964), empathy deficits (David Finkelhor & Lewis, 1988), and cognitive distortions (Abel, Becker, & Cunningham-Rathner, 1984). Over time, it was recognised that most single-factor theories lack explanatory power and, instead, there has been a move towards considering sexual offending behaviour in adults—and adolescents—to be multi-determined, focusing on how psychological factors interact with each other and with ecological factors (e.g. social and cultural environment, personal circumstances and the physical environment) and even factors such as evolutionary biology. Key theories include the four preconditions model (Finkelhor, 1984), the integrated theory (Marshall & Barbaree, 1990), the quadripartite model of sexual aggression (Hall & Hirschman, 1996), the confluence model of sexual aggression (Malamuth, 1996), the pathways model (Ward & Beech, 2006), and—for online offenders—the motivation-facilitation model (Seto, 2017).

Some of these models recognise that sexual crime is a heterogeneous phenomenon and many are underpinned by an understanding that there may be a range of different developmental pathways into sexual crime. However, despite increased theoretical sophistication and some empirical backing, aetiological theories about sexual offending are rarely used to inform primary and secondary preventions in meaningful ways. Perhaps one of the reasons for this is that the literature on the aetiology of sexual violence has—to date—been driven by psychological research, which has generally downplayed the sociological aspects of sexual crime that might prove more fruitful for identifying prevention targets. In particular, it is noticeable that contemporary empirical theories about the aetiology of sexual crime have generally shied away from the gendered nature of most crimes. Clayton, Jones, Brown, and Taylor (2018) in a discussion of the aetiology of child sexual abuse found that:

> Noticeably absent from the research is evidence pertaining to community and sociocultural factors. It is important to question critically how different factors interact. For instance, the evidence indicates that girls are more at risk of child sexual abuse, however we do not know what mechanisms are operating to produce this increased risk for girls. Feminist theory hypothesises that culture enforces an unequal social structure that disadvantages women and girls. In addition, patriarchal structures may discourage boys from reporting or recognising their experiences as abusive. However, we found no studies exploring the intersections between gender identities and sociocultural constructs.

This in turn reminds us that our current understanding of sexual violence is historically linked to the campaigning work of the 1970s that initially conceptualised this injustice as a gendered form of crime. Over time, the clinical literature in relation to sexual offending has generally ignored the fact that the majority of offenders and male and the majority of victims are female, a key factor that needs to be integrated into primary and secondary prevention approaches.

Conclusion

Prevention is always better that cure, and it is clear that the issue of how we prevent sexual crime emerging in the first place is becoming an urgent and pressing problem in contemporary society. This urgency is in part driven by an increasing recognition that current approaches to prevention focusing on what can be done after a sexual crime is reported inevitably fail to address most situations where children or adults are sexually abused or assaulted. Sexual crimes cover a wide heterogeneity of different kinds of situations, although we know that this is a gendered form of crime, where typically adult or adolescent males violate sexual boundaries with girls and women. Most sexual crime takes place in domestic contexts which provide particular challenges for prevention, although abuse in organisational, public, and online settings may be particular promising contexts for abuse to be 'designed out' of systems. Public health models, and developmental, situational and community-based approaches to prevention provide theoretical underpinnings for current prevention approaches, but to date these approaches have not been meaningfully coupled to theories of why sexual violence emerges in particular situations and contexts. Indeed, the literature on the causes of sexual violence emerges from a clinical literature on the aetiology of sexual offending that does not helpfully inform clear empirical prevention targets. Accordingly, although there is some promising emerging practice in the field of prevention of sexual violence and abuse against adults and children, we still have some progress to make before we have a unified theory of sexual crime prevention that integrates sociological, psychological and other determinants in a way that informs clear, empirically grounded prevention targets.

References

Abel, G. G., Becker, J. V., & Cunningham-Rathner, J. (1984). Complications, consent, and cognitions in sex between children and adults. *International Journal of Law and Psychiatry, 7*(1), 89–103.

Allardyce, S., Wylie, N., Ritchie, B., Sharpe, M., & Barron, I. (2016). *Preventing adolescent harmful sexual behaviour: A NOTA think piece.* Retrieved from http://www.nota.co.uk/media/1304/think-piece-preventing-adolescent-harmful-sexual-behaviour-24317.pdf. Accessed 7 May 2018.

Allnock, D., & Miller, P. (2013). *No one noticed, no one heard: A study of disclosures of childhood abuse.* London: NSPCC.

Bourke, J. (2015). *Rape: A history from 1860 to the present.* London: Virago.

Brown, J., O'Donnell, T., & Erooga, M. (2011). *Sexual abuse: A public health challenge.* London: NSPCC.

Burrowes, N., & Horvath, T. (2013). *The rape and sexual assault of men: A review of the literature.* London: Survivors UK.

Caldwell, M. F. (2016). Quantifying the decline in juvenile sexual recidivism rates. *Psychology, Public Policy, and Law, 22*(4), 414–426. https://doi.org/10.1037/law0000094

Clayton, E., Jones, C., Brown, J., & Taylor, J. (2018). The aetiology of child sexual abuse: A critical review of the empirical evidence. *Child Abuse Review, 27*, 181. ISSN 0952-9136.

Coker, A. L., Cook-Craig, P. G., Williams, C. M., Fisher, B. S., Clear, E. R., Garcia, L. S., et al. (2011). Evaluation of Green Dot: An active bystander intervention to reduce sexual violence on college campuses. *Violence Against Women, 17*(6), 777–796.

Cortoni, F., Babchishin, K. M., & Rat, C. (2017). The proportion of sexual offenders who are female is higher than thought: A meta-analysis. *Criminal Justice and Behavior, 44*(2), 145–162.

Davidson, L., & Omar, H. A. (2014). Long-term consequences of childhood sexual abuse. *International Journal of Child and Adolescent Health, 7*(2), 103–107.

Davis, R., Parks, L. F., & Cohen, L. (2006). *Sexual violence and the spectrum of prevention: Towards a community solution.* Enola, PA: National Sexual Violence Resource Center.

Dombert, B., Schmidt, A. F., Banse, R., Briken, P., Hoyer, J., Neutze, J., et al. (2016). How common is men's self-reported sexual interest in prepubescent children? *The Journal of Sex Research, 53*(2), 214–223.

Donaldson, A., McCarry, M., & McGoldrick, R. (2018). *Equally safe in higher education*. Glasgow, UK: Strathclyde University. Retrieved from https://www.strath.ac.uk/humanities/schoolofsocialworksocialpolicy/equallysafeinhigher-education/eshetoolkit/. Accessed 7 May 2018.

Doob, A. N., & Webster, C. M. (2003). Sentence severity and crime: Accepting the null hypothesis. *Crime and Justice, 30*, 143–195.

Felitti, V. J., & Anda, R. F. (2010). The relationship of adverse childhood experiences to adult medical disease, psychiatric disorders and sexual behavior: Implications for healthcare. In R. A. Lanius, V. Eric, & P. Clare (Eds.), *The impact of early life trauma on health and disease: The hidden epidemic* (pp. 77–87). Cambridge, MA: Cambridge University Press.

Finkelhor, D. (1984). *Child sexual abuse: New theory and research*. Washington, DC: Sage.

Finkelhor, D. (1994). Current information on the scope and nature of child sexual abuse. *The Future of Children, 4*(2), 31–53.

Finkelhor, D., & Araji, S. (1986). *A sourcebook on child sexual abuse*. Washington, DC: Sage.

Finkelhor, D., & Dziuba-Leatherman, J. (1995). Victimization prevention programs: A national survey of children's exposure and reactions. *Child Abuse & Neglect, 19*(2), 129–139.

Finkelhor, D., & Lewis, I. (1988). An epidemiologic approach to the study of child molestation. *Annals of the New York Academy of Sciences, 528*(1), 64–78.

Finkelhor, D., Ormrod, R., & Chaffin, M. (2009). Juveniles who commit sex offenses against minors. (Online). *Juvenile Justice Bulletin*. Retrieved from www.ncjrs.gov/pdffiles1/ojjdp/227763.pdf. Accessed 7 May 2018.

Finkelhor, D., Ormrod, R. K., & Turner, H. A. (2007). Poly-victimization: A neglected component in child victimization. *Child Abuse & Neglect, 31*(1), 7–26.

Firmin, C. (2018). Contextualizing case reviews: A methodology for developing systemic safeguarding practices. *Child & Family Social Work, 23*(1), 45–52.

Gendreau, P., Paparozzi, M., Little, T., & Goddard, M. (1993). Does "punishing smarter" work? An assessment of the new generation of alternative sanctions in probation. *Forum on Corrections Research, 5*(3), 31–34.

Greijer, S., & Doek, J. (2016). *Terminology guidelines for the protection of children from sexual exploitation and sexual abuse*. Luxembourg, Europe: ECPAT International and ECPAT Luxembourg.

Hall, G., & Hirschman, R. (1996). A quadripartite model of sexual aggression. In G. Hall (Ed.), *Theory-based assessment, treatment and prevention of sexual aggression* (pp. 51–71). Oxford, UK: Oxford University Press.

Hanson, R. K., & Bussiere, M. T. (1998). Predicting relapse: A meta-analysis of sexual offender recidivism studies. *Journal of Consulting and Clinical Psychology, 66*(2), 348.

Hanson, R. K., & Morton-Bourgon, K. E. (2005). The characteristics of persistent sexual offenders: A meta-analysis of recidivism studies. *Journal of Consulting and Clinical Psychology, 73*(6), 1154.

Harvey, A., Garcia-Moreno, C., & Butchart, A. (2007). *Primary prevention of intimate-partner violence and sexual violence: Background paper for WHO expert meeting May 2–3, 2007.* Geneva, Switzerland: World Health Organization, Department of Violence and Injury Prevention and Disability.

Heilman, B. (2018). *Masculine norms and violence: Making the connections,* Washington, DC. Retrieved from https://promundoglobal.org/wp-content/uploads/2018/04/Masculine-Norms-and-Violence-Making-the-Connection-20180424.pdf. Accessed 7 May 2018.

Higgins, D. J., Kaufman, K., & Erooga, M. (2016). How can child welfare and youth-serving organisations keep children safe? *Developing Practice: The Child, Youth and Family Work Journal, 44*(48–64).

International Labour Organisation. (2015). *Commercial sexual exploitation and trafficking of children "in a nutshell": A resource for Pacific Island countries.* Geneva, Switzerland: ILO.

Irish, L., Kobayashi, I., & Delahanty, D. L. (2009). Long-term physical health consequences of childhood sexual abuse: A meta-analytic review. *Journal of Pediatric Psychology, 35*(5), 450–461.

Jewkes, R. (2002). Intimate partner violence: Causes and prevention. *The Lancet, 359*(9315), 1423–1429.

Jones, L., Bellis, M. A., Wood, S., Hughes, K., McCoy, E., Eckley, L., et al. (2012). Prevalence and risk of violence against children with disabilities: A systematic review and meta-analysis of observational studies. *The Lancet, 380*(9845), 899–907.

Katz, J., Heisterkamp, H. A., & Fleming, W. M. (2011). The social justice roots of the mentors in violence prevention model and its application in a high school setting. *Violence Against Women, 17*(6), 684–702.

Kelly, L. (1988). *Surviving sexual violence.* Minneapolis, MN: University of Minnesota.

Kisiel, C. L., Fehrenbach, T., Torgersen, E., Stolbach, B., McClelland, G., Griffin, G., et al. (2014). Constellations of interpersonal trauma and symptoms in child welfare: Implications for a developmental trauma framework. *Journal of Family Violence, 29*(1), 1–14.

Krug, E. G., Mercy, J. A., Dahlberg, L. L., & Zwi, A. B. (2002). The world report on violence and health. *The Lancet, 360*(9339), 1083–1088.

Malamuth, N. M. (1996). The confluence model of sexual aggression: Feminist and evolutionary perspectives. In D. Buss (Ed.), *Sex, power, conflict: Evolutionary and feminist perspectives* (pp. 269–295). Oxford, UK: Oxford University Press.

Marshall, W. L., & Barbaree, H. E. (1990). An integrated theory of the etiology of sexual offending. In W. L. Marshall & H. E. Barbaree (Eds.), *Handbook of sexual assault: Issues, theories, and treatment of the offender* (pp. 257–275). Victoria, Canada: Abe Books.

McCarry, M. (2017). Sexual violence on campus: Evidence and action. *European network on gender and violence.* Paper presented at European Network on Gender and Violence, Milan, Italy.

McCartan, K. (2010). Media constructions of, and reactions to, paedophilia in society. In K. Harrison (Ed.), *Managing high risk sex-offenders in the community*. Abingdon, UK: Routledge.

McGuire, R. J., Carlisle, J. M., & Young, B. G. (1964). Sexual deviations as conditioned behaviour: A hypothesis. *Behaviour Research and Therapy, 2*(2), 185–190.

Moynihan, M. M., Banyard, V. L., Arnold, J. S., Eckstein, R. P., & Stapleton, J. G. (2011). Sisterhood may be powerful for reducing sexual and intimate partner violence: An evaluation of the bringing in the bystander in-person program with sorority members. *Violence Against Women, 17*(6), 703–719.

Office of the Children's Commissioner. (2015). *Protecting children from harm: A critical assessment of child sexual abuse in the family network in England and priorities for action.* London: Office of the Children's Commissioner.

Oxford English Dictionary. (2007). *Shorter Oxford English dictionary* (6th ed.). Oxford, UK: Oxford University Press.

Papalia, N. L., Luebbers, S., Ogloff, J. R., Cutajar, M., Mullen, P. E., & Mann, E. (2017). Further victimization of child sexual abuse victims: A latent class typology of re-victimization trajectories. *Child Abuse & Neglect, 66*, 112–129.

Pereda, N., Guilera, G., Forns, M., & Gómez-Benito, J. (2009). The prevalence of child sexual abuse in community and student samples: A meta-analysis. *Clinical Psychology Review, 29*(4), 328–338.

Rayment-McHugh, S., Adams, D., Wortley, R., & Tilley, N. (2015). 'Think Global Act Local': A place-based approach to sexual abuse prevention. *Crime Science, 4*(1), 22.

Rush, F. (1980). *The best kept secret: Sexual abuse of children.* Englewood Cliffs, NJ: Prentice-Hall.

Saied-Tessier, A. (2014). *Estimating the costs of child sexual abuse in the UK.* London: NSPCC.

Sawyerr, A., & Bagley, C. (2017). Child sexual abuse and adolescent and adult adjustment: A review of British and world evidence, with implications for social work, and mental health and school counselling. *Advances in Applied Sociology, 7*(1), 1–15.

Seto, M. C. (2017). The motivation-facilitation model of sexual offending. *Sexual Abuse.* https://doi.org/10.1177/1079063217720919.

Seto, M. C., Hermann, C. A., Kjellgren, C., Priebe, G., Svedin, C. G., & Långström, N. (2015). Viewing child pornography: Prevalence and correlates in a representative community sample of young Swedish men. *Archives of Sexual Behavior, 44*(1), 67–79.

Shannon, D. (2008). Online sexual grooming in Sweden – Online and offline sex offences against children as described in Swedish police data. *Journal of Scandinavian Studies in Criminology and Crime Prevention, 9*(2), 160–180.

Sherman, L. W., & Eck, J. E. (2002). Policing for crime prevention. In L. W. Sherman, D. L. MacKenzie, D. P. Farrington, & B. C. Welsh (Eds.), *Evidence-based crime prevention* (pp. 295–329). London: Routledge.

Smallbone, S., Marshall, W. L., & Wortley, R. (2008). *Preventing child sexual abuse: Evidence, policy and practice.* Oxford, UK: Willan Publishing.

Smallbone, S., & Wortley, R. K. (2000). *Child sexual abuse in Queensland: Offender characteristics and modus operandi.* Brisbane, QLD: Queensland Crime Commission and Queensland Police Service.

Solnit, R. (2018, March 8). Feminists have slowly shifted power, there's no going back. *Guardian.*

Stoltenborgh, M., Ijzendoom, M. H., Euser, E. M., & Bakermans-Kraneburg, M. J. (2011). A global perspective on child sexual abuse: Meta-analysis of prevalence around the world. *Child Maltreatment, 16.* https://doi.org/10.1177/1077559511403920.

Tabachnick, J. (2008). *Engaging bystanders in sexual violence prevention.* Enola, PA: National Sexual Violence Resource Center.

Tilley, N., Rayment-McHugh, S., Smallbone, S., Wardell, M., Smith, D., Allard, T., et al. (2014). On being realistic about reducing the prevalence and impacts of youth sexual violence and abuse in two Australian Indigenous communities. *Learning Communities: International Journal of Learning in Social Contexts, 14,* 6–27.

Tilley, N., & Sidebottom, A. (2017). *Handbook of crime prevention and community safety.* Abingdon, UK: Taylor & Francis.

Tonry, M., & Farrington, D. P. (1995). Strategic approaches to crime prevention. *Crime and Justice, 19*, 1–20.

UNICEF. (1989). Convention on the rights of the child. *Child Labor*, 8.

Walsh, K., Zwi, K., Woolfenden, S., & Shlonsky, A. (2015). *School-based education programmes for the prevention of child sexual abuse (1465–1858)*. Retrieved from. https://www.cochrane.org/CD004380/BEHAV_school-based-programmes-for-the-prevention-of-childsexual-abuse

Ward, T., & Beech, A. (2006). An integrated theory of sexual offending. *Aggression and Violent Behavior, 11*(1), 44–63.

Whittier, N. (2009). *The politics of child sexual abuse: Emotion, social movements, and the state*. Oxford, UK: Oxford University Press.

World Health Organization. (2013). *Global and regional estimates of violence against women: Prevalence and health effects of intimate partner violence and non-partner sexual violence*. Geneva, Switzerland: World Health Organization.

Wortley, R., & Smallbone, S. (2006). Applying situational principles to sexual offenses against children. *Crime Prevention Studies, 19*, 7.

2

Prevention in Action: Exploring Prevention Initiatives and Current Practices

Candice Christiansen and Meg Martinez-Dettamanti

Introduction to Prevention

As noted in the previous chapter, the issue of sexual violence towards children and adults has attained international attention. Professionals and policy makers in many areas have deemed sexual violence a public health issue, and prevention efforts have emerged globally with the support of governments, agencies, and communities. While tertiary prevention historically makes up the majority of services for addressing juvenile and adult sexual offences, there has been an increasing emergence of primary and secondary prevention strategies with the overarching goal of preventing sexual abuse before it occurs. This expansion in primary and secondary prevention efforts can be seen as a response to the growing epidemic that is sexual violence. Many of the programmes and projects highlighted in this chapter utilise primary and/or secondary prevention strategies, with some also employing a tertiary approach.

C. Christiansen (✉) • M. Martinez-Dettamanti
The Prevention Project™, Salt Lake City, UT, USA
e-mail: candice@thepreventionproject.org; meg@thepreventionproject.org

© The Author(s) 2018
R. Lievesley et al. (eds.), *Sexual Crime and Prevention*, Sexual Crime,
https://doi.org/10.1007/978-3-319-98243-4_2

Interest in employing these prevention strategies brought clinical and community attention to the treatment of paedophiles from a preventive perspective. From this interest, a population claiming to be "non-offending" paedophiles surfaced. Numerous members of this population appear eager to support the goals of many prevention strategies and many spearheaded prevention efforts of their own.

Introduction to the Non-offending Paedophile Population

> ...*the rights and treatment needs of an individual diagnosed with Paedophilic Disorder (except for the disturbing consequences of acting upon paedophilic urges) should be acknowledged.* (Fred S. Berlin, MD, PhD)

Research supports that "it is unknown how many people in the general population are emotionally and sexually attracted to children or pubescent adolescents... [further] suggest[ing] that many, perhaps most, adults may have a limited level of such feelings, but they are subordinate to their feelings for adults" ("Learn," 2018). Equivalently, Seto (2017) asserts in his article, *The Puzzle of Male Chronophilia*, "a sexual interest in sexually mature adolescents, though socially sanctioned in modern Western societies if under the legal age of consent, is neither uncommon nor atypical" (p. 12). Although paedophilia and the lesser known hebephilia are considered largely unfavourable, the presence of such attractions and orientations has been shown to be more common than typically thought.

In the article, *Non-Offending Pedophiles* (2016), Cantor and McPhail define non-offending paedophiles (and hebephiles) as individuals who experience sexual attraction to children but have no (known) sexual contact with a child, typically expressing a strong desire never to do so. Such expression is evident in an exclusive interview on The Prevention Podcast™, where a female paedophile, known as "Emma," describes the terms "non-offending" and "anti-contact" as related to her experience.

- Non-Offending is "indicative of behaviour so a non-offending paedophile is a person with a primary or exclusive sexual attraction towards prepubescent children, but we don't act on that attraction in any way...

so that means obviously no sexual contact with children but also extends to not possessing or consuming child pornography or doing anything to feed in that whole online child exploitation industry."
- Anti-Contact is "more a philosophy and that means that we believe, we feel that sexual contact between an adult and a child carries an immense amount of risk just of causing the child serious psychological harm, so we feel it is wrong to engage in it… there's just so much overwhelming evidence that it causes harm." (Christiansen, Martinez-Dettamanti, & Warner, 2018)

Within this population, the term "Minor Attracted Person" or "MAP" is often used by individuals who may not fully relate to the term "paedophile," but feel a sexual or emotional attraction to children or adolescents. When seeking to understand and work with MAPs, it is important to recognise that "no one chooses to be emotionally and sexually attracted to children or adolescents. The cause is unknown; in fact, the development of attraction to adults is also not understood" ("Learn," 2018). Many theories involving evolution, hormonal influence, negative socialisation, family of origin issues, and childhood sexual experiences have been considered, although most have not been tested scientifically ("Learn," 2018). None of these theories are supported by reliable evidence, including the common misconception that attraction to minors is caused by sexual abuse in childhood. Despite the lack of causal research findings, it is possible that addressing widely discussed social and clinical issues among men and women identifying as MAPs could both improve their lives and reduce the likelihood of sexual offending (Bailey & Hsu, 2016). Berlin (2014) further states that publicly acknowledging pedophilia or hebephilia as a sexual orientation can help clinically distinguish from a criminal mindset or derogatory label while supporting the need for effective psychiatric treatment for Pedophilic Disorder.

The Advancement of Actual Prevention Initiatives to Date

The prevention projects and initiatives highlighted in this chapter began as early as 1992, although prevention work began informally much earlier. In the last 20 years, the advancement of global prevention initiatives has grown to include projects that range from clinical treatment to peer led support groups, many of which will be highlighted in this chapter. Beginning with well-established and acclaimed programmes like the Prevention Project Dunkelfeld (PPD) in Germany and the Stop It Now! campaigns in the United States, the chapter guides readers through the often grass roots development of these programmes and highlights the many successive prevention initiatives and resources that have since come to fruition. This is by no means an exhaustive list of global prevention efforts. The prevention programmes, campaigns, and support services featured in this chapter were chosen based on the content of this book, the historical development of the programmes, and their impact on prevention efforts globally. It is also important to note these programmes are operational initiatives that continue to grow and evolve.

The Prevention Project Dunkelfeld, Germany

Since the late 1990s, paedophilic men have sought treatment at the Charités Institute of Sexology and Sexual Medicine outpatient clinic to understand, accept, and manage their sexuality (Beier, Neutze, et al., 2009). Through this work, it was acknowledged that paedophilic individuals often experience distressing symptoms related to the complexity of issues associated with their sexual identity. This relevant and unavoidable analysis will become an underlying thread connecting many of the prevention programmes and interventions discussed in this chapter. Therefore, the Charités Institute of Sexology and Sexual Medicines' underlying belief is that these men would be more likely than a "potential child molester" (without paedophilic attractions), to seek treatment.

The German PPD, the most well-known prevention project to date, was launched in Berlin by the Charités Institute of Sexology and Sexual Medicine, in 2005. The project's primary goal is to prevent child sexual abuse (CSA) by identifying men who are afraid they may sexually abuse a child as well as providing free and confidential treatment to those who are not mandated to seek therapeutic support (Beier, Ahlers, et al., 2009). At inception, PPD consisted of a media campaign to recruit self-identified paedophiles and hebephiles in the community and if interested, the facilitation of further diagnostics and treatment programming (Beier, Neutze, et al., 2009). With help from the German government, PPD was integrated into the health care system under the belief that costless and anonymous preventative treatment should be available ("About," 2017). Therefore, PPD allows these individuals, even those who have already offended, to seek therapeutic support without legal consequences, under doctor-patient confidentiality.

As quoted, *Dunkelfeld* translates from German to *dark field*. The term is used by PPD to refer to CSA offenders who are undetected by law enforcement and also endorse a sexual interest in children (Schaefer et al., 2010). These are individuals who have committed a sexual offence but have not been adjudicated. Between 2005 and 2011, 319 undetected "Dunkelfeld" help-seeking paedophiles and hebephiles expressed interest in taking part in a confidential anonymous cognitive behavioural treatment programme (Beier et al., 2015). About 74.5% of participants reported committing CSA or other forms of child sexual exploitation once in their life; 41% of which reported to be Dunkelfeld offenders (Beier, Ahlers, et al., 2009). Final results of the clinical diagnostic portion of the PPD found no pre/post-assessment changes in the control group, whereas, in regard to the treated group, results found that emotional deficits and offence-supportive cognitions decreased, while post-therapy sexual self-regulation increased (Beier et al., 2015).

"Kein Täter werden": The Prevention Network

PPD now has multiple sites in Germany, which comprise The Prevention Network "Kein Täter warden." Their overarching goal is to prevent CSA by providing comprehensive, qualified outpatient preventative therapy for self-identified paedophiles and hebephiles. They demonstrate that individuals with a sexual preference towards minors can be helped to not commit sex offences through adequate and accurate assessment, specialised therapy interventions, and through improving public understanding and awareness ("Goals," n.d.).

As PPD continues to grow, programme participants include individuals who have not offended and/or have never consumed CSA images (i.e.

child pornography (CP)), referred previously as "potential offenders," as well as people who have already offended and/or have consumed CP, though whose offences are not known to the legal system, referred as "Dunkelfeld offenders" ("Prerequisites for Participation," n.d.). Also, now admitted are people with relevant adjudicated sex offences, have served a sentence, or fear committing future offences, referred to as the "Hellfeld" in German, translating to "light field."

PPD demonstrates that many people with sexual attractions to minors can be motivated to make use of therapeutic interventions to prevent the commitment of both contact and non-contact child sex offences ("Results and Publications," n.d.). Although "a cure" in the sense of complete termination of a child-related sexual attraction is not possible, according to current scientific knowledge, PPD has shown the world that the objective lies in working therapeutically with individuals willing to take on this responsibility. They have served as a guiding light for many successive clinical programmes, prevention strategies, and research projects, many of which will be highlighted in this chapter.

"Just Dreaming of Them"

Our work with adults struggling with sexual preference for children… has shown that this issue should be tackled earlier in the adolescence when sexual preferences are manifested. (L. Scheling, personal communication, December 11, 2017)

While widely successful, the PPD is meant for adults. Therefore, in 2014, the Institute for Sexology and Sexual Medicine at the Charité Berlin and the Child and Adolescent Psychiatric Ward at the Vivantes Hospital am Friedrichshain established "Just Dreaming of Them" (L. Scheling, personal communication, December 11, 2017). It can be assumed that the majority of CSA that is committed by juveniles takes place in the Dunkelfeld and remains undetected (Beier et al., 2016). Therefore, PPD's creation of "Just Dreaming of Them" came from an urgent need for a primary prevention programme for juveniles.

Like PPD, "Just Dreaming of Them" started with a media campaign to encourage juveniles to seek professional help, cleverly utilising well-known dinosaur and teddy bear emojis to attract the attention of youth (Beier et al., 2016). Once they are engaged, "Just Dreaming of Them" offers help to those adolescents who experience an attraction to children through their established website and hotline which can be accessed anonymously (Beier et al., 2016). Applying the basic principle that "nobody is responsible for his/her feelings, but everybody is responsible for his/her actions," they provide costless therapy for youth feeling uncertain about their sexual feelings and/or fearful of potential actions ("Just Dreaming of Them," n.d., Section "Our Offer"). Between August 2014 and July 2015, 49 juveniles contacted the project; more than half of these individuals participated in a diagnostic assessment including the assessment of their sexual preference (Beier et al., 2016). About 82.5% of those juveniles who contacted the project had already exhibited CSA behaviours, mostly in the Dunkelfeld (Beier et al., 2016). A high quantity of comorbid psychiatric issues was found among those juveniles involved, confirming the need for these presenting disorders to be considered in the treatment of sexually offending juveniles (Beier et al., 2016).

With the interest of all children at heart, "Just Dreaming of Them" seeks to prevent child sexual victimisation while also sanctioning that "nobody should become an offender" ("Just Dreaming of Them," n.d., Section "For Adults"). Their programme helps youth not become disenfranchised because of their sexual attractions, believing that if help for adult MAPs exists, help for minor-attracted youth should too.

"Troubled Desire"

"Troubled Desire" is an online self-management treatment programme developed by the berlin-based site of the Prevention Network "Kein Täter werden" (L. Scheling, personal communication, December 11, 2017). The objectives of "Troubled Desire" are twofold: the project aims to offer online help as a minimal prevention intervention of CSA including the consumption of CP. This objective also intends to reduce the stress and discomfort associated with sexual attraction towards children (M. Schuler, personal communication, February 22, 2018). "Troubled Desire" also connects international professionals providing preventive treatment.

The "Troubled Desire" self-management tool provides strategies to improve distress symptoms in ways that validate users and integrate their sexual interests without action ("About," 2017). Specifically, this tool is available for individuals who are unable to seek help due to lack of therapeutic support in their area, or to their physical location due to mandatory reporting laws. "Troubled Desire" is anonymous, confidential, costless, and completely free from any conflict of interest. This tool exists to "contribute to the safety of children everywhere and help those with pedophilic inclinations who renounce sexual offending to live a healthy and fulfilling life" ("About," 2017, para 8).

For more information about The German PPD and the Prevention Network "Kein Täter werden" (Don't Offend), visit www.dont-offend.org and the programme specific websites https://www.just-dreaming-of-them.org/ and https://troubled-desire.com/about.html.

Stop It Now! United States

The Stop It Now! campaign, now reaching several countries, was first founded in the United States by Fran Henry, a CSA survivor in 1992. Fran's vision to "have the sexual abuse of children recognized as a preventable public health problem," ("Our Work," n.d.) stemmed from the realisation that society burdened children to recognise and report abuse. Ms. Henry recalls that child victims (and adult victims as well) may not report abuse at the time because they "just want it to stop" and do not have the power to make that happen. From this insight, came the name "Stop It Now!" and the mission directly challenges adults to accept responsibility for recognising, acknowledging, and confronting behaviours leading to abuse ("About Us," n.d.-a).

To address prevention with a public health approach, Stop It Now! uses current scientific research, market research, and programme tracking and evaluation to advance and expand its' programmes ("Our Work," n.d.). By using various methods, such as focus groups, public opinion surveys, and cooperating with leading researchers, Stop It Now! continues to build a theoretical base for practical and effective prevention programmes and materials. They identified the following five community prevention policy goals that they hope to actualise in local communities: promote accurate information, enhance services to CSA victims, provide specialised treatment programmes for sex offenders, offer timely sexuality education, and improve our understanding of behaviours that make children vulnerable ("About Us," n.d.-a).

The first campaign in 1992 was Stop It Now! Vermont, developed to answer initial questions such as *Will abusers and those at risk to abuse respond and reach out for help?* and *Can we change the social climate enough to allow talk about child sexual abuse and ultimately, question sexualised behaviours when we see them?* ("Stop It Now! Vermont," n.d.). This campaign gained state wide recognition, and in 2002 the model was adopted by the U.S. Centers for Disease Control and Prevention with Collaborative Efforts to Prevent the Perpetration of CSA. Over 20 years later, Stop It Now! campaigns exist in Philadelphia, Georgia, Minnesota, Wisconsin, and Connecticut with a sister campaign in the United Kingdom, Ireland, and the Netherlands. Campaign resources include help services in the form of a national confidential Helpline (1.888.PREVENT) and an interactive Online Help Centre; prevention advocacy, prevention education, and technical assistance and training.

Several Stop It Now! campaigns in the United States have been researched and evaluated including Stop It Now! Vermont, Stop It Now! Georgia, and Stop It Now! Minnesota. Results have shown notable success; an example being the decrease in the incidence of CSA in four of the five years that services were implemented in Georgia (Schober, Fawcett, Thigpen, Curtis, & Wright, 2012). Currently, Stop It Now! continues its mission through data analysis of individuals utilising their Helpline. This project will focus on Helpline contacts who are calling about their own thoughts, feelings, and behaviours towards children, with the goal to further expand services and research to adolescents needing support for their own concerns about minor attraction (J. Coleman, ATSA Listserv, January 16, 2018).

For more information about Stop It Now! USA, visit http://www.stopitnow.org/.

B4U-ACT, United States

In 2003, the multi-faceted programme, B4U-ACT, was established with an overall vision to: publicly promote services and resources for MAPs, educate mental health providers regarding helpful treatment approaches for MAPs, develop a pool of helping professionals desiring to serve these individuals, abide by Principles and Perspectives of Practice created by B4U-ACT, and finally, to educate the public about MAP issues ("History," 2018).

Their mission also involves referring MAPs who report suicidal ideations, depression, and/or loneliness to mental health professionals who can support them while acknowledging the impact of their attraction. They also provide answers to questions that are commonly asked by minor attracted individuals, such as *Will I be reported? What is therapy like? How will I know I am progressing in therapy?* along with guidance on questions to ask a potential therapist ("Seeking Therapy," 2018).

To support MAPs in this way, B4U-ACT compiles a list of global mental health professionals through a process where therapists can become signatories to the B4U-ACT treatment practices ("Psychotherapy for the MAP," 2018). MAP clients are also encouraged to leave feedback for signatory therapists to help other MAPs seeking therapy and improve treatment practices. Additionally, in order to educate the public and break the complicated barriers between MAPs and the general beliefs of society, B4U-ACT created an action plan that includes holding workshops for mental health professionals and MAPs together ("History," 2018).

B4U-Act Peer Support

Notably, B4U-ACT provides private and confidential peer support through a password-protected online forum created for MAPs to have the ability to talk with each other about issues related to their emotional wellbeing ("Peer Support," 2018). Topics of discussion may include coping with stigma, fear, and secrecy; finding fulfilling relationships; working with mental health professionals; and living within the law. A private forum also exists for family and friends of MAPs as a way for them to safely support each other ("Support for Family & Friends," 2018).

For more information about B4U-ACT visit http://www.b4uact.org/.

The Centre for Addiction and Mental Health: Sexual Behaviours Clinic, Canada

The Centre for Addiction and Mental Health (CAMH), established 20 years ago, is Canada's largest mental health and addiction teaching hospital, as well as one of the world's leading research centres on addiction and mental health ("Who we are," 2012).

The Sexual Behaviours Clinic (SBC) is a specialty clinic within the CAMH providing services to people with sexual behaviours, fantasies, or urges that may have resulted in personal distress and/or legal involvement. The clinic provides assessment services including pharmacological assessment, individual and group counselling including treatment related to sexual drive, family therapy, and consultation to other agencies and professionals in the field ("Sexual Behaviours Clinic," 2012). The SBC provides the following services to various adult populations:

- Individuals who have been convicted of a sexual offence (contact and/or non-contact) and are serving community sentences
- Individuals within a formal mental health diversion programme
- Individuals who are distressed by their sexual interest and/or behaviours, which may be both legal (such as excessive masturbation and pornography use) and illegal (such as CP)
- Individuals with intellectual disabilities, comorbid mental illness, and/or substance use issues, who are also experiencing underlying challenges and distress due to their sexual interests and/or behaviours.

Notably, the SBC also provides services to families of people who have been convicted of sexual offences, because they believe that stigma from the sexual offence will impact the family's friendships, home, and immigration status ("Assessing sexual re-offence risk: CAMH educates community workers," 2016).

The SBC also provides education to community parole and probation officers, child protection services, and community workers ("Assessing sexual re-offence risk: CAMH educates community workers," 2016). These educational forums provide helping professionals with an overview of assessment tools and related services. As part of a continuing education series held in September 2016, Robert McGrath, psychological services consultant, stated "Among men with a history of sexual offending, some should never have contact with certain children, some may safely have contact with certain children if adequate supervision plans are in place, and some may not pose any clear risk to children." Thus, the SBC is on par with many other prevention projects of its kind as it appears to function on the underlying premise that not all sexual offenders (minor attracted or not) can be viewed or treated with the same lens.

For more information about the SBC at The CAMH, visit http://www.camh.ca/en/hospital/Pages/home.aspx

The Moore Center for the Prevention of Child Sexual Abuse, United States

> *Our vision is a world without child sexual abuse. At the Moore Center for the Prevention of Child Sexual Abuse, we know this kind of abuse is preventable, not inevitable, which is why our work centers on developing strong prevention strategies. We believe that everyone shares the responsibility for prevention, and everyone benefits when children remain safe from abuse.* ("Our Mission, Our Vision," n.d.)

In 2012, a vision for a research centre with a public health approach for the prevention of CSA was realised in the funding of the Moore Center for the Prevention of Child Sexual Abuse by the family of Dr. Stephen and Mrs. Julia Moore ("About Us," n.d.-c). The Moore Center is located within the Johns Hopkins Bloomberg School of Public Health, which is considered an international authority on public health.

Research at the Moore Center develops and evaluates primary prevention interventions that will reduce CSA, such as those mentioned throughout this chapter. Simultaneously, this research seeks to improve understanding of the costs, causes, and consequences of CSA as well as policies that attempt to address it ("Research," n.d.).

The Moore Center's research found that the average age of someone who commits CSA against a prepubescent child is 14 years old (Johns Hopkins Bloomberg School of Public Health, 2016). Therefore, a primary focus of the Moore Center is preventing sexual violence committed by adolescents by employing web-based interventions for parents and teens. Projects at the Moore Center also advocate for the accurate treatment of juveniles, including the development and validation of an actuarial risk assessment tool for juvenile sex offenders and the evaluation of juvenile registration policies ("Moore Center Research Projects," n.d.).

Dr. Elizabeth Letourneau, Director of the Moore Center, asserts that their cutting-edge research and compelling projects will help shift national response away from "ineffective, after-the-fact policies and toward a preventive, public health focus that more effectively protects children from harm" (Johns Hopkins Bloomberg School of Public Health, 2016).

For more information about The Moore Center visit https://jhsph.edu/research/centers-and-institutes/moore-center-for-the-prevention-of-child-sexual-abuse/index.html

StopSO, United Kingdom

Formed in 2012 in the United Kingdom, the Specialist Treatment Organisation for the Prevention of Sexual Offending (StopSO) began as a charity aspiring to reduce sexual offending by providing therapy and support to potential and actual perpetrators, to prevent harm and thus protect society ("Working with sex offenders and paedophiles," n.d.). "I heard of a convicted sex offender who, during treatment, said: *'If I could have accessed help earlier, I would have stopped. I wanted to stop but I couldn't find help anywhere.'* That was the final push for me, and I got together with some colleagues in 2012 to set up StopSO" (Grayson, 2015, p. 9).

With the focus on providing therapeutic intervention and support so desperately wanted by the convicted offender that compelled Grayson to organise StopSO, the first task became training therapists. "We started running courses to teach experienced therapists how to work with this particular client group" explains Grayson (2015, p. 9). Out of the pilot project, StopSO continued training counsellors and psychotherapists. As of December 2017, StopSO had over 200 therapists trained or in training across the United Kingdom and have since opened their training resources to therapists across the globe who are interested in offering treatment to this specialised population (J. Grayson, personal communication, December 7, 2017).

StopSO connects clients with a specially trained therapist, who is geographically close, within their UK-wide independent network of qualified and experienced professionals ("Working with sex offenders and paedophiles," n.d.). Professionals in the StopSO network are supervised, and include psychologists, psychotherapists, and doctors ("About Us," 2018). Along with specialised training and supervision, StopSO provides these professionals who work with sex offenders an online support network and access to effective and applicable research. Services provided by StopSO therapists and other professionals include comprehensive risk assessments, biopsychosocial assessments; individual therapy; couples therapy; group work including Pesso Boyden System Psychomotor Therapy; advocacy and support for individuals going through the court process, and an online support network for families of offenders.

The StopSO network offers these services to individuals at risk of sexual offending or are concerned about their behaviour, non-offending paedophiles, individuals who have been cautioned, charged with, or convicted of a sexual offence, individuals fearful of reoffending, individuals who are incarcerated, and partners and families of anyone previously mentioned ("About Us," 2018). Between June 1, 2013 and August 31, 2017, 916 people contacted StopSO for help, of which 61% disclosed issues related to CSA ("Statistics3, StopSO Statistics to 31st August 2017," 2018). In August 2017, StopSO compiled the following statistics representative of the reasons why individuals seek the help of their network:

- 42% reported needing help with viewing child abuse images (i.e. child pornography)
- 13% was a family member wanting to help
- 8% reported needing help due to a "contact offense against a child"
- 6% reported troubling thoughts about an adult
- 6% reported troubling thoughts about a child
- 2% reported needing help due to a "non-contact offense against a child"
- 1% reported sexually harming a child ("Statistics3, StopSO Statistics to 31st August 2017," 2018).

While working with this population, StopSO takes a stance against the mandatory reporting of child abuse: "As we see it, it is vital that we maintain the current status of therapists in private practice not legally being required to report sexual offenders. This will enable the perpetrators struggling with their behaviour, who want to change, to come forward for help. Giving them therapy will reduce the number of victims that are created" (Grayson, 2015, p. 13).

StopSO has announced that in Summer 2018, they will expand their services to CSA survivors (J. Grayson, personal communication, December 7, 2017). StopSO will then officially change their name to StopSO: The Specialist Treatment Organisation for Perpetrators and Survivors of Sexual Offences, with the main focus of working with individuals who have sexually offended or the potential to sexually offend.

To learn more about StopSO visit https://www.stopso.org.uk/about/.

The Prevention Project™ Utah, United States

The Prevention Project™ Utah, United States, is a global prevention effort addressing risky sexual thoughts, fantasies, and non-contact problematic sexual behaviour. Candice Christiansen, CSA survivor and licensed therapist, founded and established The Prevention Project™ Utah in 2013. Their mission is to provide accurate interventions, compassionate mental health support, and psycho-educational resources with the vision of educating the global community on the importance of these resources and interventions ("A Global Prevention-Education Effort...," 2017).

The population served comprises both legally involved individuals and those seeking therapeutic services before legal involvement occurs, all with a desire to prevent offending behaviour. Specific treatment tracks offered are based on the type of sexual issue or behaviour. As part of treatment, the project also identifies and treats those who may have a sexual preoccupation. This is especially important, since, according to Marshall and Marshall (2012), a considerable number of sexual offenders meet criteria for sexual preoccupation, which has been identified as a dynamic risk factor of recidivism. Additionally, research indicates individuals on the Autism Spectrum and those suffering from a traumatic brain injury (TBI) who are involved in the criminal justice system do not have the same criminogenic factors or needs as those who are neurotypical (Mahoney, 2009; Alnemari, Mansour, Buehler, & Gaudin, 2016). Therefore, The Prevention Project™ Utah, United States, also specialises in treating offenders with neurodiverse issues.

The MAPs Programme

Officially launching in 2016 after treating MAPs individually since 2013, the MAPs Programme is a nationally recognised programme with the motto, "Everyone Deserves Support." The Prevention Project™ created a MAPs curriculum after several clients, male and female, sought them out for help with managing their attractions to minors. Some of these early clients felt addicted to CP, while others were experiencing severely distressing symptoms related to their attractions.

Believing this to be an "unchosen condition," The Prevention Project™ follows in the footsteps of programmes like the PPD, by providing global psycho-educational support for men and women who are seeking support with managing their sexual age orientation to minors and are not legally involved ("Everyone Deserves Support," 2017). The curriculum addresses several underlying issues in the treatment of non-offending, anti-contact MAPs including addressing symptoms of distress and in some cases, sexual preoccupation. Simultaneously, the project's curriculum explores sexual orientation and how to cope and manage the shame and guilt that stems from these stigmatized attractions. The heavy focus on shame resilience is also consistent with the research by Cantor and McPhail (2016), cautioning clinicians to consider the stigma-related stressors of anti-contact, non-offending MAPs. Finally, the exploration of what healthy sexuality and fulfilling relationships mean to each participant is also an integral part of the MAPs programme, similar to the compassion-focused approach of the Safer Living Foundation, a UK programme highlighted in a later chapter. The intention of the MAPs programme does not stop at prevention, but also seeks to improve the well-being of MAPs globally.

The Prevention Podcast™

In January 2018, The Prevention Project™ Utah, United States, launched The Prevention Podcast™ with the goal of educating the global community on sexual violence prevention by interviewing professionals in the field of research, individuals associated with global prevention initiatives, as well as individuals living in the midst of various issues uncovered by this research and observed by various prevention efforts ("The Prevention Podcast," 2018). The podcast began by featuring a series on "non-offending, anti-contact paedophiles." Since its' publication, this podcast has reached over 40 different countries and continues to be a source of awareness and education regarding issues that fuel the global prevention effort.

For more information about The Prevention Project™ Utah, United States and the derivative programmes, visit http://www.theprevention-project.org/ and http://www.thepreventionpodcast.com/.

Tulir: Centre for the Prevention and Healing of Child Sexual Abuse, India

"Tulir" in Tamil, a language primarily spoken by the Tamil people of India and Sri Lanka, means *"the first tender leaves of a plant; leaves fol-*

lowing a period of adversity" ("About Us," n.d.-b). For Tulir, Centre for the Prevention & Healing of Child Sexual Abuse (CPHCSA), this term symbolises children, and the belief of their inherent resilience and resurgence. India shelters 430 million children, which is approximately one in five of all children globally ("The Scene of Child Sexual Abuse in India," n.d.).

Tulir—CPHCSA is a registered, non-governmental, non-profit organisation committed to counteracting CSA in India. Their foundational belief is acknowledging CSA by creating proactive steps to respond by ensuring children benefit by feeling safe ("About Us," n.d.-b). Like many other prevention efforts, they view CSA as a serious preventable public health concern that needs addressing.

The mission of Tulir—CPHCSA states that "preventing and healing child sexual abuse require equal parts of caring, optimism and pragmatism. We must care deeply for our children, be optimistic about human being's capabilities for change and be pragmatic about how to work with children and the larger community to bring about positive transformation" ("Mission Statement," n.d.). Their primary objectives include:

- Supporting and participating in local, national, and international efforts to promote and protect the rights of children
- Raising awareness of CSA
- Improving policy and advancing the prevention of CSA with a special emphasis on the psychosocial well-being of children
- Providing direct intervention services in prevention and healing CSA
- Undertaking research, documentation, and dissemination of CSA information ("Objectives," n.d.).

Following their objectives, Tulir—CPHCSA offers the following services: resource development, personal safety education, healing and intervention, training and consultancy, advocacy, networking, and research.

Basic to Tulir-CPHCSA's philosophy of supporting abused children in their journey of healing is belief in the innate ability of the human spirit to prevail and every child's unique strengths and resilience. Furthermore, Tulir-CPHCSA recognizes the significance of family and community in a child's life and is committed to working holistically towards empowering children triumph over abuse and towards normalcy ("Mission Statement," n.d.).

For more information about Tulir—Centre for the Prevention & Healing of Child Sexual Abuse (CPHCSA), visit http://www.tulir.org/index.html.

The Association Une Vie®: PedoHelp® Project, France

The Association Une Vie® is a French non-profit association founded in 2017. They created the PedoHelp® project due to concerns of the CSA global epidemic and the myriad of associated detrimental long-term consequences (Association Une Vie, 2017). PedoHelp® is a global information and multi-targeted prevention project offering concrete and free solutions to CSA prevention.

With the mantra "No Shame, No Taboo," this costless project seeks to raise global awareness to decrease CSA internationally, guided by the belief that "the more people are informed, the fewer victims there will be" ("About the Project," 2015–2018). What was produced from the PedoHelp® project was a multi-target prevention kit, designed for inclusive, international use. This prevention kit is simultaneously a primary, secondary, and tertiary prevention measure, containing various tools on multiple medias (Association Une Vie, 2017). This kit is currently available in French and English with the goal of being translated into additional languages. The associated websites are currently available in French, English, German, Spanish, Italian, Dutch, and Polish.

Consistent with the other programmes outlined in this chapter, Association Une Vie® and the PedoHelp® project agree the majority of child sex offenders feel overwhelmed by their actions and do not agree with them morally. Thus, they believe offering accessible tools to individuals with an attraction to children may help them avoid acting on these attractions (Association Une Vie, 2017).

In addition to targeting MAPs, they believe providing training and other interventions helps expose this population to professionals and the general public. Therefore, they present locally and abroad on the PedoHelp® project and the accompanying prevention kit (Association Une Vie, 2017).

For more information about The Association Une Vie®, visit https://pedo.help/ and https://nonono.help/ (for kids).

Online Forums and Peer Led Support for MAPs

I feel very strongly that this is something that we have to raise visibility of. I know that up until now any sympathetic approach to paedophiles has always been based on the assumption that helping paedophiles helps prevent child abuse. And while that is technically correct, it misses the point that paedophiles are also human beings worthy of being helped in their own right, that we also deserve to be able to live happy lives, and that that in itself is a sufficiently good reason to help paedophiles (Personal Communication, Ender Wiggin, December 22, 2017).

Well known (by his username) non-offending, anti-contact MAP, Ender Wiggin, voices his concern about the rates of distress, particularly suicidality, among the MAP population. Undoubtedly due to the complex array of painful issues caused by having sexual attractions to children and the lack of widespread therapeutic resources, individuals like Ender, who are committed to non-offending and anti-contact, have created their own support systems. Although support forums exist, the support services to follow are highlighted for their creation by non-offending, anti-contact MAPs.

Schicksal und Herausforderung

Privately operated, Schicksal und Herausforderung (SuH) is an online support resource run by two non-offending, anti-contact paedophiles, known as Newman and Max, both of whom have participated in behavioural therapy under the PPD ("About Us," 2018). Also, on the SuH team is a former CSA victim and the site's current technical advisor, Leon ("Destiny and Challenge Living with Pedophilia," 2018). Their goal is to be a point of contact for individuals seeking advice regarding their sexual attractions, and giving a voice to those who have been affected by paedophilia, with the spirit of child protection and human dignity.

Predominantly, SuH seeks to provide users with background information on paedophilia, specifically the theories and recent understanding around cause, manifestations, and living with it ("Destiny and Challenge Living with Pedophilia," 2018). While the website adamantly informs users, it is not clinical or part of therapy services in any way, like many MAP resources, it includes information on different forms of therapy available and some address treatment centres in Germany and German-speaking countries. SuH also sponsors a support forum, dubbed "Together, not alone."

"Together, Not Alone"

"Together, not alone" is accessible to anyone over the age of 14 with a connection to paedophilia. Users may include those who are struggling with minor attractions themselves or those dealing with these issues in their lives for other reasons ("Startseite," n.d.). Through this forum, SuH recognises that dealing with paedophilia leads to both contradictory and distressed feelings. Therefore, to SuH, the "Together" platform is more than just support, but includes sharing experiences to reduce prejudice and help users feel a sense of understanding of their own reality and establish a sense of well-being. Consistent with the SuH main website, "Together" participants must accept the intolerance for sexual acts between adults and children. While factual conversations about this topic are allowed, "Together" strongly states any "pro-contact" discussion or efforts to change laws on sexual activities with children are not welcome. To keep the forum safe and consistent with SuH values, moderators exist to prevent disrespectful, inappropriate, or illegal activities from occurring within the site.

Step Out of the Shadows: Celibate Paedophiles

SuH administrators, Max and Leon, created a sister project, under the title "Step out of the Shadows" ("About Us," 2018). This long-term project began as an art project made from the global contributions of many paedophiles with the following aspirations:

- Reduce stigma by presenting a class of non-offending paedophiles; making clear that attraction or desire does not equal offending or being a "time bomb."
- Provide non-offending paedophiles the ability to express themselves through art, allowing these individuals to express the psychological burden and social strain that comes with being attracted to minors and the consequences of felt stigma.
- Encourage other paedophiles and MAPs to not offend by showing that non-offending, anti-contact paedophiles exist and live happy and fulfilling lives. ("About the Project," n.d.)

To achieve these objectives, Step out of the Shadows aims to build an online gallery made up of anonymous "self-introductions" of many non-offending paedophiles from all over the world ("About the Project," n.d.). This introduction includes who he or she is (which is requested to include nationality and identified gender), what makes up his/her personality, and insights about his or her feelings and dreams—including connection to their paedophilia or not. Participants will also design a picture or image included with their introduction creating a final piece that displays "This is me!" and in doing so, combats societal stereotypes about paedophiles; "We want to portray responsible and child-celibate pedophiles from around the world who want to step out of the dark and show the world that they are people, too" ("About the Project," n.d., para. 1).

This project was inspired by the AIDS Memorial Quilt, a large blanket made from thousands of pieces, each signifying someone who has died of AIDS during a time when communities gave no actual funerals or graves to these individuals ("About the Idea," n.d.). Step out of the Shadows believes today, paedophiles face similar discrimination. The Step out of the Shadows gallery will mirror the quilt, with each patch representing some piece of a person's life who is committed to non-offending and well-being, while faced with paedophilia.

At the time of this publication, this project was at its beginning stages, but currently has global support, including people from the United States and other countries assisting in website translation and maintaining the projects' character and vision ("About the Project," n.d.).

For more information about Schicksal & Herausforderung and their *"Together, not alone"* forum, visit http://www.schicksal-und-herausforderung.de/ and their sister project, Step Out of the Shadows visit http://www.shadowsproject.net/lang/en/index.html.

Virtuous Pedophiles

> *Virtuous Pedophiles is really just two things: a website and a peer support group. There is no formal organization or even a bank account....* (E. Edwards, personal communication, December 18, 2017)

Founded by Nick Devin and Ethan Edwards (both pseudonyms), Virtuous Pedophiles (VirPed) went live in June of 2012, as a spinoff of the B4U-ACT support group, with the intention of reducing stigma of paedophilia by advocating for the substantial number of non-offending paedophiles ("Who We Are," 2012–2018; E. Edwards, personal communication, December 18, 2017; G. Gibson, personal communication, December 7, 2017). VirPed also seeks to provide support, information, and available resources to support non-offending MAPs "remain law-abiding, and lead happy, productive lives" ("Who We Are," 2012–2018).

The VirPed website provides a "one stop shop" for information, education, and current research on paedophilia, non-offending, and/or anti-contact MAPs. Their site offers supportive pages with the following topics: "*If you are a pedophile*" advice and therapist directories; "*For young pedophiles*"; "*For partners*"; "*Advice for therapists*"; "*For everyone*"; and "*F.A.Q. and resources*" with links to research, other prevention projects, and media articles ("Getting Help & Being Helpful," 2012–2018). Correspondingly, VirPed has gathered international media attention and become a place where journalists seek individuals to interview on the subject of paedophilia (E. Edwards, personal communication, December 18, 2017).

VirPed Peer Support

Using Google Group, VirPed started a peer support group in September 2013, which as of this publication has over 2500 registered users who recognise they are attracted to minors with no desire to act on it (E. Edwards, personal communication, December 18, 2017). Of the active users, most are in their 20s, with approximately 90% being male. Additionally, members come from all over the world with considerable numbers from the United States, Canada, the United Kingdom, and Germany. Mental health professionals, researchers, and family and friends of MAPs are also allowed to join for support and information. Due to the size of VirPed's peer support, it is often where researchers go to find samples of non-offending MAPs.

Forum discussions include over 12,000 topics, including personal stories, positive and negative experiences with mental health professionals, legal ways of satisfying sexual desire, experiences with coming out, dreams for the future, and living the best life you can as a minor attracted individual (E. Edwards, personal communication, December 18, 2017). The group has no professional control of discussions; however, moderators are present to help members abide by the official rules of the discussion forum (G. Gibson, personal communication, December 7, 2017).

Founder, Ethan Edwards estimates approximately 3500 paedophiles have reached out to the VirPed website since it went live and finds many of these users report assurance by the VirPed stance and philosophy, calling themselves "non-offending" as well. Additionally, many therapists refer their MAP clients to VirPed as an added resource. Consistent with the psychological burdens of paedophilia previously mentioned, Edwards notes many VirPed users deal with depression, isolation, and for some, self-hatred (E. Edwards, personal communication, December 18, 2017).

For more information about VirPed or to become involved, visit http://virped.org/ or contact them via email at virpeds@gmail.com.

The Association for Sexual Abuse Prevention

Incorporated as a non-profit organisation in March of 2015 by Gary Gibson, his wife, Tabitha Abel, and Todd Cooper, the Association for Sexual Abuse Prevention (ASAP) is dedicated to the primary prevention of CSA ("Home," 2018; "About Us," 2017). Founded in part by MAPs, ASAP helps combat CSA by:

- Preventing CSA by making therapy accessible to MAPs
- Educating therapists and the public

- Connecting any MAPs to qualified therapists
- Obtaining funding for MAP treatment programs through donations and grant writing; and lastly
- Researching the risks leading to sexual interactions with children through their internally developed Sexual Abuse Risk Assessment (SARA) tool. ("About Us," 2017)

Individuals can contact ASAP for support through phone or email. Contact is free and confidential, although if an individual is then referred for in-person therapy, ASAP assists in making any fees set by the therapist and limits to confidentiality known ("Home," 2018). When connecting MAPs to local therapists, ASAP aligns with affirmative interventions, warning about "misguided therapy" such as "praying the paedophilia away"; conversion or reparative therapies; and the "ticking time bomb" approach, which views paedophiles as waiting for the opportunity to offend ("Affirmative Therapy," 2016).

For more information about The ASAP, visit http://www.asapinternational.org/index.html.

Czechoslovak Paedophile Community

Czechoslovak Paedophile Community (ČEPEK), an online Czechoslovak paedophile community, describes itself as a group coming together around the topic of erotic affection for children ("ČEPEK – Czechoslovak Pedophile Community," 2018). Members include both paedophilic or minor-attracted individuals, as well as MAP supporters. They astutely acknowledge that each member is a unique person and should not be defined by his or her attractions. ČEPEK makes an effort to include anyone needing help or assistance, but like forums mentioned previously, employs a strict "no tolerance" policy of illegal behaviour.

The primary mission of ČEPEK is to provide information about paedophilia, particularly to youth who feel they have minor attractions ("ČEPEK – Czechoslovak Pedophile Community," 2018). Consistent with B4U-ACT, ČEPEK targets youth who feel minor attracted and gives them resources to cope with their sexuality. Information available on their community website covers topics such as "coming out," identifying risky situations, understanding consequences, help for those seeking professional assistance, and dating and companionship. Members of ČEPEK also help each other by sharing personal stories and experiences, thus inspiring one another that it is possible to live a happy and fulfilling life without causing harm. Members also believe sharing their stories may serve as warnings about what can happen when they fail to suppress their sexuality. In some cases, they aid in the referral of distressed individuals to local sexologists via anonymous inquiries to the Advisory Centre for Czech and Slovak Paedophiles.

Like many other MAP support groups, ČEPEK also informs the public about paedophilia because vocalising the term is too often confused with the sexual abuse of children ("ČEPEK – Czechoslovak Pedophile Community," 2018). ČEPEK is adamant they are not for the legalisation of sexual acts with children, lowering the age of consent, or justifying child sex offences in any way. They are vocal about their adherence to laws and societal standards and make it a part of their mission to help others do the same.

For more information about ČEPEK, visit http://www.pedofilie-info.cz/.

Chapter Summary

The prevention initiatives presented in this chapter target a wide and varied population; however, what they all have in common is the aim to engage adults (and in some cases adolescents) who feel they are at risk to offend sexually. This advance in prevention work is different from previous efforts that focus solely on keeping children safe without addressing the individual responsible (or potentially responsible) for the abuse.

In response to research, many prevention initiatives target individuals who fear they may commit a sexual offence, specifically towards children, due to attractions towards minors, risky thoughts and fantasies, and/or sexual preoccupation. These individuals, referred to as "potential offenders" by some, while also known as "non-offending," "anti-contact," or "minor attracted" to others, have not acted on their behaviours and have no desire to do so. These individuals typically self-seek mental health intervention due to psychological burdens stemming from their attractions. Others who may self-seek any prevention projects or support services featured in this chapter include individuals who may have engaged in sexual offending behaviour but are not legally involved. The belief that individuals will self-seek services if prevention initiatives exist is foundational for the projects featured in this chapter.

Although "prevention" has the feel of a recent buzzword, the projects and initiatives in this chapter have existed for over two decades. Furthermore, the work of these programmes has influenced other countries and communities, several organisations, thousands of professionals, and undoubtedly countless individuals committed to the prevention of CSA.

References

A Global Prevention-Education Effort Addressing Risky Sexual Thoughts, Fantasies, Behavior & Mental Wellness in Adult Men and Women. (2017). Retrieved from http://www.thepreventionproject.org/
About. (2017). Retrieved from https://troubled-desire.com/about.html
About the Idea. (n.d.). Retrieved from http://www.shadowsproject.net/lang/en/About2_en.html
About the Project. (2015–2018). Retrieved from https://pedo.help/about/
About the Project. (n.d.). Retrieved from http://www.shadowsproject.net/lang/en/About1_en.html
About Us. (2017). Retrieved from http://www.asapinternational.org/about-us.html
About Us. (2018). Retrieved from http://www.schicksal-und-herausforderung.de/ueber-uns/
About Us. (n.d.-a). Retrieved from http://www.stopitnow.org/our-work/about-us
About Us. (n.d.-b). Retrieved from http://www.tulir.org/about_us.htm
About Us. (n.d.-c). Retrieved from https://www.jhsph.edu/research/centers-and-institutes/moore-center-for-the-prevention-of-child-sexual-abuse/about-us/
Affirmative Therapy. (2016). Retrieved from http://www.asapinternational.org/affirmative-therapy.html

Alnemari, A. M., Mansour, T. R., Buehler, M., & Gaudin, D. (2016). Neural basis of pedophilia: Altered sexual preference following traumatic brain injury. *International Journal of Surgery Case Reports, 25,* 221–224.

Assessing Sexual Re-offence Risk: CAMH Educates Community Workers. (2016). Retrieved from http://www.camh.ca/en/hospital/about_camh/newsroom/CAMH_in_the_headlines/stories/Pages/CAMH-educates-community-workers.aspx

Association Une Vie. (2017). PedoHelp® project 2015–2020L prevention of sexual violence against children project.

Bailey, J. M., & Hsu, K. J. (2016). An internet study of men sexually attracted to children: Sexual attraction patterns. *Journal of Abnormal Psychology, 125*(7), 976–988.

Beier, K. M., Ahlers, C. J., Goecker, D., Neutze, J., Mundt, I. A., Hupp, E., et al. (2009). Can pedophiles be reached for primary prevention of child abuse? First results of the Berlin Prevention Project Dunkelfeld (PPD). *The Journal of Forensic Psychiatry & Psychology, 20*(6), 851–867. https://doi.org/10.1080/14789940903174188.

Beier, K. M., Grundmann, D., Kuhle, L. F., Scherner, G., Konrad, A., & Amelung, T. (2015). The German Dunkelfeld project: A pilot study to prevent child sexual abuse and the use of child abusive images. *The Journal of Sexual Medicine, 12*(2), 529–542.

Beier, K. M., Neutze, J., Mundt, I. A., Ahlers, C. J., Goecker, D., Konrad, A., et al. (2009). Encouraging self-identified pedophiles and hebephiles to seek professional help: First results of the Prevention Project Dunkelfeld (PPD). *Child Abuse & Neglect, 33,* 545–549.

Beier, K. M., Oezdemir, U. C., Schlinzig, E., Groll, A., Hupp, E., & Hellenschmidt, T. (2016). "Just dreaming of them": The Berlin project for primary prevention of child sexual abuse by juveniles (PPJ). *Child Abuse & Neglect, 52,* 1–10.

Berlin, F. S. (2014). Pedophilia and DSM-5: The importance of clearly defining the nature of a pedophilic disorder. *Journal of the American Academy of Psychiatry and the Law, 42,* 404–407.

Cantor, J. M., & McPhail, I. (2016). Non-offending pedophiles. *Current Sexual Health Reports, 8,* 121–128.

ČEPEK – Czechoslovak Pedophile Community. (2018). Retrieved from http://www.pedofilie-info.cz/cepek-ceskoslovenska-pedofilni-komunita/

Christiansen, C., Martinez-Dettamanti, M., & Warner, M. (2018, January 1). Interview with a female, anti-contact pedophile named "Emma". *The*

Prevention Podcast. Podcast retrieved from http://thepreventionpodcast.com/interview-with-female-anti-contact-pedophile-emma

Destiny and Challenge Living with Pedophilia. (2018). Retrieved from http://www.schicksal-und-herausforderung.de/

Everyone Deserves Support. (2017). Retrieved from http://www.thepreventionproject.org/

Getting Help & Being Helpful. (2012–2018). Retrieved from http://virped.org/giving-getting-help.html

Goals. (n.d.). Retrieved from https://www.dont-offend.org/story/goals.html

Grayson, J. (2015). Sex offenders, pornography and the workplace. *Perspectives: Counseling at Work*, pp. 8–13.

History. (2018). Retrieved from http://www.b4uact.org/about-us/history/

Home. (2018). Retrieved from http://www.asapinternational.org/index.html

Johns Hopkins Bloomberg School of Public Health. (2016). Moore center for the prevention of child sexual abuse: Policy and prevention (2016 annual report).

Just Dreaming of Them. (n.d.). Retrieved from https://www.just-dreaming-of-them.org/

Learn. (2018). Retrieved from http://www.b4uact.org/know-the-facts/

Mahoney, M. (2009). *Asperger's syndrome and the criminal law: The special case of child pornography*. Assisted by Aygun, S., & Polen, M., Law Student Clerks. Buffalo, NY: Mark J. Mahoney.

Marshall, W. L., & Marshall, L. E. (2012). Treatment of sexual offenders: Effective elements and appropriate outcome evaluations. *Perspectives on Evaluating Criminal Justice and Corrections, 13*, 71–94. https://doi.org/10.1108/S1474-7863(2012)0000013008.

Mission Statement. (n.d.). Retrieved from About Us. (n.d.-b). Retrieved from http://www.tulir.org/mission_statement.htm

Moore Center Research Projects. (n.d.). Retrieved from https://www.jhsph.edu/research/centers-and-institutes/moore-center-for-the-prevention-of-child-sexual-abuse/research/projects.html

Objectives. (n.d.). Retrieved from http://www.tulir.org/objective.htm

Our Mission, Our Vision. (n.d.). Retrieved from https://www.jhsph.edu/research/centers-and-institutes/moore-center-for-the-prevention-of-child-sexual-abuse/about-us/mission-vision.html

Our Work. (n.d.). Retrieved from http://www.stopitnow.org/about-us

Peer Support. (2018). Retrieved from http://www.b4uact.org/attracted-to-minors/peer-support/

Prerequisites for Participation. (n.d.). Retrieved from https://www.dont-offend.org/story/prerequisites-for-participation.html

Psychotherapy for the MAP. (2018). Retrieved from http://www.b4uact.org/gallery-2-columns-filter/psychotherapy-for-the-map/

Research. (n.d.). Retrieved from https://www.jhsph.edu/research/centers-and-institutes/moore-center-for-the-prevention-of-child-sexual-abuse/research/

Results and Publications. (n.d.). Retrieved from https://www.dont-offend.org/story/results-publications.html

Schaefer, G. A., Feelgood, S., Mundt, I., Beier, K. M., Hupp, E., Neutze, J., et al. (2010). Potential and Dunkelfeld offenders: Two neglected target groups for the prevention of child sex abuse. *International Journal of Law and Psychiatry, 33*(3), 154–163.

Schober, D. J., Fawcett, S. B., Thigpen, S., Curtis, A., & Wright, R. (2012). An empirical case study of a child sexual abuse prevention initiative in Georgia. *Health Education Journal, 71*(3), 291–298.

Seeking Therapy. (2018). Retrieved from http://www.b4uact.org/attracted-to-minors/professional-support/

Seto, M. C. (2017). The puzzle of male chronophilias. *Archives of Sexual Behavior, 46*(1), 3–22.

Sexual Behaviours Clinic. (2012). Retrieved from http://www.camh.ca/en/hospital/care_program_and_services/specialty_clinics/Pages/Sexual-Behaviours-Clinic.aspx

Startseite. (n.d.). Retrieved from https://forum.schicksal-und-herausforderung.de/

Statistics3, StopSO Statistics to 31st August 2017. (2018). Retrieved from https://www.stopso.org.uk/statistics3/

Stop It Now! Vermont. (n.d.). Retrieved from http://www.stopitnow.org/our-work/about-us/prevention-advocacy/stop-it-now-vermont

Support for Family & Friends. (2018). Retrieved from http://www.b4uact.org/attracted-to-minors/support-for-family-friends-2/

The Prevention Podcast. (2018). Retrieved from http://thepreventionpodcast.com/

The Scene of Child Sexual Abuse (CSA) in India. (n.d.). Retrieved from https://www.jaagore.com/current-issues/the-scene-of-child-sexual-abuse-csa-in-india).

Who We Are. (2012). Retrieved from http://www.camh.ca/en/hospital/about_camh/who_we_are/Pages/who_we_are.aspx

Who We Are. (2012–2018). Retrieved from http://virped.org/who-we-are.html

Working with Sex Offenders and Paedophiles. (n.d.). Retrieved from http://www.thecitizenonline.net/sc-main-007.html

3

The Lucy Faithfull Foundation: Twenty-Five Years of Child Protection and Preventing Child Sexual Abuse

Alexandra Bailey, Tom Squire, and Lisa Thornhill

Introduction

The Lucy Faithfull Foundation (LFF) is the only UK-wide child protection (CP) charity dedicated solely to preventing child sexual abuse (CSA). Established in 1992, LFF takes its name from its founder, Baroness Lucy Faithfull of Wolvercote (1910–1996). Baroness Faithfull was the first ever social worker to be given a seat in the House of Lords. She created and chaired the All Party Parliamentary Group for Children, which had a huge influence on the Children Act of 1989, and earned her (playful) nickname 'Baroness Faithless' for her expert scrutiny of the country's CP policies, and ensuring the voices of children and families were heard. Those that knew her describe her as '*kind, generous and lovable*' (Philpot, 1996). As an organisation, LFF has tried to emulate Baroness Faithfull's ethics and continue to ensure the safety and welfare of children.

A. Bailey (✉) • T. Squire • L. Thornhill
Lucy Faithfull Foundation, Epsom, UK
e-mail: abailey@lucyfaithfull.org.uk; tsquire@lucyfaithfull.org.uk; lthornhill@lucyfaithfull.org.uk

For the last 25 years, LFF has worked to prevent abuse in the first instance, as well as prevent repeat victimisation. LFF delivers a wide range of services, including assessments and intervention of alleged and convicted abusers, non-abusing partners, and young people (YP) who exhibit harmful sexual behaviour (HSB). LFF also delivers training on a range of subjects, including working with offenders and families, the prevention of abuse, safer recruitment, and child sexual exploitation.

This chapter will explore LFF's services with those detected for committing sexual offences, or displaying HSB, and then move on to review LFF's prevention initiatives, aimed at averting sexual abuse in the first instance or prior to detection by law enforcement.

The Wolvercote Clinic

The first notable LFF service was the Wolvercote Clinic in Surrey, a residential assessment and treatment facility for men who had engaged in sexually abusive behaviour towards children. Referrals stemmed from statutory agencies, like the Probation and Prison Services, as well as solicitors, faith organisations, and self-referrals. Treatment would occur over, typically, a 12-month period. It would comprise group work, individual sessions, and ongoing psychological testing, with a primary cognitive-behavioural focus.

Ford and Beech (2004) cited a reconviction rate of 10% for residents who completed the programme after a two-year follow-up period, and that those who re-offended were predicted to be at high or very high risk. No residents who were 'treated' (post-treatment psychometric scores falling within the non-offending range) at the end of the programme were reconvicted of a sexual offence within the follow-up time, with 86% of those deemed to be 'untreated' also not being reconvicted. It was reported that *'the Wolvercote programme was able to effect change in 20% of High Deviance offenders for whom previous treatment had been unsuccessful'* (Ford & Beech, 2004, p. 2). As with the majority of treatment programmes, it cannot be known with certainty that this cited change was solely down to the Wolvercote programme; however, the clinic was deemed successful. It was with great disappointment that the clinic closed in 2002 due to the selling of the land for development. However, some ex-residents remain in contact with LFF and access other LFF services for support to remain offence-free.

Work with Young People Who Exhibit HSB

Since 2001, LFF has provided services for YP who exhibit HSB, within young offenders institutes and the community. Notably, LFF was commissioned by the Youth Justice Board, a contract that lasted three years, to undertake work with YP in custody. The work catered to the needs of YP who had been convicted of a sexual offence, through assessment, intervention, and case consultancy. The service developed to include a group work programme, staff training, and placement preparations.

The service was evaluated in-house, with both YP and the professionals working with them, such as Youth Offending Team (YOT) workers, being asked about their experience of the service. Feedback suggested that the service impacted issues such as release planning, supervision requirements, and risk management:

> *'I found the feedback from (LFF practitioner) was invaluable in terms of planning for (young person's) release and formulating requirements to be included in his Notice of Supervision'*. (YOT worker)

> *'We completed all targets set. I've learnt to moderate myself, learnt about my offending and lowered my risk'*. (YP)

In 2012, NatCen Social Research conducted an independent evaluation of LFF's YP services (Brown, McNaughton Nicholls, Webster, & Kenny, 2012). The evaluation stated that YP were given support and an opportunity to complete offence-related work which may not have been available to them otherwise, and that staff and agencies were better informed about the young person and HSB. The evaluation concluded that this information assisted with decision making, sentence planning, and risk management. However, the report highlighted that these particular YP often remain with challenging and complex needs, and a need for further intervention or support.

Work with Women Who Sexually Offend

The reported conviction and recidivism rates of female sexual offending are low (Cortoni, Hanson, & Coache, 2010; Ford, 2006), meaning that understanding around women who sexually abuse remains in its infancy. Additionally, male risk assessment and intervention tools are deemed inappropriate for use with women.

From the clinical histories of women who sexually offended, LFF developed an assessment coding framework (Elliott, Eldridge, Ashfield, & Beech, 2010). The framework, which is a case formulation tool, aims to aid the identification of deficits and strengths presented by women who sexually offend, which could feed into an assessment of potential harm and treatment need for use in criminal justice and family court settings.

A further aim of the assessment framework is to incorporate the women's strengths and ability to reduce her own risk. There has been increasing interest in the importance of understanding and harnessing the role of strengths, resilience, and protective factors in helping individuals develop more positive lifestyles (Masten & Obradovic, 2006).

The LFF Assessment Framework for Female Sexual Abusers version 2.0 contains five sections: Developmental Factors, Psychological Dispositions, Environmental Niche Factors, Acute Factors, and Protective Factors (Eldridge, Elliott, Gillespie, Bailey, & Beech, in press).

For intervention with women, LFF recognise the importance of a gender responsive approach (Eldridge, Bailey, & Brotherson, in press). Benedict (2005) proposes that at minimum each programme component for women should integrate five core areas: relational, strengths-based, trauma-informed, culturally competent, and holistic. LFF took a strengths-based approach with the 'New Life' programme (Eldridge & Saradjian, unpublished), highlighting the need to value and utilise the woman's positive qualities.

Although work with women is not a common occurrence for LFF, it is an area where LFF holds particular expertise.

LFF Prevention Initiatives

LFF recognises the need for more direct engagement with the public, and that the most effective CP initiatives need to engage all of society, including those at risk of causing sexual harm. LFF has always believed that addressing risk directly with those who pose a risk is important for preventing CSA. However, existing services primarily focussed on preventing abuse after it had occurred, such as traditional treatment programmes. LFF recognised the limited opportunity for those concerned about their own behaviour to seek help, without fearing the potential legal consequences. In addition, a lack of services existed to help empower other adults to protect children from harm. LFF believes that CP is the responsibility of all adults and therefore focussed its attention on developing projects aimed at preventing CSA through public engagement.

LFF projects focus across the different levels of the prevention framework and therefore include primary, secondary, and tertiary prevention initiatives. Primary prevention targets whole populations before abuse has occurred to prevent initial victimisation and perpetration, secondary prevention focuses on 'at risk' groups, whilst tertiary prevention addresses the consequences of abuse in order to prevent reoccurrence. This chapter explores the most notable LFF projects within this framework.

Stop It Now! United Kingdom and Ireland

LFF's emphasis on public engagement prevention initiatives resulted in the development of the Stop it Now! United Kingdom and Ireland campaign, and most notably, the Stop it Now! Helpline. The Stop it Now! campaign aims to increase awareness of CSA and encourage all adults to play their part in protecting children. The Stop it Now! Helpline, and its affiliate email support, is anonymous and confidential; callers do not have to identify themselves; however, if they do identify themselves and LFF is made aware that an undetected offence has been committed, or believes a child is at risk of harm, then the information must be passed onto the relevant authorities. This policy is made clear to callers on first contact.

The Helpline commenced for three target groups: adults concerned about their own thoughts or behaviour towards children, adults concerned about another adult's behaviour towards children, and parents/carers concerned about a child displaying HSB. The Stop it Now! Helpline was therefore set up as a secondary and tertiary prevention service. However, as the Helpline has grown, so has the diversity of callers, giving it a primary prevention focus, with calls from the general public asking for advice about effective child safeguarding.

An estimated seven out of eight victims of sexual abuse never come to the attention of the authorities (Children's Commissioner, 2015). Therefore, it is important for services to reach out to the public, and LFF believes that in order to protect children successfully individuals need to be offered a place to seek advice and support, and to be able to do so anonymously. By giving those worried about themselves the opportunity to discuss their concerns, they can be assisted in making changes in their life to protect children. Equally, for those who have concerns about others, the Helpline offers a place to discuss their concerns and to identify preventative action. The Helpline was launched in 2002, but was not the first of its kind, with LFF receiving support and guidance from our sister organisation; Stop it Now! United States.

The Helpline offers advice, support, and resources, which may include recommended reading, advice around self-care, the implementation of CP measures, and risk reduction strategies. As a consequence, the Helpline moves beyond considering solely the situational dynamics, but considers individuals' potential triggers and factors that may contribute to a person's abusive behaviour. The Helpline also encourages callers to consider protective factors, such as focussing time on more rewarding activities, encouraging prosocial relationships, and desistance from abusive behaviour (Brown et al., 2014; Ward & Beech, 2006). The model for the Stop it Now! Helpline has attracted international attention, with countries showing an interest in starting Stop it Now! Helplines of their own. After training with LFF, the Stop it Now! Helpline in the Netherlands was launched in 2012.

By November 2017, the UK Helpline had received 69,435 calls from individuals with concerns around CSA. The operation of the Helpline has increased steadily, with an average yearly increase in calls of 22.7%, and an average yearly increase in callers of 20%. In 2003, the Helpline received 976 calls; in 2016 the Helpline received 8083 calls. Figure 3.1

below shows the number of calls per year to the Helpline from 2002 to 2016.

It is hoped that over this time not only has the Helpline become more accessible, enabling those concerned about a child to find support, but also that the issue of CSA has become less covert. Below provides an example of a Helpline call, and the subsequent advice.

> *James, 24-years-old, called the Helpline worried about his sexual thoughts and feelings towards children. James' mother was present during the call, as he had disclosed his sexual thoughts to her. James admitted spending most of his time online, and reported looking at adult pornography because it made him feel good. He denied looking for Indecent Images of Children (IIOC), but disclosed being sent it from online friends. He was anxious that he would be arrested.*
> *Discussion/Advice:*
> *James was reassured that he had contacted the right place, and praised for disclosing to his mother. It was emphasised how she could now support him.*
> *When discussing pornography use, James was encouraged to consider why pornography might be unhelpful for some people, and how his online behaviour resulted in exposure to IIOC. James felt anxious because his mother had removed his computer from his bedroom and stopped his internet access, although he understood why. He explored how to talk with his mother about putting the computer in the living room, and only allowing internet access in the company of others; so James could spend some time online, yet his mother could feel confident he was not accessing inappropriate content.*

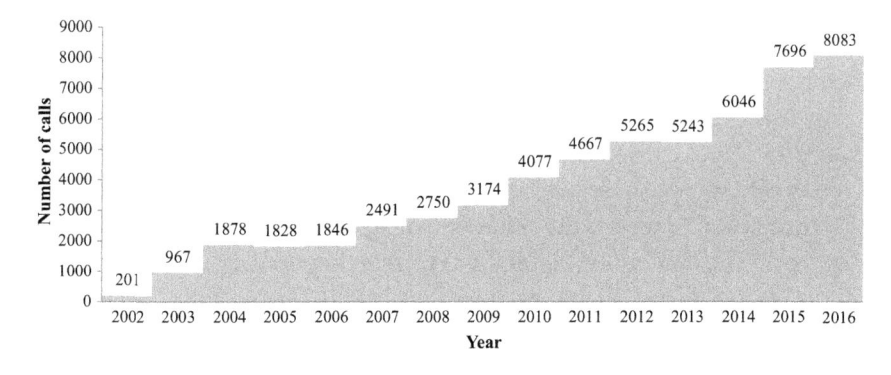

Fig. 3.1 Number of calls to the Stop it Now! Helpline from 2002 to 2016

> *James was encouraged not to masturbate to sexual thoughts of children because this can positively reinforce the behaviour. It was explored how James could implement fantasy management techniques, for example, active distraction, using self-talk, and appropriate fantasy replacement.*
>
> *It was suggested that James visit our Get Help and Get Support websites (discussed below), and that it might be helpful to work through the modules with his mother, if he felt able to, or discuss his progress with the Helpline.*
>
> *James was asked to consider his contact with children, and the importance of not being unsupervised with children whilst he had these sexual thoughts.*
>
> *James discussed spending more time offline and accessing groups, through the NHS or privately, set up for people with his interests. This would help him keep distracted from inappropriate thoughts, and develop his social network.*
>
> *Outcome:*
>
> *James called the Helpline on several occasions. In early calls James remained distressed, so he was advised to go to a GP. It was explained how a GP's confidentiality policy may be different to that of the Helpline.*
>
> *James joined a local model building group which he felt helped to reduce his internet use. James used the internet at times of stress, but his computer was in the living room so his pornography use reduced.*
>
> *His sexual thoughts about children reduced. He found the Get Help and Get Support websites useful and explored how he could use the websites to help him manage his thoughts.*
>
> *James reported no on-going concerns about his interactions with children.*

Additionally, it is common for the Helpline to receive calls from adults concerned about another adult, but unsure about where to go with their concern. There might have been unusual occurrences within the household, such as a person spending considerable time online at night, or showing an interest in a particular child.

An independent evaluation of the Stop it Now! Helpline was conducted by NatCen Social Research (Brown et al., 2014). The feedback from callers was positive, with participants citing the nature and quality of information, as well as the skills, empathy, and attitude of the Helpline operators. The evaluation highlighted factors that contributed to the prevention of CSA, such as improving callers' ability to recognise behaviour as problematic or risky, to understand that behaviour can be addressed and changed, and to implement strategies to help prevent abusive behaviour. The evaluation also highlighted economic benefits of the Helpline as a CSA prevention service.

The Helpline provides the opportunity for individuals to access other LFF services, such as a face-to-face meeting, offering a chance for individuals to meet with a practitioner. The practitioner provides advice and support and, if appropriate, suggests other services such as those discussed below. However, due to CP and confidentiality issues, those who meet with LFF must relinquish their anonymity. Therefore, those that move beyond the Helpline are typically known to the authorities; constituting a tertiary method of prevention. In the future, LFF hopes to enable undetected offenders to come forward and seek help.

Parents Protect

The Stop it Now! campaign has also galvanised other initiatives: one being the inception of the primary and secondary prevention website, Parents Protect (www.parentsprotect.co.uk), and its subsequent workshop programme.

In June 2006, the Home Secretary commissioned the 'Review of the Protection of Children from Sex Offenders', which resulted in a Stop it Now! campaign initiative piloting a public awareness campaign, Keeping the Public in Public Protection (KPPP). Following the success of the pilots, the KPPP project developed into Parents Protect; a website, leaflets for adults making enquiries under the Disclosure Scheme, a toolkit for police officers to disseminate information in their communities, and a workshop.

Parents Protect was created to aid parents and carers to better protect children and prevent CSA in the first instance. The website aims to dispel common myths around CSA and provide parents and carers with practical information to help keep children safe. The website includes a 30-minute learning video, along with resources around warning signs of abuse, internet safety, and building a family safety plan.

The website was launched in 2010, and in 2017 the website received, on average, 52,111 visits per month. Parents Protect is the LFF website with the highest number of international visits, with around 68% of users being from the United States, and 23% from the United Kingdom. A feedback form utilised on the website showed that 73% of people found the site very useful or useful, with 81% saying they found all or some of the information they were looking for.

Parents Protect was developed into a 90-minute workshop delivered to parents/carers and professionals working with children. The aim of the workshop is to increase understanding about the prevention of CSA and to empower parents to protect children. The intended learning outcomes for the workshop are to identify key aspects of CSA, develop awareness of types of abusers, explain the available systems for concerns about abuse, and explain the key principles of the Multi Agency Public Protection Arrangements (MAPPA).

An in-house evaluation found an increase in confidence for the majority of delegates in spotting warning signs of abuse in children, warning signs in abusive or potentially abusive adults, ability to keep their children safe, and ability to take action if they thought something was wrong. The workshops continue to be delivered, along with material and resource updates for the website.

Work with Internet Offenders

An issue at the forefront of CP and sexual offending is that of indecent images of children (IIOC). The internet has opened up new ways for individuals to access IIOC and, as a result, Police and CP agencies are seeing a rise in the number of people being charged for these offences (McGuire & Dowling, 2013).

This offending type has become increasingly prominent, with recognition from UK Government that more needs to be done to manage the availability of IIOC and deter individuals from accessing this material. The Prime Minister's speech on 22nd July 2013 (HM Government, 2013) called for a clampdown on internet pornography, and placing deterrents for those accessing IIOC was a point of mention. If an offender is detected for this type of offending and enters the criminal justice system, there is no guarantee that they will receive any intervention for understanding and managing their behaviour.

Due to the increase of individuals arrested for IIOC, and, as a consequence, the increase of those individuals contacting the Helpline, LFF developed a number of tertiary prevention projects to try and meet the needs of those concerned about their own behaviour, and their loved ones, after detection from law enforcement: namely Inform Plus, Inform and Inform Young People.

Prevention of Offending After Detection

Inform Plus

Around 35% of callers to the Stop it Now! Helpline in 2016 were IIOC offenders. These individuals are usually placed under investigation and are highly motivated to seek help around their behaviour, so LFF felt it was important to offer access to resources for understanding and managing their online offending. Additionally, it became widely recognised that arrests for IIOC offending were resulting in increased numbers of suicides. The Helpline became seen as an important part of suicide prevention for the Police; providing individuals with help and purpose, assisting them to feel less isolated and hopeless. A recent study on suicide prevention (Key et al., 2017) highlighted the role of the Stop it Now! Helpline, and resulted in the Helpline being entered into Police guidance when arresting IIOC offenders.

Inform Plus is a ten-week psycho-educational self-funded group course for individuals detected for offences related to accessing IIOC. The course can also be attended on an individual basis over five sessions. It provides an opportunity for individuals to explore their offending behaviour in a structured and supportive environment, to increase their self-awareness and consider actions to reduce the risk of re-offending. Sessions consist of taught models, discussions, and exercises, with between-session work. The course content focuses on offence analysis, the role of fantasy, and considers the concept of addiction. It explores the role of the Internet and offers participants information on the criminal justice process. Inform Plus focuses on improving participants' relationships, and preventing relapse, including considering risk and identifying the needs met through offending, and how these can be met in healthy ways. Inform Plus commenced in 2005, with over 1500 offenders having completed the Inform Plus course to date.

From data on 722 participants, upon commencing Inform Plus, the average amount of time offenders were spending online for a sexual purpose ranged from no time at all to 40 hours a week, with an average of 9.95 hours (sd = 8.49). What could potentially be hypothesised for some individuals is a habituation effect (Koukounas & Over, 1993; O'Donohue & Geer, 1985), as 94.2% of participants reported accessing adult pornography online prior to IIOC. Group members would often report a Coolidge effect regarding their viewing of pornography; the want for novel material.

Importantly, 77.7% stated that if they had not been arrested then they would still have been accessing IIOC. Rimer (2016) found, for Inform Plus participants, a distinction between the real world and the online world, giving focus to the impact on behaviour within an environment where people might feel they are not being 'watched'.

Group members have consistently evaluated the Relapse Prevention and Victim Awareness sessions as being the most useful. Although research indicates that victim empathy deficits do not reliably relate to sexual recidivism (Hanson & Morton-Bourgon, 2005), Inform Plus participants report this session to be the most impacting. This may relate to some of the fundamental issues of accessing IIOC; distancing themselves from the victim in the image, seeing it as 'only a picture' and not 'directly harming anyone' (Taylor & Quayle, 2003). Based on group members' self-report, being provided with the opportunity to reconnect with victims in the offline world, in a safe environment, appeared beneficial.

An evaluation of Inform Plus was completed by Gillespie et al. (2016), which included pre, post, and follow-up psychometric testing on 11 groups (92 participants). The evaluation found significant improvements post-group in depression, anxiety, stress, social anxiety, self-esteem, self-efficacy, and distorted thinking. Furthermore, these changes remained at follow-up (8–12 weeks). This indicated that, although a psycho-educational course, Inform Plus appeared to have a positive impact on psychological well-being as well as beliefs about offending. This may also have been due to the impact of the group environment, the support from others in similar situations, and non-judgemental, empathic, and non-collusive facilitators. This type of environment, especially in relation to challenging distorted thinking, could encourage change by aiding offenders to re-evaluate their minimisations, without threatening their self-image.

Additionally, a qualitative evaluation by Dervley et al. (2017) interviewed 13 Inform Plus participants, alongside eight non-offending others (partners, parents, and professionals) associated with the participants. After course completion, participants reported feeling better able to manage their thoughts, feelings, and behaviours which may have related to their offending. Inform Plus was also found to initiate a motivation for change, to facilitate communication within and beyond the group setting (with others in their life), and encourage participants to feel that a positive offence-free future was possible. The non-offending others independently validated these results.

Although the results of these evaluations are promising, more research is needed, particularly regarding whether this early intervention after detection might have an impact on re-offending, perhaps not straightforward given the low reconviction rates cited for IIOC offenders (Seto, Hanson, & Babchishin, 2011).

Inform

In parallel to services for IIOC offenders, was an increased awareness of the support needs of their family and friends. Given the secretive nature of the behaviour, loved ones play an important protective role for re-offending and CP. However, non-offending others have significant struggles, and the situation causes considerable stress. Research by Stubley (2015) with clients of LFF, found four common themes relating to shock, trying to understand/make sense of the behaviour, sensitivity to what others would think, and worrying about adverse impact on significant others. The findings indicated discovering a loved one has been accessing IIOC had a significant impact on the participants' view of the world and interfered with their ability to function normally. Additionally, from speaking with partners and family members on the Helpline, individuals often want help to understand why their loved one accessed IIOC.

For this reason, the Inform course was developed to give loved ones the opportunity to learn about the offending behaviour, consider issues of risk, and be supported by others in similar situations. The course runs over five sessions and in parallel with the Inform Plus course. This was so that offenders and those significant in their lives could learn about key issues simultaneously, with the hope that this could facilitate useful discussions around offending motivation, warning signs of relapse, and managing risk.

To date, around 300 people have attended the Inform course. One of the largest benefits appears to be meeting others in a similar situation, reducing feelings of isolation. Many Inform group members report the helpfulness of being able to share their experience with others who understand their emotional and situational strains.

Although Inform has helped support some partners and family members, not everyone is able to access the course. There is still a gap in support for families, and it is important that, in all stages of the CP process, the concerns, emotions, and stability of those who have not offended, are considered and heard.

Inform YP

Inform YP is an educative programme for YP (aged 13–21) in trouble with Police or school/colleges for inappropriate use of technology such as 'sexting' or IIOC, as well as risk-taking behaviours online, or accessing adult pornography. It also aims to support their family members, help them understand what has happened and assist them in supporting the young person. The Association of Chief Police Officers has stated it would rather not criminalise YP for internet related offences, yet they need education and help to address and modify their behaviour.

Inform YP (on average, one assessment and five intervention sessions per family) provides information, advice, and support tailored to the needs of each young person and their family to prevent a reoccurrence or escalation of the concerning behaviour.

The idea stemmed from three main sources: LFF's work with families through the Helpline, calls to the Helpline from schools concerned about a young person's sexual behaviour online, and direct communication with UK police services expressing concern about the number of YP coming to their attention. Helpline calls from families and YP themselves highlighted the distress and concern experienced by all when this behaviour came to light.

A scoping exercise indicated that there was no comparable service and no specialist support available for YP and their parents that addressed their specific needs. Below is a case example of a young person accessing the service:

> *Liam (17) was referred by the welfare tutor at his college due to concerns about his sexual boundaries and use of mobile phones. The police had been informed but there was no active police involvement.*
>
> *Five sessions were completed with Liam at his college. Liam's father had telephone contact with the practitioner, and he and the welfare tutor attended a final meeting with Liam.*
>
> *The work focussed upon issues of consent/compliance/coercion, 'OK' and 'Not' OK sexual behaviour, managing Liam's use of mobile phones and the Internet, and identifying positive activities and hobbies. A summary regarding the management of Liam's risk and situation was provided to his father and the college at the end of the five sessions.*

In this technological age, issues continue to arise with YP and sexual behaviour. Behaving inappropriately via technology, as a young person, does not mean that this behaviour will continue into adulthood, highlighting the importance of early intervention and education in order to prevent harm to others and YP themselves.

Prevention of IIOC Offending Before Detection

As the number of IIOC offenders (as estimated by law enforcement increased), so did recognition that we cannot simply arrest our way out of the problem. Therefore, a recent focus has been on deterrence, and the importance of encouraging those engaged in the behaviour, or considering engaging, to desist.

The reported rate of arrested IIOC offenders in 2011 was 2312 (Carr, 2012). This figure pales in comparison to the more recent suggestion that there could be half a million individuals accessing IIOC in the United Kingdom (NSPCC, 2016). For this reason, the role of other CP professionals is vital. This includes working towards prevention, both situational and individual, and individuals taking responsibility for their online behaviour. There are those who wish to seek help, as well as those who believe that someone they know might be engaging with IIOC. This makes providing the opportunity to seek help and advice outside of law enforcement important.

Splash Pages

As a secondary and tertiary prevention strategy, the concept of 'Splash Pages' is not new, with countries such as Norway (Wortley & Smallbone, 2012) having already utilised them as a way of deterring individuals from online IIOC. 'Splash Pages' aid in preventing IIOC access by 'removing excuses' (Wortley & Smallbone, 2012) and making individuals aware of the illegality of the website they are attempting to access.

In the previously mentioned Prime Minister's speech, 'Splash Pages' were of particular focus, where individuals are warned about the consequences of their actions, such as losing access to their children and the legal ramifications. Some IIOC offenders have reported to LFF being unaware of the consequences for their behaviour (Bailey et al., 2017).

The birth of the UK 'Splash Page' was in August 2013, with the purpose of presenting a warning to any person attempting to access IIOC hosted on a web page that had been removed by the Internet Watch Foundation (IWF). The IWF succeeds in attempting to 'increase the effort' needed to obtain IIOC, with the IWF having worked to remove 57,335 webpages containing CSA images or videos in 2016 (IWF, 2016). Unfortunately, it is unknown how many times these 'Splash Pages' have been viewed.

LFF influenced the design and wording of the 'Splash Page'. It was recognised that whilst warning individuals about the consequences of their actions could contribute towards prevention, this may not be enough, particularly for those whose behaviour may be more entrenched. Offenders often report no immediate negative consequences for their online behaviour; they felt they were anonymous online ('Triple A Engine'—sexual behaviour online offering accessibility, affordability and anonymity; Cooper, 1998) or that they justified their behaviour as being 'less serious' than other offenders' (Taylor & Quayle, 2003). All of these issues could contribute to behaviour continuing and the individual not seeking help. 'Splash Pages' help to reduce that feeling of anonymity and insignificance (Wortley & Smallbone, 2012), and for those users who require more than a warning, the 'Splash Page' directs the individual to additional help, namely the Stop it Now! Helpline.

Additionally, Google utilised measures of IIOC deterrence. When certain search terms related to IIOC are typed into Google's search engine, the person is presented with an advert for the Stop it Now! Helpline, as well as Google's own advert which directs them to a page with links to the National Crime Agency, IWF, and Stop it Now! Between November 2013 and July 2014, the Stop it Now! adverts recorded 934,209 impressions from the searching of specific terms; the adverts were clicked on 6173 times. These numbers give some idea as to the amount of times IIOC was being searched for online, whilst remembering that this is likely to be an underestimation of the total number of searches given that it included only those impressions made by the specific terms registered by Google.

The Deterrence Campaign and Get Help

Within qualitative research conducted by LFF (Bailey et al., 2017), participants were asked to identify strategies that might have encouraged them to not offend in the first place, or discouraged the continuation of their offending behaviour. Prominent themes emerged, with a particular focus on education around the legality of IIOC, being made aware of the consequences of offending, as well as being aware of access to help that they could be sure was safe (not linked to law enforcement). It was from this research that the deterrence campaign was developed.

The Deterrence Campaign

The deterrence campaign is a national primary and secondary prevention campaign aimed at discouraging individuals from accessing IIOC in the first instance by educating the public. The campaign produced and disseminated deterrence videos, which communicated key messages. For increased impact, these videos were visual prevention messages, rather than those of a text nature, as had been the main focus of previous deterrence messages such as splash pages. Additionally, the research highlighted the preventative presence of other people, so a video aimed at family and friends was produced. The deterrence videos included:

No Justification—an animated video presenting common justifications used by offenders for accessing IIOC and providing counter responses.
Very Real Consequences—presented the consequences of accessing IIOC including arrest, prison, loss of family, loss of job, and the Sex Offenders' Register. This video included actors voicing the words of convicted individuals.
Choose another path—an interactive video where the viewer could choose the direction the video took and the subsequent outcomes.
Five Steps—a video for family and friends exploring the steps that could be taken if they were concerned about someone's online behaviour.

These videos were presented to focus groups of offenders and family members, and after suggested amendments, were disseminated on social media platforms. The campaign was launched alongside media coverage.

As of November 2017, the deterrence videos had generated over 17 million views, with 13,251,331 impressions of the videos on Facebook, 2,822,737 on Instagram, and 1,919,023 on YouTube. Additionally, a survey of 215 Stop it Now! Helpline callers identified that 13% of those callers had contacted the Helpline after exposure to coverage from the deterrence campaign.

Additionally, in June 2017, the Edinburgh Offender Management Committee Prevention Sub-group launched a three-month deterrence campaign. The campaign used social media, press coverage, local radio interviews, local radio adverts, posters, and internal and external communications channels of partner agencies.

In the month after the campaign, the Stop it Now! website (www.stopitnow.org.uk) saw a 6.82% increase in new users from Scotland, increasing to 8% three months after the campaign. The Stop it Now! Helpline saw an 83% increase in new callers from Scotland in the three months following the deterrence campaign.

Although this is indicative that the message is being disseminated, more detailed research would be required in order to ascertain the impact of the project, and also the number of individuals seeking help as a result.

Get Help Website (www.get-help.stopitnow.org.uk)

Prior to 13th October 2015, LFF had direction over the CROGA website. CROGA (Quayle, 2005), originally funded by the DAPHNE project in 2001, offered anonymous online self-help to individuals concerned about viewing IIOC. The website provided information and online modules, with the aim of aiding individuals with understanding their online behaviour, and implementing management strategies. This innovative resource spent considerable time 'dormant' due to a lack of resources to update it and provide the media presence required to make its existence known to the public.

Bailey et al. (2017) highlighted the anxiety for individuals in seeking help due to their concerns about being reported should they identify themselves to a professional. This illustrated the importance of a website like CROGA, where individuals could receive accurate information about UK law and the consequences of viewing IIOC, and could obtain help in a way that did not compromise their anonymity. Therefore, LFF worked on improving the CROGA website to develop it into an effective secondary and tertiary prevention resource.

A number of significant improvements were made. First, was the inclusion of multimedia content: the deterrence videos. The self-help information was updated, with more exercises included to encourage individuals' continued engagement. The website is underpinned by The Good Lives Model (Ward, 2002), encouraging individuals to consider positive goal-

Table 3.1 Statistics from the Get Help website in comparison to the CROGA website

	April 2015–September 2015 (CROGA website)	November 2015–April 2016 (Get Help website)	April 2017–October 2017 (Get Help website)
Average users per day	35	64	99
Bounce rate	54.32%	40.64%	47.20%
Percentage of returning visitors	17.50%	30.80%	29.90%
Average time spent on website (minutes)	4.12	8.45	6.43

oriented change, rather than the relapse prevention focus of the original CROGA site. The new website also provides information for those concerned about someone else accessing IIOC and for professionals. With these changes, the Get Help website (formerly CROGA) was launched on 13th October 2015 as part of the deterrence campaign.

Since its launch, 76,889 individuals have visited the Get Help website. The table below shows the statistics of Get Help, in comparison to CROGA (Table 3.1).

The response to the site from service users has been positive, but has illustrated that, for some individuals there is need for extra assistance in understanding and applying the self-help information. Therefore, LFF have offered a callback service for detected and undetected offenders to explore the self-help modules in more detail. To date, 47 offenders have used the callback service to help them manage their online behaviour using the self-help resources.

Get Support Website (www.get-support.stopitnow.org.uk)

With the launch and success of Get Help, consideration was given to a similar resource, but one directed at those troubled by their sexual thoughts about children. The aim of this website was to offer similar information and self-help to those who had sexual thoughts about children but had not offended, or those who had committed a contact offence, in order to not reoffend. The website offers the same information about the law, as well as the opportunity for individuals to go on a self-help journey and examine ways to manage their behaviour.

This website went live in May 2017, although it remains under development in terms of its content. Evaluation data is being collected, with a view to updating and developing the site. As of November 2017, 2145 users have visited Get Support, totalling 3008 visits, with average visit duration of 5 minutes 51 seconds. Get Support has not had the media exposure of Get Help, but on the one occasion it did, the week prior saw 82 users, and 98 sessions, with the week after media exposure having 187 users and 229 sessions. This illustrates the huge impact of media and public exposure, and will be an important focus for Get Support going forward.

International Work and the Eradicating Child Sexual Abuse [ECSA] Project

In addition to undertaking Child Safety Reviews in British overseas territories, LFF has developed the ECSA website and online toolkit: www.ecsa.lucyfaithfull.org. Drawing upon the prevention framework, as set out below, the ECSA project provides a basis for discussing and identifying the most hopeful components of a strategy for the prevention of CSA on a local level. The project aims to help communities identify the nature of CSA with which they are confronted and potential strategies for prevention. The toolkit comprises hundreds of examples of CSA prevention worldwide, so that users can learn from others' experience. As part of the development of the ECSA toolkit, LFF has been involved in piloting its use in central Europe and east Africa, and hosted visits from international delegations.

The Prevention Framework (Smallbone, Marshall, & Wortley, 2008)

Figure 3.2 below presents all of the discussed LFF initiatives and their place within the prevention framework.

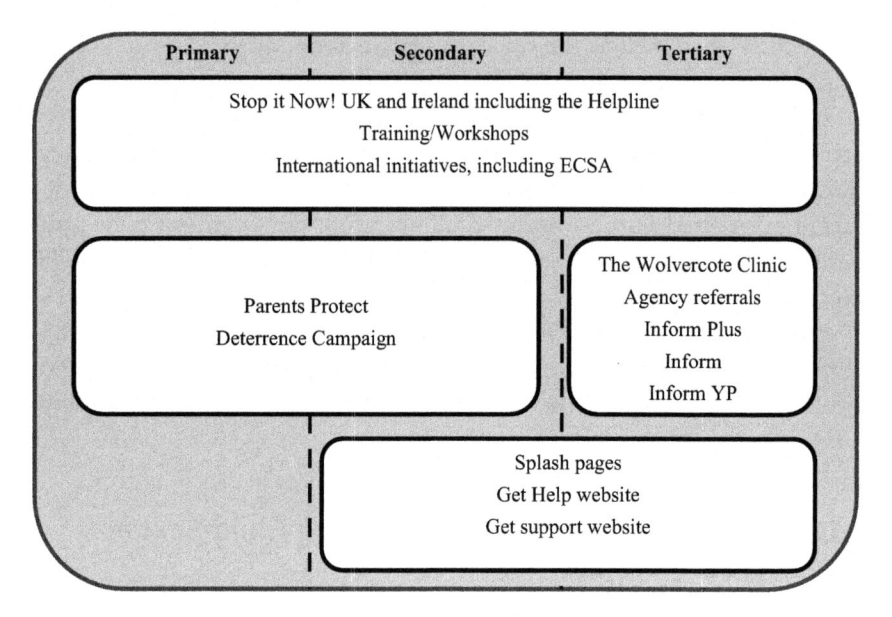

```
┌─────────────────────────────────────────────────────────┐
│   Primary      │      Secondary     │      Tertiary     │
│  ┌───────────────────────────────────────────────────┐  │
│  │  Stop it Now! UK and Ireland including the Helpline│ │
│  │              Training/Workshops                   │  │
│  │     International initiatives, including ECSA     │  │
│  └───────────────────────────────────────────────────┘  │
│                                  ┌──────────────────┐   │
│  ┌───────────────────────────┐   │ The Wolvercote Clinic│
│  │                           │   │  Agency referrals │   │
│  │     Parents Protect       │   │    Inform Plus    │   │
│  │    Deterrence Campaign    │   │       Inform      │   │
│  │                           │   │     Inform YP     │   │
│  └───────────────────────────┘   └──────────────────┘   │
│                   ┌──────────────────────────────┐      │
│                   │        Splash pages          │      │
│                   │       Get Help website       │      │
│                   │      Get support website     │      │
│                   └──────────────────────────────┘      │
└─────────────────────────────────────────────────────────┘
```

Fig. 3.2 LFF initiatives within the prevention framework

Conclusions and Future Considerations

For all those in CP, the work is never done, and although LFF firmly believes that CSA is preventable, not inevitable, there is much that needs to change in order to fully safeguard children.

Promising developments have been made, both in terms of understanding the problem, but also implementing change. The increased recognition of the importance of prevention, and the move from primarily agency referrals to more direct engagement with the public means that society is in a better position to safeguard children. CP is everyone's responsibility.

LFF continues to develop the deterrence project, with the aim of adapting this for other environments such as health care and education, as well as continuing to develop deterrence materials such as new videos and messages. Another consideration is that of online grooming. Positively, £20 million has been put forward for the police to tackle this issue (Home Office, 2017). However, while an increased police resource is essential, the question remains as to whether it will be enough to tackle this complex problem. Perhaps considering the prevention and deterrence of online grooming in alternate ways could be valuable, and potentially divert some offenders to access help. These are additional issues to consider in today's modern era.

LFF feels strongly about support and advice for non-offending partners, and as such are in the process of developing a forum for family members. It can often be difficult for partners to attend face-to-face services, so offering an online forum feels like an important service, particularly given the protective role that non-abusing others can play.

Additionally, LFF plans to continue advocating the importance of education around CSA, and its prevention. Empowering the public and professionals, helping people feel knowledgeable about the issues and able to prevent CSA, as well as able to come forward and discuss concerns; these factors help to protect children in the first instance. LFF aims to provide that opportunity, through online resources, face-to-face workshops, interactions with schools, and through the Stop it Now! Helpline.

LFF continues to invest in new projects as well as maintaining existing initiatives, in order to be innovative and influential in the prevention of CSA and the protection of children.

References

Bailey, A., Naldrett, G. A., Graham, S., Squire, T., Alladyce, S., & Johnson, A. (2017). *Prevention and intervention for indecent images of children offending: A qualitative study and service development.* Manuscript in preparation.

Benedict, A. (2005). *The five core practice areas of gender responsiveness.* COREassociatesLLC@comcast.net. Adapted from the CORE Gender-specific Programming Assessment. Retrieved from http://demoiselle2femme.org/wp-content/uploads/Five-Core-Practice-Areas-of-Gender-Responsiveness.pdf

Brown, A., Jago, N., Kerr, J., McNaughton Nicholls, C., Paskell, C., & Webster, S. (2014). *Call to keep children safe from sexual abuse: A study of the use and effects of the stop it now! UK and Ireland helpline.* Retrieved from https://www.natcen.ac.uk/media/338805/stop-it-now-uk-findings-.pdf

Brown, A., McNaughton Nicholls, C., Webster, S., & Kenny, T. (2012). *Young people with sexually harmful behaviour: Evaluation of the Lucy Faithfull Foundation assessment and intervention service in the young people's secure estate.* London: NatCen Social Research.

Carr, J. (2012, October 17). The unbelievable truth about child pornography in the UK. *The Huffington Post.* Retrieved from http://www.huffingtonpost.co.uk/john-carr/child-pornography-the-unbelievable-truth-ab_b_1970969.html

Children's Commissioner. (2015). *Protecting children from harm: A critical assessment of child sexual abuse in the family network in England and priorities for action.* Retrieved from https://www.childrenscommissioner.gov.uk/wp-content/uploads/2017/06/Protecting-children-from-harm-executive-summary_0.pdf

Cooper, A. (1998). Sexuality and the Internet: Surfing its way into a new millennium. *Cyberpsychology and Behavior, 1*(2), 24–28.

Cortoni, F., Hanson, K. R., & Coache, M.-E. (2010). The recidivism rates of female sexual offenders are low: A meta-analysis. *Sexual Abuse: A Journal of Research and Treatment, 22*(4), 387–401.

Dervley, R., Perkins, D., Whitehead, H., Bailey, A., Gillespie, S., & Squire, T. (2017). Themes in participant feedback on a risk reduction programme for child sexual exploitation material offenders. *Journal of Sexual Aggression, 23*(1), 46–61.

Eldridge, H. J., Bailey, A., & Brotherson, S. (in press). Treatment approaches for women who sexually abuse children. In J. L. Ireland, C. A. Ireland, & P. Birch (Eds.), *Violent and sexual offenders: Assessment, treatment and management* (2nd ed.). London: Routledge.

Eldridge, H. J., Elliott, I. A., Gillespie, S., Bailey, A., & Beech, A. R. (in press). Assessing women who sexually abuse children. In J. L. Ireland, C. A. Ireland, & P. Birch (Eds.), *Violent and sexual offenders: Assessment, treatment and management* (2nd ed.). London: Routledge.

Eldridge, H. J., & Saradjian, J. (unpublished). *New life manual.*

Elliott, I. A., Eldridge, H. E., Ashfield, S., & Beech, A. R. (2010). Potential static, dynamic, protective and treatment factors in the clinical histories of female sex offenders. *Journal of Family Violence, 25*(6), 595–602.

Ford, H. (2006). *Women who sexually abuse children.* Chichester, UK: Wiley.

Ford, H., & Beech, A. R. (2004). *The effectiveness of the Wolvercote clinic residential treatment programme in producing short-term treatment changes and reducing sexual reconvictions.* London: National Probation Service for England and Wales.

Gillespie, S. M., Bailey, A., Squire, T., Carey, M. L., Eldridge, H. J., & Beech, A. R. (2016). An evaluation of a community-based psycho-educational program for users of child sexual exploitation material. *Sexual Abuse: A Journal of Research and Treatment.* https://doi.org/10.1177/1079063216639591

Hanson, R., & Morton-Bourgon, K. (2005). The characteristics of persistent sexual offenders. A meta-analysis of recidivism studies. *Journal of Consulting and Clinical Psychology, 73*(6), 1154–1163.

HM Government. (2013). *The internet and pornography: Prime Minister calls for action.* Retrieved from https://www.gov.uk/government/speeches/the-internet-and-pornography-prime-minister-calls-for-action

Home Office. (2017). *Home Secretary gives £20 million boost to tackle online grooming* [press release]. Retrieved from https://www.gov.uk/government/news/home-secretary-gives-20-million-boost-to-tackle-online-grooming

IWF. (2016). *Internet watch foundation annual report 2016.* Retrieved from https://www.iwf.org.uk/assets/media/annualreports/IWF_Annual_Report_16_web.pdf

Key, R., Underwood, A., Lawrenson, J., Hawton, K., Marzano, L., Kothari, R., et al. (2017). *Managing perpetrators of child sexual exploitation and indecent images of children (IIOC): Understanding risk of suicide.* NHS, NCA, NCPP.

Koukounas, E., & Over, R. (1993). Habituation and dishabituation of male sexual arousal. *Behaviour Research and Therapy, 31*(6), 575–585.

Masten, A. S., & Obradovic, J. (2006). Competence and resilience in development. *Annals of the New York Academy of Sciences, 1094*(1), 13–27.

McGuire, M., & Dowling, S. (2013). *Cyber crime: A review of the evidence. Research report 75. Chapter 3: Cyber-enabled crimes – Sexual offending against children.* Retrieved from https://www.gov.uk/government/uploads/system/uploads/attachment_data/file/246754/horr75-chap3.pdf

NSPCC. (2016, November 3). *Child abuse images: More action must be taken for children.* Retrieved from https://www.nspcc.org.uk/what-we-do/news-opinion/child-abuse-images-more-action-taken-children/

O'Donohue, W. T., & Geer, J. H. (1985). The habituation of sexual arousal. *Archives of Sexual Behavior, 14*(3), 233–246.

Philpot, T. (1996). Obituary: Baroness faithfull. *Independent.* Retrieved from http://www.independent.co.uk/news/obituaries/obituary-baroness-faithfull-1342088.html

Quayle, E. (2005). The internet as a therapeutic medium. In E. Quayle & M. Taylor (Eds.), *Viewing child pornography on the Internet. Understanding the offence, managing the offender, helping the victims.* Lyme Regis, UK: Russell House Publishing.

Rimer, J. R. (2016). Internet sexual offending from an anthropological perspective: Analysing offender perceptions of online spaces. *Journal of Sexual Aggression, 23*(1), 33–45.

Seto, M., Hanson, K., & Babchishin, K. (2011). Contact sexual offending by men with online sexual offenses. *Sexual Abuse: A Journal of Research and Treatment, 23*(1), 124–145.

Smallbone, S. W., Marshall, W. L., & Wortley, R. (2008). *Preventing child sexual abuse: Evidence, policy and practice.* Cullompton, UK: William Publishing.

Stubley, A. (2015). He's a family man, but this is a dark side of him that I didn't know about. *The lived experience of internet offenders' partners.* Unpublished doctoral thesis, Teeside University.

Taylor, M., & Quayle, E. (2003). *Child pornography: An Internet crime.* Hove, UK: Brunner-Routledge.

Ward, T. (2002). Good lives and the rehabilitation of offenders: Promises and problems. *Aggression and Violent Behavior, 7*(5), 513–528.

Ward, T., & Beech, A. R. (2006). An integrated theory of sexual offending. *Aggression and Violent Behavior, 11*(1), 44–63.

Wortley, R., & Smallbone, S. (2012). *Internet child pornography: Causes, investigation, and Prevention.* Santa Barbara, CA: ABC-CLIO, LLC.

4

Safer Living Foundation: The Aurora Project

Kerensa Hocken

The Safer Living Foundation

The Safer Living Foundation (SLF) is a charitable incorporated organisation (CIO) based in Nottinghamshire, UK. It was founded in 2014 and is run by experts who specialise in researching, evaluating, delivering and managing rehabilitative services for men with sexual offence convictions drawn from a range of diverse backgrounds including Her Majesty's Prison and Probation Service (HMPPS), the police and Nottingham Trent University. Its charitable aims are to reduce repeat and first time sexual offending by working with those who have committed, or are likely to commit, sexual offences.

The impetus for the genesis of the SLF was the desire to deliver a Circles of Support and Accountability (CoSA) project for prisoners being released from Her Majesty's Prison (HMP) Whatton in Nottingham (UK), particularly those with learning disability or the elderly, as these groups lack the most support on release from prison into the community. HMP

K. Hocken (✉)
HMP Whatton, HMPPS, Nottingham, UK
e-mail: Kerensa.Hocken@hmps.gsi.gov.uk

© The Author(s) 2018
R. Lievesley et al. (eds.), *Sexual Crime and Prevention*, Sexual Crime,
https://doi.org/10.1007/978-3-319-98243-4_4

Whatton has long-standing experience of successful partnership working with other agencies and it was during discussions with a number of these partners that the idea to form our own charitable organisation took hold. This had appeal over and above partnering with another agency for the sole purpose of running a CoSA project as it would allow innovation for other projects that might help the prisoners of HMP Whatton. These discussions began in 2012 and, on 13th February 2014, the SLF received CIO status and began the first CoSA project that started in prison, ensuring the working relationship between the volunteers and core member was firmly established before the transitional period of release occurs. In 2015, the SLF was awarded a grant from the Big Lottery to run the traditional community-based model of CoSA in Nottinghamshire and Derbyshire and, in 2017, the SLF commenced a CoSA project for young people (under 21) with sexually harmful behaviour.

The ambition to grow the service and move into the prevention of first time sexual offending began from discussions with residents in HMP Whatton, many of whom reported that they had sought help for their sexual feelings before offending but were unable to find the right support. This triggered a research project led by the university expertise in the SLF to explore the experience of help-seeking before offending amongst the residents of HMP Whatton (Lievesley, Elliott, Barnes, & Rodgers, 2018) and highlighted the need for a free therapeutic prevention service in the UK. In 2017, the SLF were awarded funding by Nottinghamshire Police and Crime Commissioner and the Henry Smith Trust to begin a free therapy and signposting service to people who are struggling with their sexual thoughts and feelings and are concerned it may lead to a first time sexual offence. This chapter will introduce the SLF prevention intervention, named The Aurora Project (TAP); it will outline the research on intervention needs for this client group and go on to describe the therapy model and intervention aims.

Background to Prevention Work

The development of TAP drew from the research on non-offending people who self-report some type of offence-related sexual interest to help guide approach and content. This section of the chapter reviews this literature.

A key consideration for any provider looking to offer a service with the aim of preventing first time sexual offending is what to address and how to do that. In trying to establish the risk and protective factors for sexual offending, the research has almost exclusively focused on factors that predict reoffending in samples who have already sexually offended (recidivism), and there are few prospective epidemiological studies that have examined what is responsible for the initiation of sexual offending. In the absence of robust scientific knowledge about the factors that lead to a first sexual offence, the aim and content of prevention interventions cannot draw on a sound evidence base. A lack of understanding about the potential service user group is a unique and disadvantageous position when planning a psychological intervention. In seeking to understand the needs of people who may benefit from therapy to prevent first time sexual offending, researchers have more recently predominantly investigated three distinct populations: non-offending minor attracted people (MAP; an umbrella term for people who identify as being attracted to people under the age of 16 years), the general population and people who have committed sexual offences.

Until approximately 2010 very little was known about the group of the general population who have unhealthy sexual interests but choose not to offend. However, the prevailing shift to focus on prevention strategies has generated clinical and empirical interest and there is a growing body of research which aims to understand the prevalence, characteristics and needs of this group. This research is presented in depth in Chaps. 1 and 2 of this book. The nature of the sexual interests means that these clients remain largely underground due to stigma and a fear of being reported which is also a barrier to research access. The focus of research has been almost exclusively on those with paedophilic or minor attracted interests and scant attention had been paid to those who have an interest in offending against adults or other types of paraphilias that if acted on would result in an offence such as zoophilia, sadism, voyeurism and exhibitionism. The research in existence is subsequently skewed towards MAPs, and the needs of those with other interests which may lead to sexual offending are not well understood. The research on the general population has sought to measure self-identified sexual interests in a bid to understand prevalence and nature of paraphilic interests.

What We Know About the Non-offending Population

Research with MAPs and the general population indicates the presence of what might be termed 'dynamic risk factors', that is psychological characteristics that relate to sexual recidivism, suggesting there may be some overlap in the needs of the convicted and unconvicted populations. For example, studies report the presence of sexual interest in children (e.g. Cash, 2016), sexual interest in coercion (Turner-Moore & Waterman, 2017) and attitudes that are accepting of sex between adults and children (Cash, 2016). These are all factors that have been found to predict reoffending in people convicted of sexual offences (PCSOs) (Mann, Hanson, & Thornton, 2010) and are commonly targeted on interventions for people who commit sexual offences.

It is evident that some of the same factors are present in convicted and unconvicted populations; however, it has not been clearly established what differentiates non-offending groups with these characteristics from people that do offend. It is possible that established risk factors for sexual recidivism may operate differently for those who have not offended, perhaps moderated by other unknown variables. This is important to establish in order to understand what preventative therapy needs to target and to ensure preventative efforts do not accidentally disrupt the protective effects of moderating variables.

Vanhoeck, Gykiere, and Wanzeele (2014) considered the question of what should be addressed in therapy for the prevention of first time sexual offending and summarise:

> '*Langström, Enebrink, Laurén, Lindblom, Werkö, and Hanson (2013) found no published outcome research on preventive methods for adults and adolescents who have not sexually abused children but were at a higher risk of doing so. They conclude that without specific guidelines for treating individuals at risk proven to be effective, the most ethically defensible position would be to assess the presence of treatable risk factors for sexual abuse of children, including concurrent psychiatric disorder and traumas*'. (p. 38)

The conclusions of Langstrom et al. (2013) imply that prevention interventions adopt the same treatment approach as those for sexual offending. However, it may be erroneous to follow this approach and careful consideration is needed to ascertain the most evidence informed approach. The outcomes for Sex Offending Treatment Programmes (SOTPs) have not been consistently positive (Hoberman, 2016) indicating that something about programmes for sexual offending are not effective for all who undertake them. The source of ineffectiveness has not been resolved and it may be a result of methodological or outcome measures than the treatment itself, however that is difficult to establish (Walton, 2018). Furthermore, even though the non-offending population appear to have offence-related sexual interests and, in some cases, attitudes which are known to be risk factors for sexual offending, the difference between them and those who choose to offend is not well understood and it is possible that moderators such as self-regulation are more important to target. Given we do not know what to target for certain, it may be pertinent to move away from strictly manualised approaches and adopt a client-led approach more consistent with traditional psychotherapeutic approaches which empowers the client to decide what they focus on.

There are few novel approaches to prevention intervention, for example, Prevention Project Dunkelfeld offers a psychological intervention which is modelled on cognitive behavioural (CBT) for people with sexual convictions. Schulz, Palmer, Stolpmann, Wernicke, and Müller (2017) propose a therapeutic model for prevention therapy that includes aspects of Acceptance and Commitment Therapy (ACT) and Dialectical Behaviour Therapy (DBT) for developing emotional tolerance. However, these seem to form a small part of therapy and the majority of the intervention is based on treatment for people convicted of sexual offending. The authors do conclude that specific research is needed to assess the influence of these techniques with people with self-identified interest in children. The chapter will now go on to review the specific treatment needs reported for non-offending MAPs.

Trauma

In research examining predictors of sexual offending Hanson and Morton-Bourgon (2005) reported that sexual abuse history was a risk factor for first time sexual offending but not for recidivism, suggesting it may be relevant to target in prevention work. Vanhoeck et al. (2014) suggest that getting caught and thinking about own abuse is the mechanism that eliminates this as a risk factor for recidivism. They suggest a trauma informed approach should be taken to any preventative work. In a trauma informed formulation behaviours which were adaptive in an abuse situation become problematic as an adult (e.g. rejection of intimacy) but can be understood in the trauma context. Consequently, they suggest a strengths-based approach to encourage growth and mastery. The research completed on help-seeking with non-offending MAPs also highlights the need for trauma informed care in prevention services. For example, Levenson and Grady (2017) reported multiple Adverse Childhood Events (ACEs) in their online sample. Levenson, Willis, and Vicencio (2017) also demonstrated that help-seeking PCSOs had higher ACE scores (e.g. more exposure to ACEs) than those who did not seek help.

Loneliness, Isolation and Low Self-Esteem

In research with MAPs, Cash (2016) found a higher incidence of loneliness and lower self-esteem than levels reported by the general public. For those exclusively attracted to children, loneliness was greater. He found that positive disclosure experiences and having some level of attraction towards adults were related to lower levels of loneliness. In order to achieve a positive disclosure experience, Cash suggests disclosures should be met with acceptance and validation. Therefore, it is important that any prevention interventions ensure that disclosures experiences are positive for clients. It is vital that confidentiality boundaries are well understood by all so that disclosures do not result in therapists having to share information onwards.

Offence Supportive Attitudes

Cash (2016) found that more accepting attitudes towards sex between adults and children were related to higher self-esteem in MAPs. He suggests that work to change their views to acknowledge the harm caused from sex between adults and children may damage self-esteem and attributes this as the cause of the observed decreased self-esteem following therapy in the Dunkelfeld project (Beier et al., 2015). This is reminiscent of Maruna and Mann (2006) and more recently Szumski, Bartels, Beech, and Fisher (2018) who point out that PCSOs use distortions that neutralise their responsibility for offending as a form of self-protection against stigma and shame and consequently these beliefs should not be tackled in treatment. However, Maruna and Mann do suggest that attitudes which are linked to dynamic risk factors and serve to drive the offending forward should be addressed in treatment. This suggests that prevention interventions should take account of the function of the belief for the individual in order to establish its likely role in facilitating possible offending. Where the function is related to permitting sexual contact, rather than protecting the self, the attitude may be addressed in therapy, finding ways to do this without damaging self-esteem: recognising potential harm from adult and child sexual contact does not need to be equal to saying the client is causing harm by their attractions.

Sexual Interests

Several authors have proposed that minor attraction could be conceptualised as a sexual orientation because of the similarities between it and other types of sexual orientations, such as emergence in the developmental period and the concurrent romantic feelings that accompany the attraction (Seto, 2012). The research is largely consistent in the finding that a small number of MAPs are exclusively attracted whereas a larger number have co-attractions to adults suggesting that MAPs are a heterogeneous group. Cantor and McPhail (2016) argue that for some, paedophilia is immutable and not open to long-term change; therefore, prevention therapy should focus on helping individuals live and cope with their interest and to lead a fulfilling life in the presence of the interest. This is a similar conclusion to that offered by Hoberman (2016) in a review of the factors that may impede successful treatment of people with sexual convictions:

> 'The nature of both the sexual dimensions of sexual offending (e.g., paraphilias and paraphilic disorder) and the nonsexual predisposing conditions…is such

that they may be extremely difficult to change or modify; central motivators and multiple dimensions of disinhibition may represent conditions that, to date, are relatively impermeable to short-term change via time-limited psychosocial interventions and, if modified or managed temporarily, are highly likely to rebound from a modified to a risk-inducing state. The combination of constitutional or physiologically based conditions, conditions related to early adversity, and other personal elements that provide profound rewards and significant gratification may create very significant obstacles for changes as with other presenting problems'. (Hoberman, 2016, p. 679)

Hoberman's point is that some of the factors related to sexual offending may not be changeable. Thus, moving to a therapeutic model which does not seek to change, rather, accept in order to maintain functionality is the preferred approach.

Turner-Moore and Waterman (2017) explored the relationship between self-identified sexual interests and sexual behaviour comparing an online community sample and a prison sample of PCSOs. They found that PCSOs against children were more likely to experience sexual thoughts about children and that sexual thoughts about children are relevant to first time sexual offending in some cases, although they speculate that thoughts themselves may not be casual of offending and rather mediating variables such as a sexual interest in children are casual. They did not find a relationship between sexual thoughts about coercion and offending overall. However, they did find that fantasies in which the other person expresses an enduring lack of consent were commonly a feature of people who had committed sexual offences compared to those who had not.

They specifically recommend more research to understand the moderating variables for sexual offending in the presence of sexual thoughts. They speculate that a possible moderator is the experience of the sexual thought itself, for example, how vivid or frequent. Thus, it is not necessarily the sexual thought itself that causes offending but other mediating and moderating variables. This suggests that targeting the content of sexual thoughts in prevention therapy may not be necessary but work targeting the experience of the thought could be helpful.

In an earlier large-scale internet-based survey, Turner-Moore and Waterman (2013) set out to explore the offence-related sexual interests of the general population compared to a sexually convicted population. They found that 15% (approximately 1 in 7) of the general population reported sexual thoughts about children compared to 28% of PCSOs; they concluded that these thoughts appeared to be a risk factor for sexual offending, but the content of the thought differentiated between offending and non-offending groups. They found three sexual thought content themes: self, mutual and other non-specific. Self-thoughts featured pubescent females with a focus entirely on self-pleasure and were most prevalent in the non-offending sample. The mutual group focused on prepubescent children with consenting and mutually enjoyable sexual activity and was slightly more prevalent in the offending sample. The final group was present equally in both groups and included sexual activity with a known child, the focus being on sex. They considered that people reporting the mutual type of sexual thoughts may be more at risk of offending and have more treatment needs related to emotional congruence with children. Consequently, they asserted that any assessment of therapy targets should take account of the interpersonal elements of the sexual thoughts.

Dombert et al. (2016) investigated the incidence of sexual interest and behaviour against prepubescent children in the general population via online survey and found a presence of 4.1% for sexual fantasies, 3.2% sexual offending and 0.1% a paedophilic sexual preference. Critically, there was an association with reported sexual interest in children and subjectively perceived need for therapeutic help. They conclude:

'The empirical link between child-related sexual fantasies and sexual victimization of prepubescent children and high levels of subjective distress from this inclination underscore the importance of evidence-based child sexual abuse prevention approaches in the community'. (p. 3)

This suggests that prevention therapy should address the sexual interest to reduce the distress associated with it and to provide the client with the skills to manage the interest such that they do not act on it. The exact relationship between the distress at the sexual interest and perceived lack of ability to manage behaviour from the interest is unknown, but it is likely that they are inter-dependent and assisting the client with one element will see improvement in the other.

Stigma and Shame

Research on the general population has consistently demonstrated attitudes towards people who commit sexual offences are dehumanising and are accompanied by the archetypal emotion of disgust. The general population ascribe to beliefs that change is not possible and people who commit sexual offences are likely to reoffend, these being messages communicated by the media (Feelgood & Hoyer, 2008). These beliefs also seem to extend to people who have not committed sexual offences but who declare paraphilic interests, most commonly a paedophiliac one. So strong is the messaging that people who offend against children are repetitive fixated offenders that there is a conflation between paedophile and offender, the deep-seated belief being that those with paedophilia are destined to offend, and any declaration otherwise from the person is simply a sign that they are manipulating others. See Chap. 7 by Harper in this volume for detailed exploration of attitudes to MAPs.

The social responses to paraphilias are anger, disgust and social rejection. The psychological consequences of social rejection for the individual are well documented and link directly to primal emotional systems. Social rejection is possibly one of the most damaging non-physical threats that a human can experience (Williams & Nida, 2011). Loneliness, for example, seems to contribute to higher mortality (Holt-Lunstad, Smith, Baker, Harris, & Stephenson, 2015). This is understandable given humans are inherently social animals, designed to live in social groups for survival and species advancement. Shame is a social emotion and triggers defensive responses (withdrawal or attack) (Tangney, 1995) in those who experience it which further aggravates social engagement, suggesting it is not a productive emotion. Shame is a well-documented experience for those who have committed sexual offences (Bumby, Marshall, & Langton, 1999; Scheff & Retzinger, 1997). Various disabling effects of shame have been observed, such as preventing social engagement, creating defensive responses and maladaptive functioning (Tangney & Dearing, 2002). Tangney, Wagner, Hill-Barlow, Marschall, and Gramzow (1996) suggest a link between shame and anger and suspiciousness, indicating that shame may functionally maintain dynamic risk factors for offending. Cantor and McPhail (2016) highlight the salience of social stigma for MAPs and suggest that the therapy process should aim to address this as stigma results in problematic outcomes. Therefore, a prevention intervention needs to be sensitive to the social context that paraphilic interests are situated within and ensure that any associated shame is not inadvertently perpetuated in the intervention and that it aims to actively address the effects of stigmatisation on mental well-being.

Research with MAPs (see Levenson & Grady, 2017) has found that most do not seek help to prevent them offending, since they view offending as unlikely and rather want help with the stigma of living with the interest. They are particularly sensitive to the implication that they may offend and some feel that the term 'prevention programme' is insulting since it implies the primary concern is to prevent offending. This suggests that language used in the content and approach of a prevention intervention is imperative if it is not to reinforce stigma. For this reason, the SLF intervention was named The Aurora Project. The name was chosen for its multiple meanings which embody the aims of the intervention, of particular relevance being new light, and in the dream literature, it means guidance in the face of adversity, elevation of the spirit, self-esteem and love for others.

Mental Illness

MAPS report a period of depression in response to discovering their sexual interest (Cash, 2016). This is perhaps an understandable response on discovering an interest that attracts such widespread public hostility. The research by Levenson and Grady (2017) offers further understanding of the complex nature of mental illness in MAPs. In their sample, 44% said they would want to use prevention therapy to discuss their depression and anxiety and reported that distress as a result of self-hatred and lack of self-acceptance was the cause of mental illness, as one of their participants explains:

> 'The attraction is often not the problem, or what needs the focus. From my experience at least, the actual urge to have sex with a child is fuelled by self-hatred, and inability to accept the attractions. Now that I have accepted myself

as a pedophile, I am comfortable in being able to find a child attractive, enjoy that attraction, and know that I shall never act upon that attraction.'

This suggests that a key target for prevention therapy is acceptance skills in order to help clients come to terms with their sexual interests. This is likely to have a positive impact on distress and reduce incidence of depression and anxiety.

The Aurora Project

Therapeutic Approach

The research thus far illustrates that the type of service users who may want to access therapy for sexual thoughts is heterogeneous, with needs that extend far beyond simply sexual interests or sexual thoughts. The research is indicative of a need to offer therapy that helps clients to accept their sexual thoughts and to thrive in the presence of them. Consequently, it may be helpful to draw on therapeutic models that are process driven and transdiagnostic; that is, they view the reasons for human problems as resulting from common psychological processes and do not view problems as stemming from syndromes or pathologies. Typically, therapies that adopt this stance are referred to as 'third wave' CBT (Hayes, 2004). CBT models have developed from behavioural formulations of problem behaviour (considered first wave) and later the inclusion of cognitive formulations of problematic behaviour (considered second wave). CBT models in the second wave have become the dominant treatment approach for many clinical problems including anxiety disorders and depression (Nice Institute for Clinical Excellence, NICE, 2011) and sexual offending (Schmucker & Lösel, 2017).

Third wave therapies are the next evolution of CBT. There are varied definitions of third wave therapies, partly because they consist of a heterogeneous group of therapies that are not necessarily characterised by 'new' therapies and there is no agreed unifying conceptual link between all the approaches. Granthan and Cowtan (2015) propose some broad principles with which to define third wave. First is the focus on helping clients to 'thrive and flourish', as opposed to simply reducing problematic symptomology which is considered a characteristic focus of second wave. Second, is the strong focus on the function and context of behaviours and the aim to change the context in which people experience thoughts and feelings by changing the relationship to them. Finally, there is a focus on emotions and helping clients experience them and accept them, with the aim of reducing the distress at emotions rather than changing the emotions. Therefore, acceptance of thoughts and feelings is a primary agenda of the third wave. Mindfulness is a linking intervention between the different approaches, although it is conceptualised slightly differently in each therapeutic approach. A further feature of some therapies is the recognition that shame and self-criticism are counterproductive and these are actively targeted. For these reasons, Walton and Hocken (in press) argue that third wave CBT offers further ways to understand the development and maintenance of paraphilic sexual interests and propose third wave approaches as a helpful expansion of current treatment for PCSOs.

Second wave CBT has been the most prominent therapy method used with PCSOs (Schmucker & Lösel, 2017), the philosophical goals of which, to reduce problematic symptomology, align with the thinking that reducing risk factors is important to treat sexual offending (Andrews & Bonta, 2003). Yet, the shift in the current thinking that treatment of sexual offending should be strengths based and build psychological capability rather than exclusively focus on risk (e.g. Laws & Ward, 2011) has led to a disconnect with the goals of second wave CBT. The goals of third wave CBT, to help people to flourish and thrive, are far more aligned to the strengths-based approach and are well placed as a therapeutic grounding for the prevention of first time sexual offending. The philosophy of third wave CBT takes a destigmatising approach to problems and has at its heart an intention to help clients lead rich, full and meaningful lives. Inevitably, as a newer therapy approach, the evidence base for third wave CBT cannot currently equal that of second wave CBT; however, there is good evidence, within methodologically sound meta-analysis of randomised control trials, that they are effective at treating mental health problems (e.g. A-Tjak et al., 2015), including problematic sexual behaviour in the form of excessive pornography use (Crosby & Twohig, 2016).

TAP utilises three third wave CBT therapies: Compassion Focused Therapy (CFT; Gilbert, 2010), Acceptance and Commitment Therapy (said as one word—ACT; Hayes, Strosahl, & Wilson, 2012) and Functional Analytic Psychotherapy (FAP; Kohlenberg & Tsai, 1991). These, alongside mindfulness as the linking intervention, are now reviewed.

Mindfulness

Mindfulness has origins in Buddhism, but it has been used for many years as a therapeutic tool (Kabat-Zinn, 1990). There are wide and varying definitions of mindfulness but the key element is about attentional focus on the present moment, *'paying attention in a particular way: on purpose, in the present moment and non-judgmentally'* (p. 4). (Kabat-Zinn, 1994). Mindfulness aims to build capability for attention, helping to move focus from thoughts towards awareness. Two key interventions that use mindfulness to treat mental health problems are Mindfulness Based Stress Reduction (MBSR; Kabat-Zinn, 1982) and Mindfulness Based Cognitive Therapy (MBCT; Segal, Williams, & Teasdale, 2002). These techniques have been used to treat the psychological distress associated with conditions such as cancer, fibromyalgia and chronic pain as well as stress and anxiety (Fjorback, Arendt, Fink, & Walach, 2011) and the National Institute for Clinical Excellence (NICE, 2011) guidelines recommend MBCT for depression. Granthan and Cowtan (2015) summarise that one possible mechanism for the effectiveness of mindfulness is the non-reactive acceptance of thoughts and feelings which may impact on the memory specifically. For example, people with depression may encode events as being signs of their inadequacy if things don't go right ('I'm a failure'). Mindfulness teaches non-judgmentalness and thus people are able to encode and remember experiences differently ('I didn't do well in that particular situation') and the ability to disengage from thought patterns because of enhanced attentional awareness. This latter point is important because simply having insight or 'cognitive awareness' is not necessarily sufficient for managing responses to thoughts and feelings.

There is emerging evidence for the application of mindfulness with people who have committed sexual offences. Gillespie, Mitchell, Fisher, and Beech (2012) hypothesise that mindfulness works because it involves slow deep breathing which deactivates the nervous system and they suggest that this could be effective for emotional regulation for PCSOs. Other benefits of mindfulness training for PCSOs are also considered important such as developing attentional focus and the ability to defuse from thoughts and feelings.

Compassion Focused Therapy

CFT takes a neuro-evolutionary stance that psychological suffering is caused by a universal human inability to manage and respond to primal emotional drives. Human competencies for language and self-awareness are relatively new, and the integration of these 'new brain' competencies with 'old brain' drives for survival including procreation and status, are not complete. This results in a uniquely human difficulty of being aware of primal drives, itself a source of shame and self-criticism where these drives conflict with the ideals of society or the individual. CFT explicitly acknowledges that private experiences (e.g. thoughts, feelings) are a complex product of genes, environment and life experiences. As such it takes the view that thoughts, feelings, urges, sensations, perception and memories are not the fault of the individual, but there is a responsibility for how they respond to them. CFT was originally designed for depressed patients who experienced high levels of shame and self-criticism and were unresponsive to second wave CBT (Gilbert, 1992), with the aim of alleviating shame and self-criticism caused by self-blame for their difficult thoughts and feelings.

CFT proposes that the behaviours deployed by individuals to respond to difficult life circumstances can be viewed as 'safety strategies'; responses designed to ensure survival. Safety strategies are highly functional in the moment but can lead to unintended consequences further down the line. For example, an individual who experiences childhood abuse may adopt a safety strategy of withdrawal from adults. As an adult this has the unintended consequence of preventing the development of healthy adult attachments and possible healthy sexuality. Assisting individuals to understand the once functional purpose of their now unhelpful thinking and behaviours provides an unthreatening metric by which to understand the development of their problems, and destigmatises the presence of unhelpful thinking and behaviours.

The therapeutic aim of CFT is compassionate mind training (CMT). Compassion is defined as (a) a motivation to recognise suffering in the self and others and (b) having dedication and courage to act to alleviate suffering (Gilbert, 2014). Individuals can direct compassion inwards, outwards and receive compassion. In developing compassion, skills are taught to be able to view and talk to the self in kind and warm ways, helping to deactivate the sympathetic nervous system and improve abilities to self sooth. Arguably, developing skills for compassion to others may also help to moderate any unhealthy influence from offence supportive beliefs. The features of CFT indicate that it is a helpful therapeutic approach when working with traumatised populations (Taylor, 2017).

Acceptance and Commitment Therapy

In ACT, behaviours are explained in terms of contextual variables, viewing thoughts as neither correct nor incorrect but rather the human experience of thoughts, as defined via psychological inflexibility, as the source of distress. Psychological inflexibility, and its antithesis, psychological flexibility, are defined by six processes (see Table 4.1). The key therapeutic goal is to develop skills for psychological flexibility to help the client a lead rich, full and meaningful life.

In practice, these skills might require the client to notice and name (observer self) their sexual thoughts (or any other unhelpful thoughts), to be aware of their surroundings and what is happening internally (present moment awareness), be willing to allow the thoughts and feelings without changing them (acceptance), to unhook from the thoughts and feelings (defusion) and to keep clear in mind the values they are working towards and to take action towards those values. The use of ACT in TAP facilitates the ability for defusion from unhelpful sexual identities, for example (paedophile). For this reason, defusion skills are taught from the

Table 4.1 The six core processes of psychological inflexibility and psychological flexibility

Psychological inflexibility	Psychological flexibility	SLF prevention intervention application
Cognitive fusion is the belief that thoughts are fact and represent reality. We 'fuse' with thoughts and get pulled along by them	*Defusion* is the recognition that thoughts are not reality and involves the ability to step back from thoughts and observe them	Cognitive defusion skills are applied to *any* unhelpful thought including sexual, shameful and self-critical thoughts
Experiential avoidance is the process of avoiding (internal) experiences that feel uncomfortable and can lead to attempts to suppress or fight thoughts, feelings, sensations and memories	*Acceptance* is an openness to all experiences without trying to change it but at the same time behaving effectively. It is not a passive 'giving in' or letting them take over but a willingness to experience	Acceptance of all inner experiences is encouraged helping people to live with their sexual interest, or any other internal experience. Giving up the struggle allows the individual to focus on what is important to them in life
Dominance of past and future is an over focus on ruminating or worrying about what will or has happened	*Present moment contact* is bringing awareness to the here and now, noticing the experience as it unfolds	This helps to reduce anxiety, worry and build ability to enjoy experiences
Attachment to a conceptualised self is the belief that thoughts and feelings define identity and involves behaviour governed by accordance with a particular identity, e.g. being a good father, being a paedophile	*Self as context* is the recognition that thoughts and feelings do not define the identity and is closely linked to defusion since it involves the ability to observe thinking	Enables clients to step back from unhelpful identities such as 'paedophile', and the associated stigma of these identities
Lack of contact and clarity with values is not being aware of or invested in what is important or meaningful in life	*Contact and clarity with values* is about knowing what values are important to the individual, what they want to stand for in life. Values are used to guide behaviour	Enables clients to work toward a rich, full and meaningful life, not just to focus on their problems

(continued)

Table 4.1 (continued)

Psychological inflexibility	Psychological flexibility	SLF prevention intervention application
Avoidance behaviour is behaviour motivated by a desire to avoid unpleasant experiences which ends up being or leading to the problematic behaviour	*Committed action* are value-based behaviours that lead a person in the direction of their values	Clients define what actions will take them in their valued direction and are supported to build the skills necessary to achieve them

beginning of therapy. The research by Turner-Moore and Waterman (2017) speculated that the sexual thought itself may not lead to offending, but that moderating variables, such as the experience of the thought, including vividness, may be more influential. In ACT terms, this parallels the concept of 'fusion', that is thoughts are experienced as reality and things that define identity and behaviour. Thus, building skills for defusion may reduce the engagement with and likelihood of acting on any unhelpful sexual thoughts.

Psychoeducation work around likely offence supportive beliefs such can be offered but only once clients have developed skills for defusion and self as context to avoid perpetuating labels of 'paedophile'. Acceptance is also an important concept when responding to offence-related sexual thoughts and urges. Thought stopping and suppression have been tried as a means of treating offence-related sexual interests (Shingler, 2009); however, thought suppression is paradoxically more likely to increase the targeted thought and to contribute to obsessive intrusive thought patterns (Wenzlaff, Wegner, & Roper, 1988). Suppression of a sexual interest that has a biological (e.g. orientational) basis is likely to be unachievable and consequently to create feelings of shame and hopelessness, both of which will be counterproductive to recovery. Acceptance releases clients from struggling with their internal experiences, providing cognitive freedom to focus on valued behaviour.

At its core, ACT helps clients to evaluate the 'workability' of their beliefs and behaviours: that is to what degree the belief/behaviour helps them to move towards their valued direction in life. Given that ACT does not label thoughts and feelings as right or wrong, the concept of workability helps clients to discern for themselves what decisions are functional for them. Even where clients do not alter their fundamental beliefs, for example, about children and sex, if they recognise the unworkability of the belief and can apply skills to behave functionally in the presence of the belief that is likely to be sufficient.

Functional Analytic Psychotherapy

FAP takes a behavioural worldview, and as such adopts the stance that sexual thoughts, feelings and behaviours are behaviourally inputted. While not explicitly subscribing to cognitive explanations of behaviours, such as schemas, FAP acknowledges that thoughts can cause behaviour because of conditioned responses. Sexual feelings may follow sexual thoughts as a result of a stimulus responses process. However, it does not assume overt, cognitively based triggers for behaviours. While it acknowledges that cognitions such as automatic thoughts are relevant, they are not considered to be the only explanation. This is a helpful approach to take in trying to explore triggers for sexual thoughts, since it recognises that sexual thoughts could simply arise, without any observable trigger. This can be alleviating for a client who may feel the burden of shame, believing they somehow trigger their unwanted sexual thoughts.

A key concept in FAP is clinically relevant behaviours (CRBs). These are behaviours (including thoughts feelings, perceptions) that occur in therapy sessions but parallel those related to the presenting problem and are viewed as non-pathological generalisations of the client's behaviour. Some CRBs do not look the same on the surface as those behaviours outside of therapy, but they have the same function. CRBs provide ideal opportunities for real life learning. CRBs are divided into three groups: (a) those that occur in sessions, (b) clients behaviours that show improvements in session and (c) when the client begins to recognise and interpret their own behaviours successfully (showing insight). It is vital that the difference between these are spotted and understood, so that 'b' can be reinforced and 'a' not reinforced.

An important tenant of ACT, CFT and FAP is that they acknowledge the importance of the therapeutic relationship, viewing this in itself as an important context in which learning and progress occur, particularly in relation to learning about intimacy and relationships via the therapeutic relationship. FAP draws attention to the concept of hidden meanings in the client's behaviour. It suggests that these meanings might be unconscious and the client unaware of them and therapists should explore these and help develop insight. In this way, the therapist focuses attention on the dynamic of the relationship. Hidden meanings can be explored by examining the context and consequences of certain behaviours or utterances. FAP expects therapists to develop trust and safety by asking for feedback from clients on the session content, the therapists style, the therapist training and to encourage the client to ask questions about therapy, their past experience and training and to ask questions about their experience of the therapist, their age, gender etc. and how they see that playing a role in therapy. In line with the aim of building trust and safety in therapy are certain therapist behaviours that reinforce this, such as being warm and genuine, honest, consistent and deliver on promises, structuring expectations, being transparent, admitting mistakes and repairing ruptures, use of self-disclosure, treating client disclosures with respect and care, remembering client disclosures, and acting in the best interest of the client.

Paul, Marx, and Orsillo (1999) applied ACT alongside FAP, for a 12-month court mandated treatment of a male who had been convicted of exhibitionism. They report a total absence of exhibitionist behaviour at treatment completion and at six months follow-up. In addition, there were improved outcomes for social anxiety, generalised anxiety, marijuana use and depression as well as the development of functional behaviours such as healthy masturbation frequency and content, social connection and intimate relationships.

Intervention Structure

TAP does not discriminate service entry based on type of sexual interest and so offers therapy to clients no matter what the object of their interests. The nature of referrals so far is very diverse and they range from unusual sexual interests such as zoophilia (interest in animals), excessive internet pornography use, sadism and interests in children. TAP offers both group and individual therapy options. There is also an option to access medication to manage sexual arousal for those who are sexually preoccupied. The core work is undertaken in the group; however, clients will also see a therapist individually. For those unsuitable for group-based work, individual therapy is offered. The group is a rolling format intervention, meaning that it is continuous and new members begin as older remembers finish. This has the advantage of older members being able to support newer members. Typically, clients will have between 15 and 50 sessions, although the exact number is determined collaboratively with the client as therapy progresses, allowing them to decide when to finish. Clients can restart therapy again at any time. The therapy is delivered by a team of three mental health professionals (e.g. mental health nurses, psychologists, psychotherapist etc.) who are all experienced in working therapeutically with PCSOs and have received specialist training in TAP intervention. They receive clinical supervision from a forensic psychologist.

There is no requirement for clients to talk about their sexual interest in the group, although they can if they choose to. The reasoning for this is that the therapy format does not involve exploration of the detail of the sexual thought, rather it is about teaching skills for accepting and managing thoughts. A further advantage of this stance is that it minimises any 'deviancy training' that has been cited as a potential drawback of treatment programmes for PCSOs (Duggan & Dennis, 2014). Narratives relating to risk and offending are likely to perpetuate the notion that offending is likely so TAP does not use labels of 'risk' 'risk factors' or 'offending' to talk about client thoughts, feelings or lifestyle features, but instead talks about 'push' 'pull' and 'protection' factors to acting on sexual thoughts.

TAP is not a heavily manualised intervention, rather it is set of principles about how the intervention should be delivered and what to focus on, there are exercises that therapists can choose from, or they can use their own exercises to meet the client's treatment aims as long as they are consistent with the ethos of the intervention.

Assessment and Formulation

TAP accepts self-referrals as well as those from other professionals such as counsellors, healthcare professionals and educational staff. Before beginning any therapeutic work, the client will work individually with a therapist to begin to understand the nature of their problem and what they want to achieve in therapy. During this phase, some psychoeducation of the therapeutic models takes place. Agreeing behavioural goals is critical to identifying treatment targets and measuring success, a common question asked of clients is 'How will we know this therapy is working? What will we see you doing differently?' Collaboratively, the therapist and the client decide on the priorities to focus on in treatment and how that might be achieved.

Clients undertake pre- and post-therapy psychometric assessment exploring: compassion, shame and self-criticism, psychological flexibility and sexual thinking and behaviours. The change between these assessments points is used as a pre-post progress assessment and will contribute to the longer-term evaluation of the service.

Intervention

During therapy clients have the opportunity to explore and identify the origins, development and maintaining factors for their sexual interest, for example, by exploring behaviours and the value (emotional or otherwise) placed on these, which experiences were reinforced and which are punished or extinguished, to understand why some behaviours are preferred over others and what sexual things they were closed to in their lives and what they would have liked to try but never got a chance. Clients can also explore sexual self-identity including orientation, preferences for frequency and type of sex, pornography use and values about sex. The aim of TAP is not to change sexual interests but to help clients change their relationship with their thoughts and feelings and to develop compassion for themselves and others. Change to sexual interests may occur as a result of this process but that is not the aim.

Where clients have therapy needs that are more appropriate to be addressed individually such as trauma, they will have individual therapy either concurrently with group or consecutively as decided with the client. The particular therapeutic approach of the individual work is down to the therapist and client to decide, but could include third wave approaches, as well as other approaches such eye movement desensitisation and reprocessing (EMDR).

Review and Moving On

The behavioural goals clients set at the start of therapy are regularly reviewed as a measure of progress and to make decisions about therapy ending. The aim is to understand if the treatment goals have been met and if not why not. The decision to finish therapy is made collaboratively with the client and a therapist, on the understanding that the client can re-refer and enter therapy again at any point in the future. Clients are also encouraged to find ways to build and maintain their skills from therapy, for example, through self-directed reading or continuing formal mindfulness practice.

Conclusion

The requirement to provide free services to prevent first sexual offending is critical if society is to make long term, meaningful change to sexual offending prevalence. Recognition of this need has been surprisingly slow, partly because those in need of such a service are reluctant to speak out. As such, relatively little has been established about the treatment needs of this client group which has no doubt hampered the impetus to deliver these services. Far more needs to be done to encourage academic and practitioner research, debate and reflection about the best ways to help people with their unwanted sexual thoughts and feelings to prevent first time sexual offending. Through the development of TAP, the SLF is one of the first organisations in the UK to offer free therapy to people with any sexual interest that could be harmful, if acted upon. Measuring multi-level outcomes related to mental well-being, quality of life and offending behaviour are now central to testing and refining a therapeutic service that works to prevent sexual offending.

References

Andrews, D. A., & Bonta, J. (2003). *The psychology of criminal conduct* (3rd ed.). Cincinnati, OH: Anderson Publishing.

A-Tjak, J. G. L., Davis, M. L., Morina, N., Powers, M. B., Smits, J. A. J., & Emmelkamp, P. M. G. (2015). A meta-analysis of the efficacy of acceptance and commitment therapy for clinically relevant mental and physical health problems. *Psychotherapy and Psychosomatics, 84*, 30–36.

Beier, K. M., Grundmann, D., Kuhle, L. F., Scherner, G., Konrad, A., & Amelung, T. (2015). The German Dunkelfeld project: A pilot study to prevent child sexual abuse and the use of child abusive images. *Journal of Sexual Medicine, 12*(2), 529–542.

Bumby, K. M., Marshall, W. L., & Langton, C. (1999). A theoretical model of the influences of shame and guilt on sexual offending. In B. K. Schwartz (Ed.), *The sex offender: Theoretical advances, treating special populations and legal developments* (pp. 1–12). Kingston, NJ: Civic Research Institute.

Cantor, J., & McPhail, I. (2016). Non-offending pedophiles. *Current Sexual Health Reports*. Online first. https://doi.org/10.1007/s11930-016-0076-z.

Cash, B. M. (2016). *Self-identifications, sexual development, and wellbeing in minor-attracted people: An exploratory study*. Unpublished thesis, Cornell University, New York.

Crosby, J., & Twohig, M. P. (2016). Acceptance and commitment therapy for problematic internet pornography use: A randomized trial. *Behavior Therapy, 47*, 355–366.

Dombert, B., Schmidt, A. F., Banse, R., Briken, P., Hoyer, J., Neutze, J., et al. (2016). How common is Men's self-reported sexual interest in prepubescent children? *Journal of Sex Research, 53*(2), 214–223.

Duggan, C., & Dennis, J. (2014). The place of evidence in the treatment of sex offenders. *Criminal Behaviour and Mental Health, 24*(3), 153–162.

Feelgood, S., & Hoyer, J. (2008). Child molester or paedophile? Sociolegal versus psychopathological classification of sexual offenders against children. *Journal of Sexual Aggression, 14*, 33–43. https://doi.org/10.1080/13552600802133860.

Fjorback, L. O., Arendt, E. O., Fink, P., & Walach, H. (2011). Mindfulness-based stress reduction and mindfulness-based cognitive therapy systematic review of randomised controlled trials. *Acta Psychiatrica Scandinivica, 124*(2), 102–119.

Gilbert, P. (1992). *Depression: The evolution of powerlessness*. Hove/New York: Lawrence Erlbaum Associates Ltd/Guilford.

Gilbert, P. (2010). *Compassion focused therapy: Distinctive features*. London: Routledge.

Gilbert, P. (2014). The origins and nature of compassion focused therapy. *British Journal of Clinical Psychology, 53*, 6–41.

Gillespie, S. M., Mitchell, I. J., Fisher, D., & Beech, A. R. (2012). Treating disturbed emotional regulation in sexual offenders: The potential applications of mindful self-regulation and controlled breathing techniques. *Aggression and Violent Behavior, 17*(4), 333–343.

Granthan, P., & Cowtan, C. (2015). *Third wave CBT therapies brief literature review*. SDS Seminars Ltd. www.skillsdevelopment.co.uk

Hanson, R. K., & Morton-Bourgon, K. E. (2005). The characteristics of persistent sexual offenders: A meta-analysis of recidivism studies. *Journal of Consulting and Clinical Psychology, 73*, 1154–1163.

Hayes, S. C. (2004). Acceptance and commitment therapy, relational frame theory, and the third wave of behavioral and cognitive therapies. *Behavior Therapy, 35*, 639–665.

Hayes, S. C., Strosahl, K. D., & Wilson, K. G. (2012). *Acceptance and commitment therapy: The process and practice of mindful change* (2nd ed.). New York: The Guilford Press.

Hoberman, H. M. (2016). Forensic psychotherapy for sexual offenders: Likely factors contributing to its apparent ineffectiveness. In A. Phenix & H. Hoberman (Eds.), *Sexual offending*. New York: Springer.

Holt-Lunstad, J., Smith, T., Baker, M., Harris, T., & Stephenson, D. (2015). Loneliness and social isolation as risk factors for mortality: A meta-analytic review. *Perspectives Psychological Science, 10*, 227–237.

Kabat-Zinn, J. (1982). An outpatient program in behavioral medicine for chronic pain patients based on the practice of mindfulness meditation: Theoretical considerations and preliminary results. *General Hospital Psychiatry, 4*, 33–47.

Kabat-Zinn, J. (1990). *Full catastrophe living: Using the wisdom of your body and mind to face stress, pain and illness*. New York: Delacorte.

Kabat-Zinn, J. (1994). *Wherever you go, there you are: Mindfulness meditation in everyday life*. New York: Hyperion.

Kohlenberg, R. J., & Tsai, M. (1991). *Functional analytic psychotherapy: Creating intense and curative therapeutic relationships*. New York: Plenum.

Langstrom, N., Enebrink, P., Laurén, E. M., Lindblom, J., Werkö, S., & Hanson, R. K. (2013). Preventing sexual abusers of children from reoffending: Systematic review of medical and psychological interventions. *British Medical Journal, 347*, f4630.

Laws, D. R., & Ward, T. (2011). *Desistance from sexual offending: Alternatives to throwing away the keys*. New York: Guilford.

Levenson, J. S., & Grady, M. (2017, October 18). *Obstacles to help-seeking for minor-attracted persons*. Presented at the association for Treatment of Sexual Abusers (ATSA) conference, Lawrence, KS.

Levenson, J. S., Willis, G. M., & Vicencio, C. P. (2017). Obstacles to help-seeking for sexual offenders: Implications for prevention of sexual abuse. *Journal of Child Sexual Abuse, 26*(2), 99–120.

Lievesley, R., Elliott, H., Barnes, O., & Rodgers, C. (2018). *Resist not desist: An exploration of help seeking bahaviour in individuals with sexual convictions*. Manuscript in preparation.

Mann, R. E., Hanson, K. R., & Thornton, D. (2010). Assessing risk for sexual recidivism: Some proposals on the nature of psychologically meaningful risk factors. *Sexual Abuse: A Journal of Research and Treatment, 22*(2), 191–217.

Maruna, S., & Mann, R. E. (2006). A fundamental attribution error? Rethinking cognitive distortions. *Legal and Criminological Psychology, 11*, 155–177. https://doi.org/10.1348/135532506X114608.

National Institute for Health and Clinical Excellence. (2011). *Common mental health problems: Common mental health problems: Identification and path identification and pathways to care*. Retrieved from https://www.nice.org.uk/guidance/cg123

Paul, R. H., Marx, B. P., & Orsillo, S. M. (1999). Acceptance based psychotherapy in the treatment of an adjudicated exhibitionist: A case example. *Behavior Therapy, 30*, 149–162.

Scheff, T. J., & Retzinger, S. M. (1997). Shame, anger, and the social bond: A theory of sexual offenders and treatment. *Electronic Journal of Sociology*. Available at http://www.sociology.org/content/vol003.001/sheff.html

Schmucker, M., & Lösel, F. (2017). Sexual offender treatment for reducing recidivism among convicted sex offenders: A systematic review and meta-analysis. *Campbell Systematic Reviews, 8*.

Schulz, T., Palmer, S., Stolpmann, G., Wernicke, M., & Müller, J. L. (2017). Presenting a treatment concept for people with a self-reported sexual interest in children in an outpatient setting. *Open Journal of Psychiatry, 7*, 117. https://doi.org/10.4236/ojpsych.2017.71001.

Segal, Z. V., Williams, J. M., & Teasdale, J. (2002). *Mindfulness-based cognitive therapy for depression: A new approach to preventing relapse*. London: Guildford Press.

Seto, M. C. (2012). Is pedophilia a sexual orientation? *Archives of Sexual Behavior, 41*, 231–236. https://doi.org/10.1007/s1050.

Shingler, J. (2009). Managing intrusive risky thoughts: What works? *Journal of Sexual Aggression, 15*(1), 39–53. https://doi.org/10.1080/13552600802542011.

Szumski, F., Bartels, R. M., Beech, A. R., & Fisher, D. (2018). Distorted cognition related to male sexual offending: The multi-mechanism theory of cognitive distortions (MMT-CD). *Aggression and Violent Behavior, 39*. https://doi.org/10.1016/j.avb.2018.02.001.

Tangney, J. P. (1995). Recent empirical advances in the study of shame and guilt. *American Behavioral Scientist, 38*, 1132–1145.

Tangney, J. P., & Dearing, R. (2002). *Shame and guilt*. New York: Guilford.

Tangney, J. P., Wagner, P. E., Hill-Barlow, D., Marschall, D. E., & Gramzow, R. (1996). Relation of shame and guilt to constructive versus destructive responses to anger across the lifespan. *Journal of Personality and Social Psychology, 70*(4), 797.

Taylor, J. (2017). Compassion focused working in secure forensic care. *Journal of Criminological Research, Policy and Practice, 3*(4), 287–293.

Turner-Moore, T., & Waterman, M. (2017). Men presenting with sexual thoughts of children or coercion: Flights of fancy or plans for crime? *Journal of Sexual Medicine, 14*(1), 113–124 ISSN 1743-6095.

Turner-Moore, T., & Waterman, M. G. (2013, April 9–11). *Adult men's typical and atypical sexual thoughts and relationships with sexual offending*. In BPS Annual Conference 2013, Harrogate International Centre, Harrogate, UK.

Vanhoeck, K., Gykiere, K., & Wanzeele, W. (2014). How to not become a sex offender: From "offender therapy" to "offender prevention therapy". *Mental Health & Prevention, 2*. https://doi.org/10.1016/j.mhp.2014.07.003.

Walton, J. S. (2018). Random assignment in sexual offending programme evaluation: The missing method. *Journal of Forensic Practice*. https://doi.org/10.1108/JFP-08-2017-0032.

Walton, J. S., & Hocken, K. (in press). *Compassion and acceptance as interventions for paraphilic disorders and sexual offending behaviour*. Available from https://www.researchgate.net/publication/325746252_Compassion_and_Acceptance_as_Interventions_for_Paraphilic_Disorders_and_Sexual_Offending_Behaviour

Wenzlaff, R. M., Wegner, D. M., & Roper, D. W. (1988). Depression and mental control: The resurgence of unwanted negative thoughts. *Journal of Personality and Social Psychology, 55*, 882–892. https://doi.org/10.1037/0022-3514.55.6.882.

Williams, K. D., & Nida, S. (2011). Ostracism: Consequences and coping. *Current Directions in Psychological Science, 20*, 71–75. https://doi.org/10.1177/0963721411402480.

5

Mersey Forensic Psychology Prevention Service: Pilot Project

Lorraine Perry, Simon Duff, and Lisa Wright

Introduction

Mersey Forensic Psychology Service (MFPS) is a community psychology service and part of the Secure Division of Mersey Care NHS Foundation Trust. MFPS has been providing psychological interventions to adults at risk of sexual re-offending since 1986. Over the years, these interventions have evolved in order to provide a service that is responsive to clients' needs whilst aiming to reduce risk (see, e.g., Cahalane & Duff, 2018; Cahalane, Duff, & Parker, 2013; Duff & Willis, 2006; Hossack, 1999; Hossack & Robinson, 2005; Shannon, Pearce, & Swarbrick, 2013). The core service is designed for individuals who have convictions for sexual offences against children. As a highly specialised service, we only work

---

L. Perry (✉) • L. Wright
Mersey Care NHS Foundation Trust, Prescot, UK
e-mail: Lorraine.Perry@merseycare.nhs.uk; Lisa.Wright@merseycare.nhs.uk

S. Duff
University of Nottingham, Nottingham, UK
e-mail: Simon.Duff@nottingham.ac.uk

with individuals who are motivated to attend treatment, have a desire to change, are psychologically minded, and acknowledge their offence and/or attraction to children. These are important components for success, particularly as research has demonstrated that withdrawing from an intervention programme prior to completion can negatively impact upon risk (McMurran & Theodosi, 2007).

The development of our new Prevention Service is based broadly on our work and experience working with men who have offended; therefore, we will provide an account of that work prior to discussing the details of the Prevention Service.

MFPS: Reducing Risk of Re-offending

The MFPS intervention is a multi-theoretical approach that has been developed over a number of years. Ultimately, the approach is shaped by findings that cognitive behavioural therapy (CBT) group interventions alone will not bring about the changes needed in all offenders to reduce their risk of reoffending (Dennis et al., 2012; Schmucker & Lösel, 2015; Walton & Chou, 2015); therefore, methods that produce enduring emotional and physiological change have been employed as a part of our practice. This is in line with earlier studies that have suggested that UK Prison-based Sex Offender Treatment Programmes (SOTP), which are predominantly CBT in nature, show most effect in those identified as of medium risk, but little change in those considered high risk (Friendship, Mann, & Beech, 2003). Furthermore, recent evaluation of Core SOTP in prison has found that it has had little effect on re-offending rates (Mews, Di Bella, & Purver, 2017). Service user evaluation is consistent with this: individuals who have re-offended following our previous CBT-based interventions have reported that the feelings driving the offending behaviour had not changed and, when active, had led to reoffending. There are also individuals who identify as being incapable of change following CBT-based interventions (Walton & Duff, 2017). We therefore have included alternative theoretical models in all of our interventions, based on evidence of their effectiveness in mental health settings.

There are five integrated elements to the MFPS reducing risk of re-offending service: the Introductory Group, the Intermediate Group, Individual Therapy, the Relapse Prevention Drop-in Forum, and a Non-Offending Partners Group (NOP group) (Duff et al., 2017; Perry, Wright, & Duff, 2013). Men who have offended against children will be offered the Introductory, Intermediate, and Individual Therapy elements and when these are complete they will be offered the Drop-in Forum, which is a monthly support group. If they have children or stepchildren, their partners will be offered the NOP group, which improves their ability to protect children from sexual abuse. Interventions for the men are based on an idiosyncratic collaborative formulation, which is developed for each client and informs their specific needs during each phase of the intervention.

The Introductory Group

The Introductory Group is the start of the treatment journey and has a focus on offending behaviour. The aim is to introduce clients to the notion that there is a process to their offending. The group is fundamentally CBT in approach and identifies the thoughts, feelings, and behaviours that were active at the time of offending. This aids in the development of explicit risk management strategies, which is a primary focus as clients are living in the community, by identifying the issues that maintain the risk of recidivism in order to pre-empt them and take evasive action, based on the risk-need model (Ward & Beech, 2006).

This 16-week programme helps clients identify their own individual process of offending using Finklehor's Precondition Model (Finkelhor, 1984). It also gauges their level of insight into victims' experiences and explores and discusses victim experiences using a variety of media. Although Finkelhor's Precondition model is over 30 years old (and thus does not account for many of the twenty-first -century methods of sexual offending), and, additionally, has been criticised in the literature (Ward & Hudson, 2001), it has enormous utility in group settings with our service users. It is a simple framework to work with, both for the therapists and clients, and the flexibility and inclusiveness that Ward and

Hudson identify as a potential source of inconsistency allow for broad and deep discussions in order to uncover the (i) motivations, (ii) cognitions, (iii) planning, and (iv) behaviours that overcome victim resistance, helping individuals both understand the various aspects of their offending process and to be able to verbalise it. Understanding gained from using the Finkelhor model can be used to identify areas of focus for the next phases of intervention. This may be the first time the participants have spoken about their offending in detail with others who are not part of the criminal justice system. Past service users have reported that a non-judgemental, non-confrontational stance presented by facilitators allowed them to speak more openly and honestly about their offending and that shame could be a barrier to engagement. Clinicians need to recognise and acknowledge this and pace the sessions such that the service users feel safe enough to disclose. Clients report that previously they may have minimised or denied their behaviour in order to achieve lesser sentences, to have minimal disruption in their lives, and through fear of societal reprisals or negative responses from partners or family. These are understandable concerns as the label of 'sexual offender' can impact upon one's access to one's own children, bring about the ending or changing of relationships, and can lead to threats of harm in prison and in the community. Professionals need to be responsive to the very real negative consequences that may impact upon how the men perceive and describe themselves, engage with services, and have the capacity to work within a group setting with other offenders. Hence the therapists should be warm and empathic, and offer some flexibility in approach (Duff, Perry, Wright, & Jackson, 2014; Marshall, 2005) in order to develop a good quality therapeutic relationship and an emotionally safe environment that the men can then use to explore their behaviour (Gilbert, 2009).

The Intermediate Group

Phase two of the programme is the 18-week intermediate group; clients begin to explore their lifelong psychological development in more depth whilst identifying the origins of emotional and sexual factors linked to risk. As the group progresses, a collaborative formulation is developed, helping individuals to understand the impact of their early experiences on their subsequent development and encouraging them to understand their offending behaviour as part of a wider context, involving personality traits, coping styles, attachment issues, and inter-relational difficulties.

We began to incorporate Schema Therapy (Young, Klosko, & Weishaar, 2003) into our programme in 2010 after learning from men who had re-offended after completing CBT-based interventions. They reported that, although they had learned more healthy ways of thinking and behaving from these interventions, when distress or other difficult emotions had been active in their lives, this new way of thinking and behaving had been too difficult to access. Reoffending had occurred as a result. Schema Therapy recognises that emotions drive behaviour and can override rational thinking. It has been used in mental health settings to produce long-term emotional and personality change (Giesen-Bloo et al., 2006) and, more recently, in forensic settings to alter the personality factors associated with risk of re-offending (Bernstein, Arntz, & de Vos, 2007). We therefore use it with our clients to change the emotional factors linked to risk of sexual re-offending.

The schema model explains that when needs for safety and acceptance, autonomy, freedom of expression, spontaneity, and appropriate boundaries are not met adequately during childhood, early maladaptive schemas begin to develop (Young et al., 2003). Schemas are a mixture of emotions, physical feelings, memories, beliefs, and expectations clustered around a specific theme (e.g. an 'emotional deprivation' schema involves the expectation that one's emotional needs will not be met by others, that one is unimportant or unloved). These schemas are activated by particular situations, which then propel the individual into specific modes that allow them to cope with the schema and get their needs met. However, these modes involve either 'surrender' (going along with the schema), 'avoidance' (attempts to detach from the schema) or 'overcompensation' (trying to fight the schema but going too far), which can involve problematic thinking and behaviour and eventually result in reinforcement of the schema. Just as schemas have originated in unmet childhood needs, modes are a development of the ways that the child had learned to cope with the pain and distress of the unmet need.

The Schema Therapy model allows the client to understand their offending behaviour as having its origins in their unmet childhood needs and coping strategies. Conceptualising offending behaviour as part of a specific coping mode brings a little distance and a perspective that can reduce shame and defensiveness, which is common in this client group, allowing them to explore their offending behaviour more easily. It identifies targets for risk management, initially, and risk reduction, over time, as the clients become more familiar with their own schemas and modes and engage in change work.

After having gone through each client's childhood experiences, we educate them on the Schema Therapy model, help them to identify the schemas and modes that they experience and the origin of these in their unmet childhood needs. As they become more familiar with the model, and in recognising the activation of the schemas and modes in their day to day living, we teach them methods to stop the reinforcement of the schemas and modes and to engage in alternative 'healthy adult mode' responses. However, this, in itself, is not enough to significantly reduce risk of reoffending. We go on to produce a Schema Therapy offending formulation together. This is an understanding of the schemas and modes that were involved in the offending behaviour and were active at the time of offending and is represented in a diagram. This is consistent with the information gathered from the Finkelhor process (e.g. cognitions identified using the Finkelhor process can be seen as part of a mode). This formulation is then used in individual therapy to guide progress. In this one-to-one work, the schemas and modes linked to risk are weakened through imagery re-scripting and chair work, the main mechanisms of emotional change. Imagery re-scripting involves reprocessing of the memories of the childhood experiences that led to the development of the schemas, leading to weakening of the feelings, attributions and expectations that make up the schema.

Schema theory can also be used to understand unhealthy or risk related sexual fantasy as often one's schemas, modes, and unmet needs are evident in fantasy. Insight into these processes helps the individual to perceive their fantasies in an alternative way, at times reducing the attraction to them. The underlying principle that links the Intermediate Group to the Introductory Group is that both stages seek to help individuals notice elements of their inner lives that are linked to their offending and, in becoming aware of them, be able to monitor when they might become 'active' (i.e. when particular offence-supportive thoughts are in mind or when particular modes are being acted out). The progression through the stages of intervention recognises and acknowledges the increasing sophistication with which clients are able to analyse their feelings, thoughts, and behaviours, the greater extent to which they can be considered as psychologically minded, whilst continuing to encourage the same principles of awareness and management. Thus, there are transferable skills from one group environment to another.

Empathy is revisited in more depth, with clients being encouraged to connect emotionally with victims of sexual abuse, using the knowledge gained from the schema theory, for example, how abusive experiences may be linked to the victim's pre-existing or developing schemas. A reflective diary is introduced with the aim of promoting insight and self-awareness, using this to record schemas and modes, to reflect on responses to situations between sessions and monitor risk management. Sessions explicitly focusing on emotional regulation are also covered, the extent and detail dependent on group need, which includes education on the function of emotions, encouraging greater recognition and awareness, and teaching of new coping strategies.

The reality of the sex industry is explored and discussed; the notion that what you see is not necessarily what is happening behind the camera is introduced. This is particularly useful for those who have accessed illegal images of children or used pornography to reinforce risk related fantasies. Research has demonstrated that there are associations between self-reported exposure to soft-core pornography and sexual attitudes, where currently the attitudes relate to adult women (Daniels & Duff, 2015, 2017). Child and adult pornography may also impact upon sexual attitudes towards children.

This group is the stepping stone from a more educational and risk management focused group to Phase 3 of the programme, individual therapy. The Intermediate Group helps clients develop the reflective capacity, communication skills, and a willingness to share and trust the clinicians which is necessary for individual work. They become more knowledgeable about a range of psychological strategies for attending to, critically analysing, and making informed decisions about their behavioural choices in different contexts.

Individual Work

Individual work was introduced into the programme at MFPS in order to complete the process of change. Inclusion of individual sessions has been found to deliver improved outcomes in this client group (Schmucker & Lösel, 2015) and individual therapy is used in mental health settings to alter psychological functioning. We found that individuals were generally reluctant to discuss their own traumatic experiences in a group setting; however, their own trauma is understood to play an important role in many aspects of development, including sexual and social development (Duff, Perry, Wright, & Wakefield, 2015). Research has found that adult males who offend sexually are three times more likely to have experienced childhood sexual abuse (CSA) than other non-sexual offenders (Jespersen, Lalumière, & Seto, 2009). In order to explore this, and bring about lasting sexual, social, and emotional change, individual work is necessary.

It has been suggested that intervention to address the effects of historical trauma and adverse childhood experiences should be undertaken prior to any offence-focused work (Reavis, Looman, Frabco, & Rojas, 2013). However, we have found it beneficial to start with the offence-focused work for two main reasons; clients find it relatively easier to explore their own offending than their own abuse and, as they are living in the community, risk management strategies derived from an understanding of the offending behaviour are important to establish as soon as possible. Furthermore, a non-judgemental and compassionate approach to the client's offending nourishes the beginnings of a trusting relationship, which is a necessary precursor to trauma-focused work.

Individual work is based on the idiosyncratic formulation developed over the previous groups. This allows the therapy to be tailored to each individual's needs, with the aim of a lasting change in the underlying feelings and psychological processes that drove the offending behaviour. Schema Therapy can be continued, building on the work begun in the Intermediate group, the emphasis on weakening the schemas and modes linked to offending. Eye Movement Desensitization and Reprocessing (EMDR) can be used to reprocess memories of past experiences thought to be linked to offending behaviour. The approach chosen is based on the individual's formulation, needs, abilities, and the nature of the issues to be addressed.

EMDR is frequently used in mental health settings to address the effects of childhood events on current functioning (Shapiro, 1995, 2001). It alters perceptions, attributions, and beliefs and produces change in emotional and physiological functioning, resulting in more adaptive behaviour in a variety of client groups (De Jong, Ten Broeke, & Renssen, 1999; Gauvreau & Bouchard, 2008; Grant & Threlfo, 2002; Jaberghaderi, Greenwald, Rubin, Zand, & Dolatabadi, 2004; Proudlock & Hutchings, 2016; Ray & Zbik, 2002; Soberman, Greenwald, & Rule, 2002). It has been used effectively in forensic populations, including individuals who cause sexual harm, producing cognitive, emotional and physiological change (Ricci & Clayton, 2008; Ricci, Clayton, & Shapiro, 2006; Ten Hoor, 2013).

EMDR makes use of a naturally occurring process, referred to as adaptive information processing (AIP), which is the normal and intrinsic process of linking new experiences with relevant stored information, to produce adaptive learning and resolution. AIP can be interrupted when experiences are accompanied by strong and overwhelming emotions, which 'block' normal processing and lead to memories of the experience (trauma) being stored in a fragmented way. This means aspects of the memory such as thoughts, emotions, images, sounds, and physical sensations are dysfunctionally stored in isolation to each other. These can then be triggered by similar situations, leading to affect, cognition, and physical sensation associated with the original event being experienced as happening again or influencing present perceptions. EMDR allows the individual to engage in AIP so that the traumatic memory can be reprocessed in connection with existing stored information to produce an adaptive resolution (Shapiro, 1995, 2001). Ricci and Clayton (2016) developed the 'offense drivers' model to guide therapists in their use of EMDR to change the factors that motivated the individual's offending behaviour, by resolving the past experiences linked to these factors.

EMDR has been used to alter deviant sexual arousal in individuals who cause sexual harm and have a reported history of CSA. Ricci et al. (2006) provided EMDR in addition to standard CBT-based group interventions for people with sexual offences. A significant reduction in deviant sexual arousal was reported, as measured by penile plethysmography, compared to a control group who only received the CBT intervention (these changes were maintained at follow-up between 6 and 12 months later). The study also found that offenders receiving EMDR verbalised and demonstrated increased remorse, in addition to increased empathy for their victims and improved motivation to engage in intervention. The authors explain that beliefs, emotions, and physical sensations experienced at the time of CSA remain unchanged as they have not been processed in an adaptive, healthy manner. These are then re-triggered in the present by particular stimuli, for example, the sight of a child that is reminiscent of their abuse. It was noted that each participant of their study had at least one victim the same age the participant was when he was sexually abused.

As in other client groups that have found EMDR effective in altering the physiological sensations associated with the traumatic memory, it is possible that the sexual feelings associated with sexual abuse trauma could be altered by this therapeutic process. For example, EMDR with one previously sexually abused individual, who sexually harmed a child, produced self-reported changes in emotional, cognitive, and physiological functioning, including reductions in the frequency and strength of sexual arousal to children, which was maintained at 12 month follow-up (Wright & Clarke, under review).

Prevention Service

Development of the Service

The new Prevention Service is an addition to the core service and has been developed in collaboration with Merseyside Police. The aim is to work with individuals who experience a sexual attraction to children and are concerned that they may offend or engage in sexually inappropriate activities. The intervention is designed to prevent them from offending or from their behaviours escalating. Identifying and working with people when their sexualised behaviour is considered concerning or antisocial rather than reaching the level of an offence means that they are less likely to be labelled as a sexual offender, a label that can impact upon their social experiences and opportunities for meaningful activity. The Prevention Service was proposed by Merseyside Police as a way of reducing the number of sexual crimes committed. This was born out of their experiences of arresting individuals who they felt may not have offended if they had received support and intervention in relation to their sexual thoughts and feelings earlier on. We used our experience of working with our core client group to design interventions aimed at preventing sexual offending. However, there were a number of questions to answer prior to starting the service, for example: How involved would the police be? Who would the client group be? What would the referral criteria be? Where would the sessions be run? Group or individual work? How would referrals to safeguarding work? What issues would be referred to safeguarding? The notion of working with non-offenders to prevent offending also necessitated an exploration of the potential differences and similarities to working with those who had already offended. Would the knowledge we have accrued from our core service be applicable to this new client group? Would they have particular strengths when compared to those who had offended? Would they be on an offending trajectory? Additionally, treatment and its effects should be measured and disseminated; this is ground-breaking work in potentially preventing sexual harm and keeping children safe; hence the need to ensure treatment is recorded appropriately, its effects assessed robustly and then publicised. Little is known about the trajectory of individuals who engage in concerning sexual behaviours or experience sexual attraction to children and the factors that are associated with its cessation, maintenance, or escalation (Wynn & Duff, 2015). The literature shows that issues of criminal trajectories are complex and require greater investigation (Cale, Smallbone, Rayment-McHugh, & Dowling, 2016; Lussier, Tzoumakis, Cale, & Amirault, 2010).

Recruitment and Referral

During the design and implementation of the prevention service, our current core service users were asked their views relating to recruitment and engagement of this new client group. Many of them thought back to the time before they had offended; some had been aware that their feelings, fantasies, or behaviours were potentially harmful and they considered how they may have responded to an offer of attending the Prevention Service at that time.

Initially, it was envisaged that the police would identify potential clients who had engaged in unusual sexual activities—for example, exposure, voyeurism, or considered to be at risk of accessing illegal images of children—and been subject to some investigation but not been prosecuted or convicted. However, such individuals approached by the police were not willing to engage. Clients attending MFPS' core service were asked their opinion on the police being actively involved in the service, identifying potential clients, recruiting, and assisting in assessments. Their feedback suggested that, even if they had not yet offended and wanted help, they would be reticent about sharing information with police for fear of a punitive response. Hence, the main role of the police in addition to recommending the service to potential clients and other professionals is to provide ongoing consultation regarding legal issues, supporting the clinicians with potential safeguarding referrals, and assisting with the development of publicity material.

The service is up and running; however, obtaining referrals was a challenge initially. This was addressed by publicising the service within the NHS Trust, and informing professional organisations and services who may be the first point of contact for individuals with issues regarding an attraction to children or inappropriate sexual behaviour of the service. This includes GPs, counselling services, Community Mental Health Teams, Sexual Health Services, and others.

Clients who have offended are generally referred by police, probation, MAPPA, or Social Services and have been directed to attend treatment in order to reduce their risk of reoffending, to gain more contact with family or to fulfil requirements of the court. Some clients are willing to engage in whatever is required in order to achieve their goals, others are more resistant and are difficult to engage. Often those who have offended have been to prison and are adamant that they do not want to return, which can increase motivation. Many state that they would not have sought the referral to such a service voluntarily but often report that once engaged with the service and realising the benefits to psychological change are pleased that they participated. However, prevention clients are not exposed to the same level of encouragement or direction. Those who have offended may have also undertaken work previously or discussed their offending to some degree with professionals and may understand they will have to discuss difficult issues, and be more prepared and accustomed to doing this. However, conversely having been through the Criminal Justice System, they may have found this unhelpful, shaming and distressing, which may increase their resistance to discuss issues and motivation to change. They have also had opportunities to talk to others with similar offences and had time to rationalise their offending, maintaining a particular narrative of their behaviour that may be difficult to shift, should it be unhelpful. Clients referred to the Prevention Service have the autonomy to decide whether they attend or not and are therefore more willing to engage and have the desire to make changes.

Referral criteria were based on our knowledge of working with adults who had offended and our current expertise in order to minimise the differences in working with this new client group. Prevention Service clients should be aged 18 or over; be motivated to participate in intervention aimed at reducing risk of sexually offending; not have any convictions for sexual offences; be able, emotionally and practically, to engage in psychological therapy that may involve the exploration of potentially distressing childhood experiences; and have a GP that we can liaise with if necessary for safeguarding issues, including risks of self-harm. This client group, as an unknown set of people, may come with a range of risks to themselves and others. We have worked with a number of service users who have attempted suicide due to the shame and distress of being sexually attracted to children, have disclosed situations that need to be reported to safeguarding services and have found it difficult to cope with their feelings in between therapy sessions. We therefore place importance on having an agreed safety procedure for all clients that includes the option of contacting GPs, Social Care, Safeguarding Services and Police if necessary. Based on our work and knowledge of our core service users, clients are expected to engage in fairly intense, challenging and at times distressing therapy, dependent on their individual formulation; hence they need some level of resilience, reflective capacity, and psychological thinking. This is aided by the therapists being psychologists with experience of appropriately challenging, supporting, containing, and grounding clients when they are distressed, detached, or dissociated. Poor emotional regulation and resilience leaves clients susceptible to possible abreaction between sessions, whilst limited reflective capacity means clients have difficulty engaging with therapy and struggle to understand themselves, which impacts on their ability to develop the insight necessary for change. This is explored during the assessment phase following referral, as are protective factors and safeguarding issues; if a referrer or a client discloses any illegal activity a referral to the appropriate service is made.

Safeguarding Issues

Careful consideration was given to safeguarding and managing risk; the referral criteria for potential clients include no convictions for sexual offences. This means that generally they are not known to the Police, and this might be their first contact with services. The assessment process involves detailed exploration of the client's thoughts, feelings, and behaviour including formulating the potential risks to any children they have contact with. Given some individuals are unaware of the legality of certain activities it is imperative that clients displayed a clear understanding of what would happen should clinicians be concerned regarding their behaviour.

Although it was not possible to provide an exhaustive list of illegal activities and our planned responses to them before they were encountered, a number of situations are clear: if someone discloses they are downloading illegal images, this will be referred to the Police. If sexual attraction to their own children or step children is disclosed and the client is living in the family home, a discussion with Safeguarding Services ensues following a thorough assessment of the situation. This assessment includes the details of any children, for example, their names, ages, date of birth, cognitive, emotional, behavioural development, any health problems, and school attendance. The client's relationship with that child and contact is discussed. Information regarding their partner or the children's carer is also gathered, including mental health problems, drug or alcohol use, employment, parental discord, past convictions, and sources of support. Essentially information would be gathered in order to engage in discussion with Safeguarding Services and make an informed decision together in relation to management of any risk the client poses to children. Sometimes the client is asked to leave the family home, reduce or stop contact with children whilst being assessed or undergoing therapy. Where therapy is exploring and reprocessing CSA or seeking to understand the origin of their attraction to children, feelings can re-emerge that can temporarily increase risk.

Therapy Models

The majority of clients referred to MFPS have had a conviction for a sexual offence; however, clients referred to the Prevention Service, by the nature of the service, do not have a conviction. Does this mean the clients will need different interventions? Will the therapeutic approach need to be altered?

The original intention was to offer a combination of group and individual therapy as we do in our core service. Core service users felt that having to discuss sensitive issues in a group setting may increase the shame of the people we were attempting to recruit, reducing engagement and that given the choice of individual or group intervention, individual therapy would be a preference to those people considering a referral to the service. This, we felt, may be an area where the difference between those who have offended and are referred by outside services as part of a multi-agency risk management plan and the prevention clients, who are under no obligation to attend, may be significant. Therefore, we offer individual therapy with the option available to undertake group work if it appears that this would be helpful as the service develops. Furthermore, individual therapy is needed to work on the various traumas that may be linked to risk of offending. The various topics covered and introduced in the group phases are included in the individual work, as appropriate and as suggested by the client's formulation.

During the assessment process, the development of an idiosyncratic formulation of the client's sexual difficulties begins. This is a collaborative understanding with the individuals of the origin of their problematic thoughts, feelings, and behaviours and based on psychological theories. This formulation is used to guide therapy to produce enduring psychological change that reduces risk of offending. This can involve reprocessing past adverse childhood experiences which impact on their current functioning, for example, abuse, neglect, difficult family experiences, and experiences of or acting out bullying. These experiences influence sexual and emotional development and hence behaviour (Jespersen et al., 2009). Using therapy to change the current impact of past trauma in these cases may therefore promote lasting change that can reduce risk of offending (Reavis et al., 2013).

In order to benefit from the intervention, clients need to be able to discuss these experiences and emotionally connect with their own trauma in order to reprocess it in a more adaptive way within a safe therapeutic relationship, thereby altering its current impact on their functioning (emotional, relational, behavioural, sexual), and understanding the potential effects on others and themselves of offending. This is a very psychologically demanding process that can lead to ambivalence for most individuals. It can involve significant cognitive and emotional upheaval as individuals have often managed their emotional responses to their own abuse by detachment or disconnection. Some develop beliefs that they were responsible for their own abuse, which supports beliefs that their (potential) victims are also responsible for their abuse. Connecting with the trauma and betrayal of their own childhood helps individuals empathise with others and take responsibility for their own behaviour. Some may have become sexually aroused or associated positive emotions with their abuse that can be subsequently linked to a sexual attraction to children.

The change in perspective of their own abuse can have a number of consequences, for example, having believed they were responsible for their abuse they may never have reported it. However, the recognition of their own vulnerability and powerlessness as a child may lead them to decide to report their abuser. This may not always produce a desired conclusion—the abuser may not be prosecuted or may be found not guilty—this can be stressful and unhelpful for clients. New understanding of their own abuse can result in questioning the nature of other childhood relationships and absent protection, which can lead to family conflict. Anger at an abuser or failed protector is a common consequence and often an important part of the process of change but, particularly in those with emotional regulation difficulties, can necessitate further risk management and work on processing this appropriately. Therefore, time is needed to assist the individual with these secondary issues.

Some find that undertaking trauma-focused work feels as though they are reliving the trauma and they have little resilience to rely upon. Prevention clients can sometimes be very reluctant to revisit their own abuse. Some believe it could strengthen feelings related to risk of offending and have previously detached from it as a conscious strategy. Alternatively, those who have offended have already recognised that detachment is not effective; they have some awareness that it may be linked to their offending, so are more motivated to undertake the work that is needed to make changes.

As Schema Therapy and EMDR have been found to be effective in our core client group in addressing and significantly changing the feelings, beliefs, physiological sensations, and behaviour patterns linked to offending, they are used to understand and change the emotional and sexual factors linked to problematic sexual functioning, attraction to children and risks of offending in the Prevention Service.

We work on the basis that the clinicians' experience and expertise of working with men who have offended is applicable when working with Prevention Service clients, which is a valid assumption at the time of designing the Prevention Service. In time, we will be able to adapt our approach (if required) as we learn more from our new client group. However, clinicians are mindful that the clients have not offended and may have particular strengths and protective factors that reduce the likelihood of offending being their trajectory. These are explored in therapy and, as with all individuals engaging in psychological therapy and working from an individualised formulation, adaptive and protective factors are incorporated into any risk reducing intervention.

In order to ascertain the efficacy of the intervention and the prevention service as a whole, a number of outcome measures are employed. The aim is to determine change in specific domains linked to sexual attraction to children, these being psychosexual characteristics, interpersonal functioning, shame, self-esteem, emotional processing, and wellbeing (Cortoni, 2009; Tangney, Stuewig, & Martinez, 2014). Also, as part of a research project to further understand the process of change, some clients will participate in semi-structured interviews. As a new service we are yet to be at the stage where we can examine the effectiveness of our work.

Summary

This chapter details the services offered by MFPS specifically its work with adults who have sexually offended against children in the community including the development of the new Prevention Service. The ethos and practice of the core service and how this has informed the new Prevention Service has been discussed, particularly the potential differences of working with clients with a conviction for a sexual offence and those who have not offended. Details of the new Prevention Service in Merseyside (UK) are described, including information on the client group, the intervention methods and the outcome measures. The challenges of setting up a service that works with non-offenders regarding a very stigmatising subject are also discussed.

References

Bernstein, D. P., Arntz, A. R., & de Vos, M. (2007). Schema focused therapy in forensic settings: Theoretical model and recommendations for best clinical practice. *International Journal of Forensic Mental Health, 6*(2), 169–183.

Cahalane, H., & Duff, S. (2018). A qualitative analysis of nonoffending partners' experiences and perceptions following a psychoeducational group intervention. *Journal of Sexual Aggression: An International, Interdisciplinary Forum for Research, Theory and Practice, 24*, 66–79.

Cahalane, H., Duff, S., & Parker, G. (2013). Treatment implications arising from a qualitative analysis of letters written by the nonoffending partners of men who have perpetrated child sexual abuse. *Journal of Child Sexual Abuse, 22*(6), 720–741.

Cale, J., Smallbone, S., Rayment-McHugh, S., & Dowling, C. (2016). Offense trajectories, the unfolding of sexual and non-sexual criminal activity, and sex offense characteristics of adolescent sex offenders. *Sex Abuse: A Journal of Research and Treatment, 28*(8), 791–812.

Cortoni, F. (2009). Factors associated with sexual recidivism. In A. R. Beech, L. A. Craig, & K. D. Browne (Eds.), *Assessment and treatment of sex offenders*. West Sussex, UK: Wiley.

Daniels, S., & Duff, S. (2015, June). *The effect of newspaper soft-core pornography on attitudes towards women and rape*. Division of Forensic Psychology annual conference. Manchester Metropolitan University, Manchester, UK.

Daniels, S., & Duff, S. (2017, June). *The effects of short-term exposure to soft-core pornography on males' attitudes towards sexual aggression and rape proclivity*. Division of Forensic Psychology annual conference, Bristol, UK.

De Jong, A., Ten Broeke, E., & Renssen, M. R. (1999). Treatment of specific phobias with Eye Movement Desensitization and Reprocessing (EMDR): Protocol, empirical status and conceptual issues. *Journal of Anxiety Disorders, 13*, 69–85.

Dennis, J. A., Khan, O., Ferriter, M., Huband, N., Powney, M. J., & Duggan, C. (2012). Psychological interventions for adults who have sexually offended or are at risk of offending. *Cochrane Database of Systematic Reviews, 12*. Art. No.:CD007507.

Duff, S., Perry, L., Wright, L., & Jackson, P. (2014, June). *Working with difficult clients*. Symposium, Division of Forensic Psychology annual conference. Glasgow Caledonian University, Glasgow, UK.

Duff, S., Perry, L., Wright, L., & Wakefield, N. (2015, June). *Trauma: Not just for the victims*. Division of Forensic Psychology annual conference, Manchester Metropolitan University, Manchester, UK.

Duff, S., Wakefield, N., Croft, A., Perry, L., Valavanis, S., & Wright, L. (2017). A service for non-offending partners of male sexual offenders. *Journal of Forensic Practice, 19*(4), 288–295.

Duff, S., & Willis, A. (2006). At the precipice: Assessing a non-offending client's potential to sexually offend. *Journal of Sexual Aggression, 12*(1), 43–51.

Finkelhor, D. (1984). *Child sexual abuse: New theory and research.* New York: The Free Press.

Friendship, C., Mann, R. E., & Beech, A. R. (2003). Evaluation of a national prison-based treatment program for sexual offenders in England and Wales. *Journal of Interpersonal Violence, 18*(7), 744–759.

Gauvreau, P., & Bouchard, S. (2008). Preliminary evidence for the efficacy of EMDR in treating generalized anxiety disorder. *Journal of EMDR Practice and Research, 2*, 26–40.

Grant, M., & Threlfo, C. (2002). EMDR in the treatment of chronic pain. *Journal of Clinical Psychology, 58*, 1505–1520.

Giesen-Bloo, J., van Dyck, R., Spinhoven, P., van Tilburg, W., Dirksen, C., van Asselt, T., et al. (2006). Outpatient psychotherapy for borderline personality disorder, randomized trial of schema focused therapy vs transference focused psychotherapy. *Archives of General Psychiatry, 63*, 649–658.

Gilbert, P. (2009). *The therapeutic relationship in the cognitive behavioral psychotherapies.* London: Routledge.

Hossack, A. (1999). The professional the paraprofessional and the perpetrator. *Journal of Sexual Aggression, 4*(1), 15–21.

Hossack, A., & Robinson, J. (2005). Treated sex offenders as "paraprofessional" co-workers in the treatment of the sex offender. *Journal of Sexual Aggression, 11*(1), 103–113.

Jespersen, A. F., Lalumière, M. L., & Seto, M. C. (2009). Sexual abuse history among adult sex offenders and non-sex offenders: A meta-analysis. *Child Abuse & Neglect, 33*, 179–192.

Jaberghaderi, N., Greenwald, R., Rubin, A., Zand, S. O., & Dolatabadi, S. (2004). A comparison of CBT and EMDR for sexually abused Iranian girls. *Clinical Psychology and Psychotherapy, 11*, 358–368.

Lussier, P., Tzoumakis, S., Cale, J., & Amirault, J. (2010). Criminal trajectories of adult sex offenders and the age effect: Examining the dynamic aspect of offending in adulthood. *International Criminal Justice Review, 20*(2), 147–168.

Marshall, W. L. (2005). Therapist style in sexual offender treatment: Influence on indices of change. *Sexual Abuse: A Journal of Research and Treatment, 17*(2), 109–116.

McMurran, M., & Theodosi, E. (2007). Is treatment non-completion associated with increased reconviction over no treatment? *Psychology, Crime & Law, 13*(4), 333–343.

Mews, A., Di Bella, L., & Purver, M. (2017). *Impact evaluation of the prison-based Core Sex Offender Treatment Programme*. Ministry of Justice Analytical Series.

Perry, L., Wright, L., & Duff, S. (2013, June). *A multi layered approach to sex offender group intervention*. Symposium, Division of Forensic Psychology annual conference, Queens University, Belfast, UK.

Proudlock, S., & Hutchings, J. (2016). EMDR within crisis resolution and home treatment teams. *Journal of EMDR Practice and Research, 10*, 47–56.

Ray, A. L., & Zbik, A. (2002). Cognitive behavioral therapies and beyond. In C. D. Tollison, J. R. Satterthwaite, & J. W. Tollison (Eds.), *Practical pain management* (3rd ed., pp. 189–209). Philadelphia: Lippincott Williams and Wilkins.

Reavis, J. A., Looman, J., Frabco, K. A., & Rojas, B. (2013). Adverse childhood experiences and adult criminology: How long must we live before we possess our own lives? *The Permanente Journal, 17*(2), 44–48.

Ricci, R. J., & Clayton, C. A. (2008). Trauma resolution treatment as an adjunct to standard treatment for child molesters: A qualitative study. *Journal of EMDR Practice and Research, 2*, 41–50.

Ricci, R. J., & Clayton, C. A. (2016). EMDR with sex offenders: Using offense drivers to guide conceptualization and treatment. *Journal of EMDR Practice and Research, 10*, 104–118.

Ricci, R. J., Clayton, C. A., & Shapiro, F. (2006). Some effects of EMDR on previously abused child molesters: Theoretical reviews and preliminary findings. *The Journal of Forensic Psychiatry and Psychology, 17*, 538–562.

Schmucker, M., & Lösel, F. (2015). The effects of sexual offender treatment on recidivism: An international meta-analysis of sound quality evaluations. *Journal of Experimental Criminology, 11*(4), 597–630.

Shannon, K., Pearce, E., & Swarbrick, R. (2013). Factors influencing the development of an innovative service for women non-offending partners (NOPs) of male sexual offenders. *Journal of Sexual Aggression, 19*(3), 357–368.

Shapiro, F. (1995). *EMDR: Basic principles, protocols, and procedures*. New York: Guilford Press.

Shapiro, F. (2001). *Eye movement desensitization and reprocessing: Basic principles, protocols and procedures* (2nd ed.). New York: Guilford Press.

Soberman, G. B., Greenwald, R., & Rule, D. L. (2002). A controlled study of Eye Movement Desensitization and Reprocessing (EMDR) for boys with conduct problems. *Journal of Aggression, Maltreatment and Trauma, 6*, 217–236.

Tangney, J. P., Stuewig, J., & Martinez, A. G. (2014). Two faces of shame: Understanding shame and guilt in the prediction of jail inmates' recidivism. *Psychological Science, 25*(3), 799–805.

Ten Hoor, N. M. (2013). Treating cognitive distortions with EMDR: A case study of a sex offender. *International Journal of Forensic Mental Health, 12*, 139–148.

Walton, J. S., & Chou, S. (2015). The effectiveness of psychological treatment for reducing recidivism in child molesters: A systematic review of randomized and nonrandomized studies. *Trauma, Violence & Abuse, 16*(4), 401–417.

Walton, J. S., & Duff, S. (2017). "I'm not homosexual or heterosexual, I'm paedosexual": Exploring sexual preference using interpretive phenomenology. *Journal of Forensic Practice, 19*(2), 151–161.

Ward, T., & Beech, A. (2006). An integrated theory of sexual offending. *Aggression and Violent Behavior, 11*, 44–63.

Ward, T., & Hudson, S. M. (2001). Finkelhor's precondition model of child sexual abuse: A critique. *Psychology, Crime & Law, 7*(1–4), 291–307.

Wright, L., & Clarke, H. (under review). EMDR with a sexually abused child sex offender: Self reported changes in sexual arousal.

Wynn, C., & Duff, S. (2015, June). *Offence patterns in repeat sexual offenders: An examination of escalation, de-escalation, and stability across sexual offence categories.* Division of Forensic Psychology annual conference, Manchester Metropolitan University, Manchester, UK.

Young, J. E., Klosko, J. S., & Weishaar, M. (2003). *Schema therapy: A practitioner's guide.* New York: Guilford Publications.

6

The Need for Prevention: A Service-User's Perspective

Peter Binks

Introduction

In this chapter, I explain my life journey so far in battling with my unwanted sexual thoughts and feelings. I explore the effect of the different forms of treatment I undertook and consider some of the underlying factors that contributed to my problems becoming as severe as they did and how I came to commit offences. I put forward the reasons why I believe that prevention would have been effective for me and why it is vital to the safety, health and well-being of society as a whole.

I work with the Safer Living Foundation (SLF) prevention project and am writing this chapter because I believe that preventative work can provide help to people in their struggles to deal with undesirable sexual thoughts and feelings. This timely assistance will help them to lead a constructive offence-free life with far greater ease than they would without this support.

P. Binks (✉)
Safer Living Foundation (SLF), Nottingham, UK
e-mail: peter.binks@ntu.ac.uk

My Background

I was raised by my genetic middle-class well-educated parents. Home life was comfortable, safe, and without any serious problems. I was moved to different areas of the country at ages four, six and eight. I was bullied throughout my school life, both inside and outside school. Consequently, I struggled to form and retain friendships. My parents are caring but not demonstrative. I was raised at a time when sex education was not present in schools. Discussion or information about sex in the home was completely taboo. Not having close friends or relatives my age meant that I only learnt from snippets I overheard or observed, which I was not mature enough to process effectively.

I spent a long time struggling to deal with my sexual thoughts and feelings alone and in secret. I was finally able to access treatment after I was arrested years ago. I have been offence-free ever since and remain committed to not reoffending.

Sexual Development

Being somewhat isolated, distressed and baffled by my peers' behaviour towards me, I sought some form of comfort and compensation. I grew up at a time when the impact of bullying was little understood. It was considered just a normal part of school life. I could not talk to my parents or anybody else about sexual matters. I did not dare tell them about the bullying for fear of it escalating, or of being ridiculed. This left me without a suitable outlet for my distress. Many children discover their genitalia in childhood and find some pleasurable sensations from it. This became my prime source of comfort and relaxation; it was a substitute for thumb-sucking. I began masturbating frequently when I was somewhere between the ages of four and seven and this continued throughout my life. The techniques I used were not fundamentally different to those I experienced through puberty and into adulthood. Although I did not develop erections until late puberty and did not ejaculate until age 16, the pleasurable feeling was nonetheless intense. Occasionally I was caught by my parents, but they mostly did not realise what I was doing. When mum caught me masturbating as a teen she just said "don't do that". I felt embarrassed at being caught but did not think of using the bathroom to avoid this. Since nobody talked to me about what I was doing, I did not really understand what was happening.

At about age seven, I extracted my penis in the classroom and was masturbating, as I did at home. The boy sat next to me noticed and called it to the attention of the two girls sat opposite. I was embarrassed and tried to hide myself, but the boy held my hands away and the girls saw me. Their reaction was childish, interested curiosity, as might reasonably be expected from girls their age. This was the first time I had encountered peers seeming pleased and interested in anything to do with me. This was a great surprise and became subconsciously embedded as a means of gaining pleasant attention from peers of the opposite sex. I displayed my penis to girls on several other occasions during childhood. They responded with smiles, wide eyes and other apparent signs of interest and enjoyment. This was a very pleasing reaction for me. There was also an occasion when another boy, of eight or nine years old, exposed himself and most of the girls in the class swarmed round him trying to get a better look. On odd occasions, I did not get the good reaction to exposing myself to same age girls, but they never reacted badly or rejected me. There was no fear in their eyes or screams or running away. They would continue to treat me the same and play board games with me in private subsequently.

At this time, adults were much less well-informed about the potential dangers of exhibitionism. Although teachers became aware of my behaviour on at least two occasions, nothing was done to help address this and it was not made clear to me that it was wrong.

I was late developing and did not understand what was happening with my body and emotions during puberty. I was vaguely aware that males developed erections and produced something which made females pregnant, but that was about the extent of my understanding.

I developed desires for my female peers but did not dare to approach anybody to ask them out. I had no idea how to go about this and few hobbies or interests that I could involve anybody in. I was also sure that I would be rejected. Consequently, I did not experience normal interaction with peers—no kissing, cuddling, chatting, hand-holding, shared activities or other ways in which people normally develop an understanding of intimate and sexual relationships.

Some of my female friends were younger. Having had pleasing reactions from exposing myself to girls of around the ages of nine to twelve, when I was of a similar age, I continued doing this when opportunity presented. This remained my only outlet for obtaining sexual gratification with others. I never intended any harm and the girls were never scared by my behaviour. They knew me and I made it appear I did not know I was exposed. This meant that even as I grew older the girls continued to react with smiles, bright eyes and appreciative comments. Consequently, I developed a strong desire for exposing myself to girls in this age range for the pleasant attention it gave me and appeared to give my victims.

In my teens, I became increasingly aware that there was something wrong with my behaviour. Having nobody to talk to, and no idea how to form normal relationships, masturbation and exposure remained my sole means of gaining pleasure and attention from my peers. This was my compensation for the otherwise unpleasant experience of school. I increasingly relived memories of the girls' reactions to my exposure in my frequent masturbation. This continued after I started getting erections and ejaculating. This masturbatory reinforcement, the intermittent pleasing reactions, accompanied by the lack of any adverse response from my victims, together with adults not tackling this, resulted in the behaviour becoming very deeply ingrained.

After leaving school, my opportunities to expose to younger girls in situations where I could make it seem accidental and remain otherwise unobserved, diminished drastically. Thus, the behaviour subsided. It was always strictly an opportunistic activity without advance planning to create the situation, only to exploit the opportunity.

I am embarrassed and ashamed of both the masturbation and the exposure. Would attending a preventative programme at around age ten to twelve have helped? I have no doubt it would. Qualified therapists treating me compassionately as an individual facing an unwanted and complex dilemma could have provided the help and support I needed to change my behaviour. With the right advice and education at this early stage, I might even have gone on to develop normal relationships with peers. Although this would already have been too late for some victims, at least it could have prevented any further victims. There is some hope that these early victims were not too badly damaged as we were of the same age and it was not, at that time, considered dangerous.

In later life, my marital relationship suffered with difficulties. I was petrified of producing offspring. I feared for the safety of a daughter and was concerned that a son would inherit my difficulties and perpetuate the problem through another generation. My wife found physical protection measures interrupted the flow of sex, but her health problems meant we did not feel it would be safe for her to take the pill. My wife wanted full penetrative sexual intercourse, believing that other forms of sex were just child's play. I have sexual hang-ups left over from my upbringing which means it is difficult for me to commit to sexual intercourse, even with a stable partner. It is no surprise that sexual activity rapidly vanished from our relationship. Let me be absolutely clear that my wife was not aware of my predilections. These preceded her and she was not in any way responsible for my actions. That responsibility rests solely with me.

Offending

As I approached middle age, I was working long hours in a high stress role and my wife suffered significant mental health difficulties. I had still been unable to find any help with my distressing sexual thoughts and feelings. I encountered a girl's school close to where I sometimes worked. With masturbation being my sole stress-relief technique, and with my history, this situation proved too much of a temptation. My past exposing behaviour resurfaced. I was still able to make it appear that I was unaware of being exposed, so even at this age some of the girls did not respond at all whilst others again smiled, looked and appeared to pass pleasing comments to each other on what they had seen. I passed the girls walking normally and so was long gone by the time any adverse reaction set in. Ultimately, I was caught in the act by police and was arrested. This meant I was finally able to access treatment but by this time there had been far too many victims. I live with the pain of knowing I have caused distress to my victims and that my actions have caused suffering to those close to me. If this treatment had been available, without me having to offend to receive it, then life would have been much better for everybody concerned.

Personal Development

When I grew up, the emphasis in school was on learning academic abilities. Whilst educational systems now have a greater focus on skills that could lead to jobs, there still needs to be further development in teaching children how to cope with the pressures of life in modern society.

My parents did not challenge each other, me or anybody else, so I never experienced the need to assert myself, negotiate or compromise. Having no siblings, cousins living many miles away and my poor experiences of peer interaction, meant I did not learn the ways of sharing and interacting socially.

Despite my parents being kind, caring, well-educated and well-meaning, I did not manage to learn effective ways of dealing with life either through upbringing or schooling. There are many children who do not receive the best guidance in their early life. A prevention service can provide an alternative safe environment for learning. People can express their needs and wants in a constructive way, listen to other's views and find ways for everybody to get some of what they want and to feel valued and understood.

Relationship Skills

My parents lack of demonstrativeness towards each other and myself contributed to my difficulty in forming typical teenage experimental relationships with members of the opposite sex, which is my preferred sexual orientation.

Would a prevention service have helped me learn the rudiments of how to build friendships and deal with the inevitable changes that life brings? Would it have helped me to cope with the problems at school? I believe it would.

My first normal relationship came when I was 20. I formed a close friendship with a girl of the same age at college. She did not want to be publicly known as my girlfriend only as a friend. During our five-year relationship, we privately indulged in mutually consenting pleasurable masturbatory exploration. Neither of us at any stage in the relationship sought to engage in other sexual activity. This was confusing for me. I have had only one other relationship in my life. I was married for over 15 years until I was arrested, at which point we separated. We still remain close friends and regular companions.

Would attending preventative treatment have assisted me in learning how to approach members of the opposite sex and what is and is not appropriate? Surely it would. Would this also have helped me to deal with the inevitable emotional problems, conflicts, compromises and breakups of normal relationship development cycles? How could it not? Would this have given me a better chance of forming a successful intimate relationship? I think it would.

Emotional Coping Strategies

Emotions were not outwardly displayed in the home and I was brought up in an era when "men don't cry". As a result, I have always struggled to acknowledge, accept, express and cope with my changing feelings. Strong emotions that come up when in a situation of conflict or with someone of deep importance are especially difficult for me to handle.

Since showing distress to bullies caused the bullying to escalate, I learnt not to display any distress ever to anybody and thus nobody could know I needed help to cope.

Would seeing people expressing difficult emotions and receiving appropriate support have assisted in learning to effectively express feelings in an assertive way, without fear of reprisal? I believe it would.

Could having somebody to discuss my emotions with have helped me better understand the ebb and flow of challenging emotions that everybody experiences? Surely everybody can benefit from having someone to talk to. Would techniques used in preventative treatment have helped me better understand my abnormal desires and enabled me to manage them without acting out and causing harm to others? Given my response to treatment it seems clear it would.

General Coping Strategies

It is to be expected that people will encounter setbacks, disappointments, frustrations, relationship difficulties and breakups during their life. My parents shielded me from being aware of any problems they encountered and over-protected me as a child. I, therefore, never developed the abilities to cope with these inevitable life buffeting events.

Could prevention have shown me that significant changes and setbacks are just part of life and can be overcome? I believe so. Would I then have developed better strategies for coping with these unfortunate events and been more able to recover and move on? It could only have helped. As it is, the pain I experienced from the persistent bullying and the breakup of my first relationship have had lifelong impacts on me that I still struggle with today.

Shame and Isolation

Although I was ashamed of my sexual behaviour, I dared not talk to anybody about it for fear of potential adverse consequences. I was aware that people who knew me would be shocked and disappointed in me if they found out. This fear forced me into trying to deal with these problems alone. A task for which I was very ill-equipped.

Based on the benefits I have gained from treatment since conviction, I firmly believe that prevention assistance at an early stage would have enabled me to lead a constructive, happy and offence-free life, as I would have wished to do. This would have benefited my subsequent victims, myself, those close to me and wider society.

People who are ashamed of themselves or their actions will be very reluctant to come out into the open, particularly in a society that instantly condemns somebody for an inappropriate sexual desire, no matter how committed they are to not acting upon it. By shaming and judging people, irrespective of their true motives and desires, society is compounding the problem.

I am not suggesting that it is right to act on these desires or that these desires are a good thing, but it is better to help people to live with them, without harming others, than to frighten them to the extent that they dare not get help. Fear and isolation are likely to result in them acting out.

Past Versus Future Focus

When training a dog or a child it is more effective to concentrate on praise and reward for good behaviour and to educate about why bad behaviour is unacceptable and what to do instead. Those who continually punish bad behaviour, but ignore good behaviour are likely to exacerbate the problem. Previous Sex Offender Treatment Programmes (SOTP) concentrating on the offence are less likely to be effective than the more enlightened approach of looking at the values and talents the individual has, and the ways they can capitalise on those to get the things they really want out of life. For most people, these focus around a purpose, meaningful work, strong intimate relationship, caring for others, strong friendships and broad interests. The sexual gratification obtained by committing offences is a poor substitute for these life-enhancing experiences.

As a child, it was rare for me to see excitement in the family, and pleasant expectations were often not fully realised. From this, I learnt not to strive or hope for things in the future. Consequently, I struggle to recognise my aims and values and work towards acquiring the "goods" of life in an effective and appropriate way.

Would prevention have shown me how to achieve things and that striving for them could be rewarding in itself? I say yes. Could these help people to find meaningful ways to achieve self-gratification, instead of relying solely on masturbation? Why don't we try it and see? Would prevention have helped me overcome the feeling that the normal things in life were not ones that I could reasonably expect to be able to obtain? Surely it would provide hope.

What Causes Sexual Offending?

There are a wide range of contributing factors. In my case, I had very poor sexual education and developed a high level of deeply ingrained offence-related sexual thought patterns in childhood. In addition, my social skills are underdeveloped due to significant childhood isolation, disruption and bullying. A natural shyness, and poor peer relations, makes it exceptionally difficult for me to form normal relationships. Fear of conflict and lack of examples, from parents, peers or responsible adults, of how to overcome life obstacles leaves me struggling when things go wrong in life. Being ashamed of the way my sexual thoughts and behaviours failed to evolve makes it hard for me to talk about this. An inability to keep up with my peers in any field at school means that I lost hope and ambition and accepted that life would never be fun. None of this excuses my behaviour.

Need for Prevention

I was unable to access help in time and, as a result, there have been victims. I believe that I would have been receptive to support and able to adapt successfully had the right assistance been available early enough. The help I finally received, from a Compassion-Focussed Therapist (CFT), has enabled me to develop better coping strategies and to begin to slowly rebuild a meaningful, socially acceptable and valuable life. This process would have been much easier had it begun a lot earlier in my life, before problems became so deeply ingrained and at a time when I was young enough to be more adaptable.

Pornography, adverts, TV and films give people misleading information about the role of sex in relationships. Human sexuality is highly diverse, and several aspects are illegal and harmful. I don't think many people genuinely want to cause harm and distress to others. If the right help is available, at the right time, then it must surely be possible to prevent a lot of the harm that is currently caused through ignorance and lack of life skills.

People may say that all men experience some form of sexual thought or feeling regularly but do not act on it. Of course, many men do act on their sexual impulses frequently, but it is with consenting adults and, as such, perfectly reasonable. However, the following statistics on sexual harassment in the workplace make it clear that inappropriate actions also follow thoughts and feelings on significantly more occasions than is generally accepted. This suggests there are a lot more people who could benefit from preventative treatment than is widely recognised. In October 2017, Channel 4 (Worrall, 2017) and BBC (2017) both reported over half of women had experienced some form of sexual harassment in the workplace. In November 2017, the Telegraph newspaper reported one in five women had suffered physical sexual harassment. This was followed up in February 2018 by both the Independent and the Guardian newspapers reporting the same statistics. The Guardian (Williams, 2017) additionally stated that 63% of women and 79% of men who had been sexually harassed at work did not report it. The Telegraph (Kirk, 2017) also stated that 12% of those who reported the action to their company found that the incident was not even acknowledged and 31% that no action was taken. In February 2018, the American National Public Radio station (Chatterjee, 2018) reported 81% of women and 43% of men had experienced some form of sexual harassment in the workplace. Could prevention help to reduce the level of abuse women receive in the workplace? Something certainly needs to be done.

Why I Would Have Accepted and Responded to Prevention Treatment

I was never happy with my aberrant sexual thoughts/feelings or behaviour and did seek help prior to conviction. If that help had been available, I would have jumped at the chance. Since conviction, I have been able eventually to find treatment that has helped me enormously, but this was very expensive at a time when I could no longer earn money. Had the treatment been provided when I was in my early teens, then I have no doubt that a lot of harm would have been avoided, and that my life would have taken a more socially constructive route. Whilst I am now able to move in a better direction, and am committed to desistance, it is already too late for many victims. This has caused great heartache for myself and those close to me, as well as the distress to the victims and their families and carers.

My Experience of Treatment

Following conviction, I voluntarily consulted three psychiatrists and two Cognitive-Based Therapists. These all felt that they could not assist with this problem and that it was better dealt with through legal channels. However, the compulsory old-style SOTP I attended caused me more distress than help. I finally tracked down a CFT, who I paid privately, and who was able to offer significant assistance. In this section, I pass comment on what the various forms of therapy involve and how they helped me.

Compassion-Focussed Therapy

This technique helps people understand that instinctive thoughts and feelings have complex roots and are not wholly under the control of the individual. Individuals do not choose their genetic background, upbringing or environmental experiences but are still shaped by them. It is possible to break the cycle between thought/feeling and action. CFT helps to achieve this by encouraging the acceptance of thoughts and feelings as just thoughts and feelings that arise and pass away. It uses mindfulness meditation techniques to help get away from the mind traps and instead focus on the experiences of the five senses.

My therapist also encouraged me to read and practise the exercises in "The Compassionate Mind" by Paul Gilbert and to join a mindfulness group, both of which have helped me to further develop my life skills.

CFT recognises that we cannot always control the events that happen to us, but that we can choose to act in line with our moral values, rather than just responding instinctively to stimuli. It also recognises that fighting against unwanted thoughts and feelings is ineffective. It is better to simply acknowledge that the thought or feeling has arisen, however undesirable it may be, name it, take a breath and then turn attention to something more constructive. This helps to strengthen the self-sooth system and reduce the feelings of fear and panic that can so easily arise when these unwanted sexual desires surface. The threat system is designed to cause instinctive action, so the more this is triggered the greater the risk that the action will be damaging.

Acceptance and Commitment Therapy

My therapist also introduced me to Acceptance and Commitment Therapy (ACT). Reading several books on this ("Get Out of Your Mind and Into Your Life" by Steven C. Hayes and "The Reality Slap", "The Confidence Gap" and "The Happiness Trap" all by Russ Harris) enabled me to find ways to focus more on living in line with my values, irrespective of what thoughts, feelings and events may arise.

ACT acknowledges the difference between instinctual uncontrollable feeling and the choice on what action to take. It helps to instil the ability to pause between the feeling and the physical act. This allows the making of a value-based conscious decision on how to act, instead of expressing the feeling by its natural action. It is also important for people to understand that it is the chosen action that is potentially problematic, rather than condemning people merely for having the thought or feeling, even if they do not act on it.

Peer Support

Peer mentors have proved effective in treating addiction, through the likes of Alcoholics Anonymous. They have also helped to support people with mental health difficulties, through groups like Mind and Depression Alliance. A survey by Positively UK (2014) showed a 12% improvement on the Warwick Edinburgh Mental Well-Being Scale following peer support, for people with HIV.

A man cannot fully understand the process of pregnancy and childbirth. Similarly, we cannot expect people who have no aberrant sexual thoughts to be able to fully understand what it feels like to experience these. Involving people who have similar thoughts and feelings, but are committed to not acting on them, can provide additional support. Listening to someone who has been there telling you how they maintain control is far more powerful than just listening to people who have never had these aberrant thoughts.

Old-Style Treatment

After conviction, I was permitted to attend the judicial community-based SOTP. This was the first time I met other people with similar problems and became aware that it was not just me who struggled with these thoughts and feelings.

The old-style treatment focussed heavily on getting offenders to realise the enormity of their crimes and taking full responsibility. This is not always the best approach, as it focusses too much on the problem, rather than the solution. Dwelling on the problem is likely to exacerbate it. The more we dwell on something, the stronger the mental pathways become. The modern approach of focussing much more on how people can gain the things they want in acceptable ways, whilst still taking responsibility for future behaviour is much more productive.

Since I was already distressed by my behaviour, focussing on the offence continually activated my threat system and just made me more frightened and upset, and consequently less able to think clearly about ways to alter my behaviour.

Would discussing painful sexual thoughts and feelings, especially with peer support help people? Most people find that problems are reduced by talking through them. Virped.org is an organisation that provides an online peer support forum for people who are sexually attracted to children but would never consider acting on this as it is against their moral values. This kind of support can be immensely helpful. Realising that you are not alone, and having examples of people living decent lives, whilst still being plagued by unwanted thoughts, provides hope. Seeing that it was possible to live normally, in spite of these aberrant desires, would have made it much easier for me to cope with these problems. Humans are sociable animals. Being able to talk openly about difficulties with supportive people makes it much easier to cope with challenges, without harming others.

Therapeutic Relationship

Some of the Sex Offender Group Treatment Programme facilitators were easier to work with than others. Having somebody recognise that you are trying to deal with your problems and providing helpful support in that aim is vitally important. A good teacher can inspire a pupil to great heights whilst a bad teacher can put a pupil off a subject for life. The relationship between the people delivering the treatment and the individual receiving it is crucial to its success. I found it helpful to have people treat me as an individual who wanted not to harm others and needed help and guidance to realise this aim. People who judged me solely on my aberrant behaviour were much harder to work with. Some facilitators seemed more interested in ensuring that people were punished for heading the wrong way rather than encouraged to head the right way.

Desistance Theory and Good Lives Model

Very few people commit offences when they are content with their life in its current state and have plans for how to continue to develop and improve their lives.

Instead of focussing on what factors led to offending, it is more constructive to focus on what factors can lead away from offending. This helps the individual understand appropriate ways to get their needs met. Theory alone is not sufficient. Just understanding that something is wanted is not enough. There also needs to be some practical assistance in establishing a realistic way to obtain it.

The core factors identified through The Good Lives Model and Desistance theory are paraphrased here.

- Meaningful work
- Self-control
- Financial independence, assertiveness

- Positive intimate relationship
- Friendships and community belonging
- Contributing to others' well-being
- Development of values
- Self-acceptance and enjoyment of life
- Creative expression

Potential "offenders should be viewed as someone attempting to live a meaningful worthwhile life … not moral strangers. …(*Potential to commit harmful acts*) does not suggest that they are intrinsically bad or destructive … it is only the rarest of individuals whose motives are purely psychopathic or sadistic" (Laws & Ward, 2011) (italicised sections are mine).

Helping people to acquire these life-enhancing features is much more likely to enable them to desist or avoid offending than condemning them for having undesirable sexual thoughts and feelings.

Somebody believing in you and your ability helps provide encouragement for growth as a person. Discovering ways to live with potentially harmful sexual thoughts and feelings without acting on them removes some of the fear. Being assisted to find more normative ways to attract the things I really wanted enabled me to change my behaviour.

Societal Awareness

During my developmental stages, indecent exposure was still legally dealt with under the vagrancy act. There was far less awareness of the serious impact of any form of child sexual exploitation, or of the extent to which this behaviour was carried out. Subsequent historical investigations have indicated that there was much more widespread sexual abuse of children than was generally acknowledged.

Media portrays the idea that people who commit sexual offences are compulsive recidivists. In fact, Ministry of Justice (2018) reports that for April to June 2016 only 14.7% of sexual offenders reoffended, compared to 30.1% (robbery) and 51.3% (theft). This indicates that more than twice as many people continue committing other offences than sexual ones. There is general misunderstanding about the motivation of people who commit sexual offences, particularly those who harm children. Some target children, not because they see them as vulnerable and easy to exploit, but rather because they identify with that level of maturity in themselves and struggle to cope with appropriate adult relationships.

The way in which sex is presented in adverts, films and books is also potentially harmful. I recently watched a series about a Marvel comic-book heroine, called Jessica Jones, on Netflix. I was saddened to see this character portrayed as ready to jump in to bed with men after very little contact and that this seemed to be a coping strategy for her. In particular, I felt it was inappropriate that in one scene a man in a bar complimented Jessica on her backside. She asked him to repeat the statement, which he gleefully did, and in the next scene they are having sex together in a public toilet. Is this an appropriate example to set for young people?

Usually, when someone is revealed to have committed a sexual offence, the neighbours, family and friends are shocked and would never have expected it of that individual. It is unfortunate that they typically then dismiss everything they previously knew about the individual and focus only on this new revelation, rather than seeing it in the context of the whole person. Whilst it is easy to judge people, this has never proved effective in enabling people to change, or to live constructive lives in spite of what they are judged for. Changing the emphasis to look at condemning isolated behaviours, rather than dismissing the entire person, provides scope for the individual to accept the error of their action and move on to better behaviour in the future.

Legal System

There are significant inconsistencies in the way punishments are administered for sexual offences. It is essential that adequate measures are taken to protect society, but imposing unlimited term restrictions, or failing to reduce restrictions when individuals show commitment to desistance from offending, is counter-productive. Imposing an indefinite term sends the subliminal message that the individual cannot change, which could easily result in the person giving up on themselves. A better method is to impose appropriate restrictions for a sensible period of time. These should then be reviewed periodically to see if they are still necessary. Individuals who show clear progress and commitment to desistance should be rewarded. Where there is evidence of diminished risk, restrictions should be reduced or lifted. There always remain Disclosure and Barring Service (DBS) checks to ensure that individuals cannot put themselves in situations that are potentially dangerous, even without additional sanctions.

Societal Attitudes

Child sexual exploitation in all its forms, whether internet-based, contact or my non-contact offending is wrong and causes harm to victims. It is entirely right that this behaviour should be condemned and prevented. However, society's tendency to condemn the whole individual for the action, rather than seeing this as one aspect of their personality and behaviour is actually detrimental to the prevention of this behaviour. Condemnation of the person pushes the behaviour further into the shadows, increases the perpetrators shame and isolation and reduces their opportunity to talk to others about the problem. This weakens their ability to learn how to control the unwanted urges, instead of acting on them.

"Failure to grant sex-offenders the basic entitlements of citizenship and the conditions required to live fulfilling lives is ethically unjustified as well as practically self-defeating" (Laws & Ward, 2011).

During group treatment, I encountered other service users. My impression of most of these individuals is that they were not predators wanting to cause harm to vulnerable children. Instead, they seemed to be as human as anybody else I met. They were people who had unwanted desires that they did not have the skills and understanding to be able to control, in the way they would have preferred. I saw significant change in many of these individuals during treatment and I see no reason why they would not have been equally able to respond effectively to preventative treatment.

It is a great deal easier to help people to learn effective coping strategies for difficult emotions when they are still young, and prior to committing an actual offence.

My local paper has at least one article a week about somebody behaving in a sexually inappropriate way. I believe that many people are struggling to avoid offending. The increased awareness of the problem will only yield solutions if people are guided to appropriate assistance before it is too late.

It is possible to prevent harm, at much lower cost, through early preventative intervention, rather than the much more painful, complex and expensive process of attempting to treat people post-offence. By which time, they have already inflicted distress and potential serious harm on others.

Permanent imprisonment of those who have gone beyond assistance is extremely expensive. The earlier effective intervention is provided the cheaper this will be and the less overall harm there will be to society. People who are treated successfully early in their lives will inevitably cause far less problems. They are much more likely to make valuable contributions to society, thereby increasing, instead of depleting, the overall resources available.

Many people who have dangerous desires do not want to commit sexual offences. It is possible to control these desires, just as people learn to control their temper, without hitting others. People can be aware of a strong sexual desire for a relative's partner or a work colleague without acting on that impulse. If, as a society, we accept that some people want to change and avoid offending, then we can much more effectively address this ever-increasing problem.

If we continue to treat people as irredeemable predators, who are inevitably going to harm children, then the chances are high that this is exactly what they will become. Instead, we can treat people as humans, who want to behave morally but need help to develop effective strategies to cope in life. This is more likely to create a better society in which we all want to live and where we can all make valuable contributions. We have come a long way in reducing stigma and persecution associated with race, sexual orientation, colour and disability. Now we need to extend this to not judging people solely on the basis of a particular set of thoughts or desires, or even on a single aberrant action, but recognising that there are good and bad parts to everybody.

I acknowledge that there are individuals who do want to harm others or see nothing wrong in their actions. However, in my experience, most people who have undesirable sexual thoughts and feelings and worry about their risk of committing a sexual offence are not happy with how they are feeling and would much prefer to have normal sexual desires and behaviour. I believe that it is more productive to help these people to live normal lives, without harm, despite their urges, than to continually imprison them. Prison offers little opportunity for them to build a life in which they can readily avoid acting on their urges.

By enhancing public services through offering prevention treatment, we provide people another opportunity to develop. Some people's childhood experiences do not equip them well to deal with the problems that are part of human existence.

Practical Steps

Although sex education in schools has come a long way, I suspect that there is still no discussion of sexual thoughts/feelings that it would be inappropriate or illegal to act on. I think introducing this into sex education would help children to discuss why certain actions must not be done. It could help them to understand what the consequences for victim and perpetrator would be. Above all, it could teach how these difficult thoughts/feelings can be successfully managed without acting out and causing harm. Discussion about sexual thoughts/feelings that people don't want or like would help understanding. Given the right support, it is possible for these people to find appropriate ways to live worthwhile lives in the community. Problems that remain taboo tend to remain problems. Circles of Support and Accountability (CoSA) help people to accept responsibility for their behaviour but also offer encouragement in finding workable solutions. This helps individuals with these problems to develop effective coping strategies and be less marginalised and isolated. It is vital that we do not condone the actions of those who harm others, but it is more effective to treat people as humans with difficulties than to dismiss these people.

Adults involved with children, whether as parents, teachers or in social activities, could be more aware of the quiet ones. If somebody is not talking to others, then whatever problems they have, they are having to deal with alone. Few children have the capacity to cope with their problems alone, if they did, then they would not be problems. It is most definitely not the case that all introverts need assistance to avoid committing a sexual offence. However, in my opinion, there are few people who are part of mainstream social peer interaction at school who go on to commit sexual offences, unless they suffer major tragedy in adulthood. Those who are on the periphery of their peer group are more likely to suffer isolation and loneliness. This increases the probability that they will struggle with future relationships and consequently need more assistance to avoid sexual offending.

Film, TV and book authors should be encouraged to present the downsides of casual sex, to advocate use of appropriate protection and to reveal consequences of risky or inappropriate sexual behaviour. This would help to combat the glorification of sex and general encouragement to indulge. Most films/TV series and books include scenes where people become involved in sexual encounters with little evidence of any initial relationship formation or any intention to commitment.

There was a time when people thought it was fine to have a few beers and then drive home from the pub. The majority of people now would not consider drinking and driving and this is generally frowned upon by modern society. Smoking is now considered antisocial. Homosexuality is now legal and is appropriately accepted as a perfectly reasonable sexual orientation and way of behaving. Most of these changes have come about through government campaigns, education and media activity. There is now emphasis on dealing more effectively with domestic violence and, again, attitudes are changing on this front too. Societal attitudes can be improved which would lead to a more humane value-driven society.

Conclusion

Puberty can be difficult for many young people. The better they are prepared for possible problems, the more likely they are to come through those problems as mature responsible adults.

Relationships are complex and fraught with problems. Understanding this makes it easier to work through problems that arise and thereby strengthen the relationship.

Men are especially prone to struggle with effectively expressing emotions. Shame is not conducive to growth.

Focussing on ways to help people develop the skills that are needed to survive in the modern world will build a stronger, more humane society.

According to the latest statistics from the Ministry of Justice, only a minority of people convicted of a sexual offence reoffend. This proves that behavioural change is possible.

I don't want people to cause harm to others, as I did, due to the lack of preventative assistance. It is challenging dealing with distressing sexual thoughts and feelings on your own and acting on them just makes things infinitely worse.

We need to offer a prevention service instead of just relying on treating people after they have harmed others. This service needs to be provided by trained therapists with experience of supporting people with offence-related sexual thoughts.

In all areas of life, prevention of harm is far superior to restitution or punishment.

Acknowledgements With thanks to Emma Allen, Dr. Kerensa Hocken and Mrs. Pat Taylor for their assistance in editing this ready for publication.

References

BBC. (2017). *Half of women sexually harassed at work.* http://www.bbc.co.uk/news/uk-41741615

Chatterjee, R. (2018). 81 Percent of women have experienced sexual harassment. https://www.npr.org/sections/thetwo-way/2018/02/21/587671849/a-new-surveyfinds-eighty-percent-of-women-have-experienced-sexual-harassment

Kirk, A. (2017). *One in five women have been sexually harassed.* https://www.telegraph.co.uk/news/2017/10/25/two-five-women-have-sexually-harassed-workplace-poll-shows/

Laws, R., & Ward, T. (2011). *Desistance from sex offending.* New York: Guilford Press.

Ministry of Justice. (2018). *Proven Re-offending statistics quarterly bulletin – April 2016 to June 2016, England and Wales*. https://www.gov.uk/government/statistics/proven-reoffending-statistics-april-2016-to-june-2016

Positively UK. (2014). *Improving well-being: The effectiveness of peer support*. http://positivelyuk.org/wp-content/uploads/2014/01/Evaluation-report-web.pdf

Williams, Z. (2017). *Sexual Harassment 101: What everyone needs to know*. https://www.theguardian.com/world/2017/oct/16/facts-sexual-harassment-workplace-harvey-weinstein

Worrall, P. (2017). *How many women face sexual harassment in the workplace?* https://www.channel4.com/news/factcheck/factcheck-how-many-women-face-sexual-harassment-in-the-workplace

7

Social and Professional Attitudes in the Prevention of Sexual Abuse

Craig A. Harper

Introduction

Several key organisations, such as the Association for the Treatment of Sexual Abusers (ATSA), have designated the prevention of sexual abuse as one of the most pressing public health issues facing modern societies. However, there is a raft of research evidence that suggests the manner in which we discuss such offending behaviour, and our responses to those at risk of becoming abusers, hinders such prevention efforts. This chapter explores the role of public attitudes in various prevention processes.

'Prevention' is a broad and catch-all term for a myriad of initiatives geared towards the reduction of the incidence of sexual abuse. That is, prevention can take three distinct forms. *Primary prevention* refers to broadscale societal initiatives aimed at reducing the societal prevalence of sexual abuse. Examples of such schemes include the National Society for the Prevention of Cruelty to Children's (NSPCC's) 'pants' initiative (designed to teach children about the importance of keeping private parts

---

C. A. Harper (✉)
Nottingham Trent University, Nottingham, UK
e-mail: Craig.Harper@ntu.ac.uk

private) and Stop it Now! United Kingdom's advertisements describing the damaging nature of accessing indecent images of children via the internet. *Secondary prevention* is more focused and refers to targeted initiatives that aim to access individuals who are at risk of becoming sexual abusers and working with them to stop abuse before it occurs. An example of secondary prevention is Project Prevention Dunkelfeld (from here 'the Dunkelfeld Project'; Beier et al., 2009; Beier, Özdemir, Schlinzig, Groll, & Hellenschmidt, 2016; see also Christiansen, this volume), which offers anonymous therapy to people who self-identify as having paedophilic sexual interests. Finally, *tertiary prevention* refers to more traditional rehabilitative initiatives whereby people who have already committed acts of sexual abuse are provided with treatment input in order to reduce the chances of such behaviour being repeated.

The aim of this chapter is to provide a critical review of the academic literature surrounding both attitudes towards sexual offenders and the stigmatisation of people with sexual interests involving children, and to link this research base to ongoing prevention efforts. Opportunities for developing more effective communication strategies geared towards the prevention of sexual abuse are also outlined in detail.

In this chapter, the order of prevention schemes will be reversed (first examining tertiary prevention, then secondary prevention, and finally primary prevention) in order to best reflect the expanding nature of societal conversations about reducing the incidence of sexual abuse.

Attitudes and Their Effects in Tertiary Prevention (Offender Treatment) Services

As noted in the introductory comments to this chapter, tertiary prevention in this area of work refers to the treatment of those who have already committed acts of sexual abuse. A range of recent research has highlighted the potential importance of attitudes in this important process.

In a review of this literature by Harper, Hogue, and Bartels (2017), professionals' attitudes were reported to affect decision-making in a number of domains. For instance, negative staff attitudes may play an important role in the effectiveness of treatment via a construct referred to as 'therapeutic climate' (Hogue, 2015). Blagden, Winder, and Hames (2016) used the social psychological dichotomy of 'entity' and 'incremental' implicit theories of behaviour (Dweck, Chiu, & Hong, 1995) to assess whether forensic professionals' views about the core nature of sexual offending were associated with (1) their attitudes towards their clients, and (2) the rehabilitative climate in which they were working. For clarity, those who hold an entity-based implicit theory about sexual offending would be said to assume that this behaviour is fixed and stable over time, and that offenders would be unlikely to change their behaviour as a result of treatment efforts. In contrast, people with more incrementally based implicit theories about sexual offending are likely to endorse the idea that this behaviour is changeable through rehearsal or treatment.

Consistent with their hypotheses, Blagden et al. (2016) reported a positive relationship between attitudes towards sexual offenders and incremental implicit theories about sexual offending, indicating that positive attitudes were associated with the belief that offenders do have the potential to eventually desist from crime. Further, qualitative analyses suggested that positive attitudes from staff allowed sexual offenders to have the required 'headspace' (p. 380) to engage in treatment, and experience a sense of relative safety while doing so. These findings were heightened among offenders who were in treatment groups led by facilitators with incremental implicit theories about sexual offending.

These results are consistent with earlier work conducted by Beech and Hamilton-Giachritsis (2005), who found that a supportive therapeutic climate within treatment groups was associated with greater levels of interpersonal communication within groups, group cohesiveness, and, in turn, treatment effectiveness (as measured through significant reductions in offence-supportive cognitions).

Within the social domain, attitudes towards sexual offenders and those with paedophilic sexual interests may play an important role in desistance and abuse prevention processes. A framework for understanding how these difficulties play is described by Göbbels, Ward, and Willis (2012) in their Integrated Theory of Desistance from Sexual Offending (ITDSO).

This is a four-phase theory describing the processes by which people who have committed sexual offences can transition from criminal behaviour, through incarceration and formalised treatment, to eventually living as non-offending members of society.

Phases one and two refer to processes whereby individuals make the conscious decision to change their ways and engage in formal treatment programmes, with attitudes of staff playing an important role here, as outlined above. However, phases three and four of the ITDSO adopt a more social perspective, and describe the desistance-strengthening (or desistance-impeding) influences of the external social environment. Göbbels et al. (2012) identified the importance of a rehabilitation-reinforcing social environment, such as the maintenance of positive social relationships and a strong non-offender identity. However, they also point out the difficulties associated with achieving these social conditions with a history of sexual offending, through the processes of stigmatisation, labelling, and strict probation restrictions.

One tertiary prevention initiative that operates within the community is Circles of Support and Accountability (CoSA). This approach involves people who have convictions for sexual offences (or 'core members', as they are referred to within the programme) being provided with practical and pastoral support as a means of reducing re-offence risk upon the completion of their formal criminal justice sanctions. This support is provided by a small number of community-based volunteers (the 'inner-circle'), who are supported in turn by trained professionals (the 'outer-circle'). The role of the inner circle is to meet regularly with the core member, and to provide them with practical (e.g., arranging medical appointments, and assisting with finding housing and employment opportunities) and emotional support as they seek to successfully reintegrate into the community upon the completion of formal criminal sanctions.

Evaluations of CoSA appear promising with respect to (re)offending rates, with Wilson, Cortoni, and McWhinnie (2009) reporting a rate of reoffending approximately 70% lower among Core Members when they are compared to matched controls. A randomised controlled trail conducted by Duwe (2018) has further reported that CoSA initiatives can reduce sexual reoffending by up to 88%, general reoffending by 49–57%, and provide a justice system financial benefit of $3.73 per $1 spent on the scheme.

Broadly, there is strong support for schemes such as CoSA among the general population. According to a range of surveys, around 70% of people see value in this type of approach to preventive sexual abuse, with only small numbers being suspicious about its potential effectiveness (e.g., Wilson, Picheca, & Prinzo, 2007). Nonetheless, in spite of general level of support, there is also a reluctance to actively and personally engage in CoSA procedures. In one survey conducted by Höing, Petrina, Duke, Völlm, and Vogelvang (2016), over half of respondents (55%) said that they would support a friend who wanted to volunteer with CoSA, though only 12% would consider doing so themselves.

Understanding public attitudes may shed light on this lack of willingness to actively engage with CoSA initiatives. Richards and McCartan (2018) have suggested that the framing of information about CoSA has an impact here. They examined social media comments made in response to online posts about the launch of a CoSA initiative in Australia. They found that comments about the scheme were overwhelmingly hostile when the framing of the initial news posts were negatively valenced (e.g., 'Controversial paedophile support program to launch in South Australia in a national first', and 'Stop the COSA Trial in South Australia Immediately').

It may be, then, that the acknowledgement of the potential usefulness of socially based tertiary prevention initiatives is widely held, but there are other societal pressures—such as personal reputational concerns—that stop people from actively supporting them. That is, people may be dissuaded from participating in CoSA schemes due to the 'strong negative reaction to the image of "supporting" child sex offenders' (Richards & McCartan, 2018, p. 13). With this in mind, a societal shift in the ways in which we view sexual abuse prevention may be required to improve engagement with progressive tertiary prevention programmes.

Attitudes as a Barrier to Secondary Prevention of Sexual Abuse

As we move towards ideas of secondary and primary prevention, it is important to explicitly state a shift in emphasis. The majority of the empirical work conducted in this area is focused around the reduction of child sexual abuse, as such, the remainder of this chapter will be focused around this area. This is not to downplay the importance of preventing the sexual abuse of adults, and addressing cognitive distortions and thinking styles that are invoked as causal factors for sexual assault in the general population. However, a review of this comprehensive literature is beyond the scope of this chapter (though interested readers may be interested to read some recent theorising by Nunes, Petterson, Hermann, Looman, & Spape, 2016).

Definitional Issues in the Secondary Prevention Domain

Before exploring the secondary (and subsequently primary) prevention of child sexual abuse, defining some key terms—specifically 'paedophilia'—is necessary.

Paedophilia is generally defined by sexologists and forensic professionals as a primary or exclusive sexual interest in pre-pubertal children, typically aged between three and ten years. While this type of sexual interest is implicated as an important risk factor in predicting reoffending among convicted child abusers (Helmus, Ó Ciardha, & Seto, 2015), recent research conducted by Schmidt, Mokros, and Banse (2013) has demonstrated that fewer than half of all child abusers actually meet the criteria for being accurately labelled as paedophilic. Further, data from the German government-funded MiKADO project has suggested that approximately 4% of adult men (based on a sample of almost 9000 non-offenders) self-report to masturbating to sexual fantasies involving children (Dombert et al., 2016). This figure is consistent with Seto's (2009) upper estimate of 5% as a general prevalence rate for paedophilia within the general (male) population.

While this almost 1 in 20 may feel like a concerning prevalence rate to a large proportion of people, it is small in comparison to men's self-reported sexual attraction to people who are legally under the age of consent. Again using German data, Ahlers et al. (2011) reported that around 10% of adult men admitted to some degree of sexual attraction to children (i.e., they gave a response to images of children that was not an emphatic 'this image is absolutely not sexually arousing', or admitted to engaging in sexual fantasies involving children). This rate of interest rises again to 25% when analysing online chat room transcripts (Bergen,

Antfolk, Jern, Alanko, & Santtila, 2013). That is, 1 in 4 men continued to sexualise conversations with somebody who revealed themselves as being between the ages of 10–12 years.

These data suggest that the rate of paedophilic sexual interests (as a broader concept than 'paedophilia' as a clinical label) is much higher than many members of the public may realise, and that this may represent a pressing public health issue. In spite of this, there is still a popular conflation of 'paedophilia' with 'child sexual abuse' within contemporary society and the popular media (Feelgood & Hoyer, 2008). In practice, what this means is that those who identify as having a paedophilic sexual orientation are automatically assumed to be child molesters. This leads to those who are labelled as paedophiles (either accurately as a result of their sexual interests, or inaccurately as a result of index offences for which they may have been convicted) facing substantial amounts of stigmatisation and hatred in contemporary society. In turn, this response may act as a potential hindrance to the accessibility of effective prevention services for those who are struggling with sexual fantasies or thoughts involving children.

This point was stressed by clinical sexologist Dr. James Cantor in the Canadian documentary, *I, Pedophile*:

> The day before somebody gives in to his sexual interest in children, he was a person who was struggling with his sexual interest in children. And that was the day we failed him.

With this in mind, formulating effective communication strategies in order to promote a more reasoned conversation about paedophilia and the prevention of child sexual abuse is of great social importance.

Social Attitudes and the Stigmatisation of (Non-offending) Paedophiles

The stigmatisation of people with paedophilic sexual interests (even in the absence of any history of offending behaviour) has recently become a growing and vibrant area of empirical inquiry. Jahnke and Hoyer (2013) identified this area as a 'blind-spot' in contemporary stigma research, and suggested several potentially important effects of widespread stigmatisation of this group.

In relation to paedophilia, stigmatisation takes the form of stereotyping, emotional responses (e.g., fear, loathing, and hatred), and a belief that paedophiles should be incarcerated as a preventative measure. It is clear from a cursory analysis of the literature that these responses are remarkably similar to those directed towards those who have been tarnished with the 'sex offender' label (Bastian, Denson, & Haslam, 2013). Indeed, King and Roberts (2017) observed that 'when asked about "sex offenders" many are inclined to envision the media-proliferated stereotypical image of a violent, predatory male p[a]edophile' (p. 72).

As an example of these extreme responses, a substantial proportion of both German and American participants in a survey-based study conducted by Jahnke, Imhoff, and Hoyer (2015) believed that paedophiles (irrespective of whether they had committed a sexual offence) should be incarcerated for reasons of sexual abuse prevention. Further, a significant minority even suggested that such people 'should better be dead'. This final statement, at best, appears to endorse or encourage suicidal behaviours among people with paedophilic sexual interests, and at worst endorses lethal physical violence against them.

In the same samples as those described above, a paedophilic sexual interest was seen as something that a person chooses for themselves. These findings highlight why stigmatisation towards paedophiles may be heightened. Given the conflation of 'paedophilia' (as a sexual interest or orientation) with 'child sexual abuse' (as a criminal behaviour), the attribution of controllability over paedophilic interests may reinforce the view that paedophiles (as a homogeneously labelled group) purposively seek out children to abuse in a predatory manner.

The Sources and Effects of the Stigmatisation of (Non-offending) Paedophiles: Implications for Secondary Prevention Initiatives

As in many areas of the psychology of public attitudes, the mass media—particularly newspapers—have been implicated as the drivers of such opinions. In some of the most thorough analyses of press coverage about paedophilia, Harper and Hogue (2014) reported how this label was commonly associated with child sexual abuse, which in turn was substantially over-represented as a criminal category in news stories. Further, child sexual abuse is also associated with dehumanising descriptions of the (typically) men involved in this type of offending (Harper & Hogue, 2017). For instance, people convicted of child sexual offences are referred to as 'beasts', 'fiends', and 'monsters'.

Bringing this work together with the theorising discussed above, it is clear that the mass media play at least some role in perpetuating the previously mentioned conflation between 'paedophilia' and 'child sexual abuse'. This is not a new argument. For example, McCartan (2010) set out an argument that placed media constructions of paedophilia within the sociological literature on moral panics. That is, the social construction of 'the paedophile' portrays this group as a collective of predatory child sexual offenders, consistent with the arguments subsequently advanced by King and Roberts (2017). In doing so, the media encourages reactionary decision-making, typically in the form of stigmatisation and punitive responses to a group that is homogenously defined, but in need of a carefully considered and nuanced social treatment.

The roots of such emotional responses may also be based on fundamental aspects of our moral psychology. Jahnke (2018) reported how anger and disgust are emotions associated with more punitive responses to non-offending paedophiles, with these emotions being heightened when motivations for non-offending were extrinsic (i.e., a fear of incarceration or punishment) than intrinsic (i.e., the paedophile morally knowing that offending would be wrong). This corresponds closely to Harper and Harris' (2017) observations that moral foundations could guide personal and social responses to themes related to sexual offending. That is, sexual relations between adults and children are seen by the vast majority of society as being impure from a moral standpoint. Those who entertain these relations, either in a non-offending way through sexual fantasy or through sexual offending behaviour, elicit these instinctual responses, with these cascading into support for punitive policies directed towards paedophilic individuals.

In addition to the stigmatisation coming from the wider community, some people with paedophilic sexual interests may take on these societal views as a part of their self-concept. Moreover, self-stigmatisation among paedophiles has been found to contribute to a fear of discovery by the wider community, as well as reductions in cognitive and emotional functioning (Jahnke, Schmidt, Geradt, & Hoyer, 2015). In a practical sense, these effects manifest themselves as enhanced levels of depression, anxiety, and perceived loneliness.

Given that these factors have been identified by Gillespie, Mitchell, Fisher, and Beech (2012) as potential risk factors for the commission of sexual offences against children, there is a potential argument to be made that reducing societal levels of stigmatisation of those individuals who do have sexual interests in children non-offending paedophiles could contribute to reductions in sexual offending behaviour. For example, self-stigmatisation was implicated by Jahnke and Hoyer (2013) as a possible cause of social isolation among paedophiles, and this was suggested as a barrier to self-seeking behaviour (e.g., approaching medical professionals or support groups for support with managing sexual interests). Thus, it appears logical to argue that reductions in levels of self-stigmatisation among the paedophilic community (possibly via the reduction of wider social stigmatisation at the population level; Harper, Bartels, & Hogue, 2016) might have unintended positive implications for the reduction of sexually abusive behaviour.

In support of this idea, self-stigmatisation has been implicated as a possible cause of social isolation among people with paedophilic sexual interests, with this linked to a lack of willingness to actively seek therapeutic support for these sexual interests (Jahnke & Hoyer, 2013). Further, Cantor (2014) argued that examining how we (as a society) can help those with such interests live productive and law-abiding lives free from stigma might be a more productive way to prevent the sexual abuse of children. This is consistent with broader arguments about the potential use of acceptance-focused therapeutic practices with those who have unwanted sexual interests in children (Hocken & Taylor, 2018; see also Chap. 4 of this book).

It is here where research into attitudes towards people with paedophilic sexual interests could be useful and lead to the development of public interventions for improving such views. By improving public attitudes (or, as a minimum, developing a more evidence-based understanding of the true nature of paedophilia), a social environment that is supportive of rehabilitative efforts may be fostered, and efforts to prevent the incidence of child sexual abuse could be made more likely to be a success.

One such initiative that has had relative success in this regard is the Dunkelfeld Project, which offers support to men who self-identify as being sexually attracted to children. Using national television advertisements, this initiative has been able to attract hundreds of self-identifying paedophiles into anonymous treatment programmes, which have demonstrated reductions in the expression of offence-supportive cognitions among people engaged in the programme (Amelung, Kuhle, Konrad, Pauls, & Beier, 2012), as well as improved sexual self-regulation (Beier et al., 2015). The advertisements used by the Dunkelfeld Project directly address some of the stereotypes identified through the research of Jahnke and colleagues (reviewed above). They are explicit about framing paedophilia as a form of sexual orientation that is unchosen, but place personal responsibility on people with such sexual interests to take control of their behaviour. In doing so, these advertisements humanise paedophiles, and encourage them to use their personal agency to seek support, if required, in order to reduce their likelihood of committing an act of sexual abuse.

Similarly, Stop it Now! United Kingdom has launched a national drive to encourage 18–30 year old men who feel troubled by their sexual interests to come forward for support. Using a similar approach to that developed by the Dunkelfeld Project, Stop it Now! have produced a series of videos that tell the stories of people who have been through the criminal justice system after committing sexual offences. These films were viewed more than two million times in the first 12 months of release (2015–2016) and have contributed to more than 4000 people calling an anonymous support line each year to access help (Allardyce, 2018).

Taking the above ideas into account, it is clear that our current approach to paedophilia lies at the punitive end of the response continuum, in spite of emerging examples of progressive policies that both assist in the reduction of offending behaviour and improve the psychological well-being of people with paedophilic sexual interests. What this indicates is that we may require a cultural shift in the ways in which we conceptualise paedophilia, with this being a necessary first step in changing more formalised approaches to sexual abuse prevention at the legislative level.

A Cultural Shift: Changing Social Attitudes in the Primary Prevention of Sexual Abuse

In the previous sections of this chapter, attitudes towards people with paedophilic sexual interests, and their broader societal stigmatisation, have been discussed within the specific context of preventing sexual abuse. However, as noted earlier, it is important to acknowledge the nature and prevalence of paedophilic sexual interests within the general population, and how many of these individuals may not actually be at an increased risk of committing sexual offences. With this in mind, and given the relatively high base rate of paedophilia in the broader male population (upper estimates of around 5%; Seto, 2009), it may be possible to contextualise responses to paedophilia, and the legal protections afforded to people with these sexual interests, within the broader picture of anti-discrimination laws as they apply to other sexual minorities.

For instance, the United Kingdom's Office for National Statistics (2017) recently reported the prevalence of non-heterosexuality as 6.6%, while Collin, Reisner, Tangpricha, and Goodman (2016) estimated the prevalence of self-reported transgender identity to be 0.2–0.6%. Recent decades of campaigning have rightly led to the rolling out of legal protections for lesbian, gay, bisexual, and transgender (LGBT) identifying individuals, meaning that discrimination on the grounds of these aspects of identity is illegal, and attacks based on these factors can be classified as hate crimes. However, these protections do not apply equally to those who identify as having paedophilic sexual interests.

This line of argumentation may seem odd, though this may be more of a reflection of the popular conflation between paedophilia (the sexual interest or orientation) and child sexual abuse (the criminal act) than the validity of the point being advanced here. However, let us briefly consider the philosophical basis for hate crime laws, and evaluate whether they could conceivably be extended to those with paedophilic sexual interests.

In his paper titled 'Is pedophilia a sexual orientation?', Seto (2012) reviewed the relevant evidence to answer this specific question. Seto set out three criteria that characterise a sexual orientation: early onset, persistence over time, and resistance to change. For example, those who identify as being homosexual typically report recognising this in early adolescence, at around the age of 10 (Herdt & McClintock, 2000), their interests are stable throughout puberty and into adulthood, and efforts to 'reverse' homosexuality (so-called conversion therapy) have been consistently found to be unsuccessful (Flentje, Heck, & Cochran, 2014).

The nature of paedophilia, and the difficulty in accessing community samples of people who identify as having these interests as a primary sexual orientation, makes it difficult to design and execute studies that would map on to these studies on homosexuality. That said, we can infer this information from historical studies on those who have been found to be paedophilic after being convicted of sexual offences against children.

Freund and Kuban (1993) and Marshall, Barbaree, and Eccles (1991) reported that offenders within their samples reported experiencing sexual urges involving children before the end of adolescence, while Bernard (1985) argued that a substantial proportion of paedophiles recognise this sexual interest before the age of 15. Seto, Lalumière, and Blanchard (2000) also reported that paedophilic sexual interests can be detected using phallometric techniques before the onset of adulthood. With modern advances in social media, we also now have access to self-identifying paedophiles on online platforms. Anecdotally, it is clear that a large significant percentage of these accounts either (a) are still adolescents, or (b) recognised their sexual orientation during this point in their lives.

In relation to temporal stability, Seto (2012) reports that paedophiles continue from adolescence and into adulthood having a greater emotional congruence with children than non-paedophiles. In addition to this, Houtepan, Sijtsema, and Bogaerts (2016) found that those who self-identify as paedophiles were less interested in sexual relationships with adults than they were with having emotional relationships with children (which they also report as being just as important as any potential sexual relationship with their preferred sexual targets; see Cantor & McPhail, 2016). These findings indicate that self-identified paedophiles' general preference for intimate partners does not typically fluctuate between children and adults across different time points.

Paedophilic sexual interest also appears to be resistant to treatment and change over time. For instance, Grundmann, Krupp, Scherner, Amelung, and Beier (2016) found that self-reported high levels of stability in relation to self-reported sexual fantasies involving children in a group of paedophiles recruited via the Dunkelfeld Project. In their study, they administered a series of repeated questionnaires asking about sexual fantasies used during masturbation among a sample of self-identifying paedophiles and hebephiles over a period of more than two years, finding no significant differences in the prevalence or arousal levels of a range of sexual fantasies between the first and last questionnaires that were completed.

Given that paedophilic sexual interests appear to satisfy Seto's (2012) criteria for classification as a sexual orientation, we are left with an ethical conundrum regarding the most appropriate social response to people who identify as being paedophiles—particularly those who desire support in a bid to prevent sexual abuse. From a legal perspective, we have protections to safeguard people against discrimination and harassment on the basis of sexual orientation (as operationalised through LGBTQ+ legislation). While some have argued for paedophilia to be added to this list, their motivations have typically been seen as opening the door to the normalisation and eventual legalisation of adult-child sexual relationships (for a thorough review of legal debates about paedophilia, see Kaplan, 2015).

This 'normalisation' hypothesis may also be associated with the fears that some have about the effects to their reputation if they became involved in tertiary prevention initiatives, as discussed previously in this chapter. This would be the incorrect way to deal with the issue of paedophilia and may be related to the popular definitional conflation of 'paedophilia' with 'child sexual abuse'. However, to navigate this issue, any legislative movement could be framed around the prevention of child sexual abuse, rather than the promotion of 'paedophile rights'.

This cultural change in how we view paedophilia should be front-and-centre of the efforts being made by initiatives trying to facilitate the (primary) prevention of child sexual abuse. For instance, as a society we are able to separate normative sexual interests (e.g., heterosexuality and homosexuality) from the criminal act of rape. Similarly, we should be able to separate the sexual orientation of paedophilia from the criminal act of child abuse and molestation. In doing so, it is possible to simultaneously acknowledge the inherent vulnerabilities of the targets of paedophilic sexual interests, and offer preventative schemes to support those paedophiles who desire support in living with their sexual interests. Alongside these schemes, the promotion of the scientific argument about paedophilia as a sexual orientation offers an opportunity to simultaneously educate the wider population about the dangers of stigmatising paedophiles (in line with the arguments made earlier with regard to discouraging help-seeking behaviour; Jahnke & Hoyer, 2013).

Using Psychological Research in the Primary Prevention of Child Sexual Abuse

Perhaps surprisingly, relatively few studies have sought to establish the routes by which we may be able to harness intuitive and largely automatic psychological processes in an attempt to improve social attitudes towards people with paedophilic sexual interests. Specifically, two studies have sought to examine rehumanisation in relation to paedophiles. This work was undertaken in response to the growing awareness of implicit and automatic information processing with regard to issues related to sexual crime (Harper & Hogue, 2017; Harris & Socia, 2016). In the first of these studies, participants (who were trainee psychotherapists) presented with information about paedophiles from the perspective of somebody with a sexual interest in children expressed significant improvements in their explicit (self-reported) attitudes towards this group as compared to a control group, who were presented with a video about violence-free parenting (Jahnke, Imhoff, & Hoyer, 2015). Moreover, this effect was still present in follow-up testing six weeks after the experimental manipulation, indicating a stable change in viewpoints over time as a result of this intervention.

Harper et al. (2016) went further by directly isolating the source of the message from the message itself. That is, they divided their sample of 100 students into two conditions. In the first condition, participants were presented with a short video clip from the British documentary *The Paedophile Next Door*. This was a mainstream, primetime television documentary that told the story of 'Eddie'—a man living every day as a non-offending self-identifying paedophile. Eddie spoke to camera about the social stigma that he faces about the need for greater levels of social and professional support for people with paedophilic sexual interests, and about how policies could be put in place to prevent sexual offending before it occurs. This represented a 'narrative humanising' approach. A separate group of participants were presented with a video clip of an expert (Dr. James Cantor) speaking about the sexological and biological nature of paedophilia, and concluding with similar claims about the best ways to prevent sexual abuse. By adopting such an approach, Harper et al. were able to identify whether it was indeed the humanisation element of Jahnke et al.'s manipulation that led to attitude improvement, rather than these changes merely being a reflection of the different messages being conveyed within the Jahnke et al. research.

Both groups demonstrated significant reductions in negative attitudes towards paedophiles, though this effect was far greater in the humanising condition. Even more interestingly, the narrative-based humanisation of Eddie's clip led to more positive responding at the implicit level than did the expert-delivered information. This result highlights the potential utility of direct exposure to examples of potential offenders that run counter to media stereotypes when attempting to influence attitudes.

This idea supports theoretical arguments made by some criminologists, who have highlighted society's lack of a desistance narrative for individuals who have committed sexual offences (e.g., Farmer, McAlinden, & Maruna, 2015). That is, we typically do not hear from those who have been convicted for these types of offences—either about the precursors to their offending behaviour, or their journeys towards desistance. The same principle potentially applies to those who have not yet committed an offence, but whom society views as being at risk of doing so (i.e., paedophiles). Again, this has links to the heuristic-based information processing strategies discussed previously in this chapter. If all that is available is a punitive and dehumanised 'monster' narrative (Harper & Hogue, 2017; King & Roberts, 2017), it is no surprise that members of the public jump to conclusions and make snap judgements about paedophiles and the prevention of sexual crime based on this stereotype. By incorporating the voices of individuals who have paedophilic sexual interests into more mainstream and broader societal discussions about the prevention of sexual abuse, it may be possible to disrupt this tendency of heuristic decision-making and facilitate more rational discussions about this area of public policy.

Conclusions

This chapter has discussed the role of social attitudes towards sexual offenders and those with paedophilic sexual interests in the context of sexual abuse prevention. It is clear from this review of the literature that the stigmatisation of these groups is widespread in contemporary society, and is most likely based around an emotional response to the common conflation between 'paedophilia' and 'child sexual abuse'. This conflation is driven, at least in part, by misrepresentative and dehumanising media presentations of sexual offending and the individuals who perpetrate such crimes.

A number of recommendations have been put forward as a result of this review. For clarity, these are that:

1. The lay social framing of sexual abuse prevention creates a barrier to the active support of the public in tertiary prevention of sexual abuse. That is, by reconceptualising these services as efforts to reduce victimisation (vs. helping sexual offenders), it may be possible to encourage more members of the public to come forward to assist with schemes such as CoSA, for which there is already widespread support.
2. We need a re-evaluation of how we view paedophilia at a societal level. That is, there is a case to be made to categorise the stigmatisation and public attack of *non-offending* paedophiles as hate, consistent with existing human rights laws. This is because paedophilia appears to conform to empirical definitions of sexual orientation and could therefore be afforded the same legal protections as other groups who are already afforded such protections on this basis.
3. Changing the public view of paedophilia may be possible via the process of narrative humanisation. Several studies have demonstrated how the presentation of first-person narratives of people with paedophilic sexual interests can have statistically significant effects in the form of reducing both explicit (self-reported) and implicit levels of

stigmatisation. More research is needed in order to establish whether this approach is as effective when examining attitudes towards people who have already committed sexual offences.
4. By reducing stigmatisation, it may be possible to encourage those (typically men) with paedophilic sexual interests to access help and support through secondary prevention initiatives to refrain from sexually abusive behaviour, should they feel that they require it.

The enactment of these recommendations requires vast amount of bravery on the parts of public intellectuals, researchers, and advocates in this area of work, such is the extent to which stigmatisation of sexual offenders and paedophiles is entrenched in contemporary society. However, the pay-offs for this bravery are just as great. By addressing the stigmatisation of the paedophilic sexual orientation, and by encouraging the use of effective sexual abuse prevention services, it is possible to achieve some of the key aims of organisations in this sector: keeping society safe, and the realisation of the mantra of 'no more victims'.

References

Ahlers, C. J., Schaefer, G. A., Mundt, I. A., Roll, S., Englert, H., Willich, S. N., Beier, K. M. (2011). How unusual are the contents of paraphilias? Paraphilia-associated sexual arousal patterns in a community-based sample of men. *Journal of Sexual Medicine, 8*, 1362–1370. https://doi.org/10.1111/j.1743-6109.2009.01597.x.

Allardyce, S. (2018, April). *Current directions in the prevention of child sexual abuse: The work of Stop it Now! UK*. Paper presented at the Safer Living Foundation 'Prevention in the UK' conference, Nottingham Trent University, Nottingham, UK.

Amelung, T., Kuhle, L. F., Konrad, A., Pauls, A., & Beier, K. M. (2012). Androgen deprivation therapy of self-identifying, help-seeking pedophiles in the Dunkelfeld. *International Journal of Law and Psychiatry, 35*, 176–184. https://doi.org/10.1016/j.ijlp.2012.02.005.

Bastian, B., Denson, T. F., & Haslam, N. (2013). The roles of dehumanization and moral outrage in retributive justice. *PlosONE, 8*, e61842. https://doi.org/10.1371/journal.pone.0061842.

Beech, A. R., & Hamilton-Giachritsis, C. E. (2005). Relationship between therapeutic climate and treatment outcome in group-based sexual offender treatment programmes. *Sexual Abuse, 17*, 127–140. https://doi.org/10.1007/s11194-005-4600-3.

Beier, K. M., Ahlers, C. J., Döcker, D., Neutze, J., Mundt, I. A., Hupp, E., & Schäfer, G. A. (2009). Can pedophiles be reached for primary prevention of child sexual abuse? First results of the Berlin Project Prevention Dunkelfeld (PPD). *The Journal of Forensic Psychiatry & Psychology, 20*, 851–867. https://doi.org/10.1080/14789940903174188.

Beier, K. M., Grundmann, D., Kuhle, L. F., Scherner, G., Konrad, A., & Amelung, T. (2015). The German Dunkelfeld project: A pilot study to prevent child sexual abuse and the use of child abusive images. *Journal of Sexual Medicine, 12*, 529–542. https://doi.org/10.1111/jsm.12785.

Beier, K. M., Özdemir, U. C., Schlinzig, E., Groll, A., & Hellenschmidt, T. (2016). "Just dreaming of them": The Berlin project for primary prevention of child sexual abuse by Juveniles (PPJ). *Child Abuse & Neglect, 52*, 1–10. https://doi.org/10.1016/j.chiabu.2015.12.009.

Bergen, E., Antfolk, J., Jern, P., Alanko, K., & Santtila, P. (2013). Adults' sexual interest in children: A quasi-experimental study. *International Journal of Cyber Criminology, 7*, 94–111.

Bernard, F. (1985). *Paedophilia: A factual report* [English edition]. Rotterdam, The Netherlands: Enclave Press.

Blagden, N., Winder, B., & Hames, C. (2016). "They treat us like human beings" – Experiencing a therapeutic sex offenders prison impact on prisoners and staff and implications for treatment. *International Journal of Offender Therapy and Comparative Criminology, 60*, 371–396. https://doi.org/10.1177/0306624X14553227.

Cantor, J. M. (2014). "Gold-star" pedophiles in general sex therapy practice. In Y. M. Binik & K. S. Hall (Eds.), *Principles and practice of sex therapy* (5th ed., pp. 219–234). New York: Guilford Publications.

Cantor, J. M., & McPhail, I. V. (2016). Non-offending pedophiles. *Current Sexual Health Reports, 8*, 121–128. https://doi.org/10.1007/s11930-016-0076-z.

Collin, L., Reisner, S. L., Tangpricha, V., & Goodman, M. (2016). Prevalence of transgender depends on the "case" definition: A systematic review. *Journal of Sexual Medicine, 13*, 613–626. https://doi.org/10.1016/j.jsxm.2016.02.001.

Dombert, B., Schmidt, A. F., Banse, R., Briken, P., Hoyer, J., Neutze, J., & Osterheider, M. (2016). How common is men's self-reported sexual interest in prepubescent children? *The Journal of Sex Research, 53*, 214–223. https://doi.org/10.1080/00224499.2015.1020108.

Duwe, G. (2018). Can circles of support and accountability (CoSA) significantly reduce sexual recidivism? Results from a randomized controlled trial in Minnesota. *Journal of Experimental Criminology.* Advance online publication. https://doi.org/10.1007/s11292-018-9325-7.

Dweck, C. S., Chiu, C., & Hong, Y.-Y. (1995). Implicit theories and their role in judgments and reactions: A world from two perspectives. *Psychological Inquiry, 6*, 267–285. https://doi.org/10.1207/s15327965pli0604_1.

Farmer, M., McAlinden, A.-M., & Maruna, S. (2015). Understanding desistance from sexual offending: A thematic review of research findings. *Probation Journal, 62*, 320–335. https://doi.org/10.1177/0264550515600545.

Feelgood, S., & Hoyer, J. (2008). Child molester or paedophile? Sociolegal versus psychopathological classification of sexual offenders against children. *Journal of Sexual Aggression, 14*, 33–43. https://doi.org/10.1080/13552600802133860.

Flentje, A., Heck, N. C., & Cochran, B. N. (2014). Experiences of ex-ex-gay individuals in sexual reorientation therapy: Reasons for seeking treatment, perceived helpfulness and harmfulness of treatment, and post-treatment identification. *Journal of Homosexuality, 61*, 1242–1268. https://doi.org/10.1080/00918369.2014.926763.

Freund, K., & Kuban, M. (1993). Toward a testable developmental model of pedophilia: The development of erotic age preference. *Child Abuse and Neglect, 17*, 315–324. https://doi.org/10.1016/0145-2134(93)90051-6.

Gillespie, S. M., Mitchell, I. J., Fisher, D., & Beech, A. R. (2012). Treating disturbed emotional regulation in sexual offenders: The potential applications of mindful self-regulation and controlled breathing techniques. *Aggression and Violent Behavior, 17*, 333–343. https://doi.org/10.1016/j.avb.2012.03.005.

Göbbels, S., Ward, T., & Willis, G. W. (2012). An integrative theory of desistance from sex offending. *Aggression and Violent Behavior, 17*, 453–462. https://doi.org/10.1016/j.avb.2012.06.003.

Grundmann, D., Krupp, K., Scherner, G., Amelung, T., & Beier, K. M. (2016). Stability of self-reported arousal to sexual fantasies involving children in a clinical sample of pedophiles and hebephiles. *Archives of Sexual Behavior, 45*, 1153–1162. https://doi.org/10.1007/s10508-016-0729-z.

Harper, C. A., Bartels, R. M., & Hogue, T. E. (2016). Reducing stigma and punitive attitudes toward pedophiles through narrative humanization. *Sexual Abuse.* Advance online publication. https://doi.org/10.1177/1079063216681561.

Harper, C. A., & Harris, A. J. (2017). Applying moral foundations theory to understanding public views of sexual offending. *Journal of Sexual Aggression, 23*, 111–123. https://doi.org/10.1080/13552600.2016.1217086.

Harper, C. A., & Hogue, T. E. (2014). A prototype-willingness model of sexual crime discourse in England and Wales. *The Howard Journal of Criminal Justice, 53*, 511–524. https://doi.org/10.1111/hojo.12095.

Harper, C. A., & Hogue, T. E. (2017). Press coverage as a heuristic guide for social decision-making about sexual offenders. *Psychology, Crime & Law, 23*, 118–134. https://doi.org/10.1080/1068316X.2016.1227816.

Harper, C. A., Hogue, T. E., & Bartels, R. M. (2017). Attitudes towards sexual offenders: What do we know, and why are they important. *Aggression and Violent Behavior, 34*, 201–213. https://doi.org/10.1016/j.avb.2017.01.011.

Harris, A. J., & Socia, K. M. (2016). What's in a name? Evaluating the effects of the "sex offender" label on public beliefs and opinions. *Sexual Abuse, 28*, 660–678. https://doi.org/10.1177/1079063214564391.

Helmus, L., Ó Ciardha, C., & Seto, M. C. (2015). The Screening Scale for Pedophilic Interests (SSPI): Construct, predictive, and incremental validity. *Law and Human Behavior, 39*, 35–43. https://doi.org/10.1037/lhb0000099.

Herdt, G., & McClintock, M. (2000). The magical age of 10. *Archives of Sexual Behavior, 29*, 587–606. https://doi.org/10.1023/A:1002006521067.

Hocken, K., & Taylor, J. (2018, April). *Compassion-focused therapy: A promising treatment approach to prevent first time sexual offending*. Paper presented at the Safer Living Foundation 'Prevention in the UK' conference. Nottingham Trent University, Nottingham, UK.

Hogue, T. E. (2015, June). *Attitudes to sex offenders*. Paper presented at the British Psychological Society's Division of forensic psychology annual conference. Manchester Metropolitan University, Manchester, UK.

Höing, M., Petrina, R., Duke, L., Völlm, B., & Vogelvang, B. (2016). Community support for sex offender rehabilitation in Europe. *European Journal of Criminology, 13*, 491–516.

Houtepan, J. A. B. M., Sijtsema, J. J., & Bogaerts, S. (2016). Being sexually attracted to minors: Sexual development, coping with forbidden feelings, and relieving sexual arousal in self-identified pedophiles. *Journal of Sex and Marital Therapy, 42*, 48–69. https://doi.org/10.1080/0092623X.2015.1061077.

Jahnke, S. (2018). Emotions and cognitions associated with stigma of non-offending pedophilia: A vignette experiment. *Archives of Sexual Behavior, 47*, 363–373. https://doi.org/10.1007/s10508-017-1073-7.

Jahnke, S. & Hoyer, J. (2013). Stigmatization of people with pedophilia: A blind spot in stigma research. *International Journal of Sexual Health, 25*, 169–184. https://doi.org/10.1080/19317611.2013.795921.

Jahnke, S., Imhoff, R., & Hoyer, J. (2015). Stigmatization of people with pedophilia: Two comparative surveys. *Archives of Sexual Behavior, 44*, 21–34. https://doi.org/10.1007/s10508-0140312-4.

Jahnke, S., Schmidt, A. F., Geradt, M., & Hoyer, J. (2015). Stigma-related stress and its correlates among men with pedophilic sexual interests. *Archives of Sexual Behavior, 44*, 2173–2187. https://doi.org/10.1007/s10508-015-0503-7.

Kaplan, M. (2015). Taking pedophilia seriously. *Washington and Lee Law Review, 72*, 75–170.

King, L. L., & Roberts, J. J. (2017). The complexity of public attitudes toward sex crimes. *Victims & Offenders, 12*, 71–89. https://doi.org/10.1080/15564886.2015.1005266.

Marshall, W. L., Barbaree, H. E., & Eccles, A. (1991). Early onset and deviant sexuality in child molesters. *Journal of Interpersonal Violence, 6*, 323–336. https://doi.org/10.1177/088626091006003005.

McCartan, K. (2010). Media constructions and reactions to, paedophilia in modern society. In K. Harrison (Ed.), *Managing high-risk sex offenders in the community: Risk management, treatment and social responsibilities* (pp. 248–268). Abingdon, UK: Willan Publishing.

Nunes, K. L., Petterson, C., Hermann, C. A., Looman, J., & Spape, J. (2016). Does change on the MOLEST and RAPE scales predict sexual recidivism? *Sexual Abuse, 28*, 427–447. https://doi.org/10.1177/1079063214540725.

Office for National Statistics. (2017). *Sexual identity, UK: 2016*. London: Author.

Richards, K., & McCartan, K. (2018). Public views about reintegrating child sex offenders via Circles of Support and Accountability (COSA): A qualitative analysis. *Deviant Behavior, 38*, 400–416. https://doi.org/10.1080/01639625.2017.1304800.

Schmidt, A. F., Mokros, A., & Banse, R. (2013). Is pedophilic sexual preference continuous? A taxometric analysis based on direct and indirect measures. *Psychological Assessment, 25*, 1146–1153. https://doi.org/10.1037/A0033326.

Seto, M. C. (2009). Pedophilia. *Annual Review of Clinical Psychology, 5*, 391–407. https://doi.org/10.1146/annurev.clinpsy.032408.153618.

Seto, M. C. (2012). Is pedophilia a sexual orientation? *Archives of Sexual Behavior, 41*, 231–236. https://doi.org/10.1007/s10508-011-9882-6.

Seto, M. C., Lalumière, M. L., & Blanchard, R. (2000). The discriminative validity of a phallometric test for pedophilic interests among adolescent sex offenders against children. *Psychological Assessment, 12*, 319–327. https://doi.org/10.1037/1040-3590.12.3.319.

Wilson, R., Picheca, J., & Prinzo, M. (2007). Evaluating the effectiveness of professionally-facilitated volunteerism in the community-based management of high-risk sexual offenders: Part one: Effects on participants and stakeholders. *The Howard Journal of Criminal Justice, 46*, 289–302. https://doi.org/10.1111/j.1468-2311.2007.00475.x.

Wilson, R. J., Cortoni, F., & McWhinnie, A. J. (2009). Circles of support & accountability: A Canadian national replication of outcome findings. *Sexual Abuse, 21*, 412–430. https://doi.org/10.1177/1079063209347724.

8

Future Directions: Moving Forward with Sexual Crime Prevention

Rebecca Lievesley, Helen Elliott, and Kerensa Hocken

Introduction

As has been discussed in considerable detail within this book, it is well recognised that there are a number of individuals in the community who have concerns about their sexual interests, for example, a sexual attraction towards children, who are (a) not offending, and (b) actively working to manage their sexual attraction and/or reduce their risk of offending. Whilst a number of intervention initiatives and support groups exist

R. Lievesley (✉)
Nottingham Trent University, Nottingham, UK

Safer Living Foundation, Nottingham, UK
e-mail: Rebecca.Lievesley@ntu.ac.uk

H. Elliott
Bishop Grosseteste University, Lincoln, UK
e-mail: Helen.Elliott@bishopg.ac.uk

K. Hocken
HMP Whatton, HMPPS, Nottingham, UK
e-mail: Kerensa.Hocken@hmps.gsi.gov.uk

© The Author(s) 2018
R. Lievesley et al. (eds.), *Sexual Crime and Prevention*, Sexual Crime,
https://doi.org/10.1007/978-3-319-98243-4_8

specifically to work with this population (for examples, see Chaps. 2, 3, 4, and 5 of this book), this is a considerably new arena, and this chapter aims to explore some of the issues faced in providing support to this group. This will include an overview of some of the recognised barriers to accessing support for this population, before moving on to consider some of the future directions for prevention efforts and the factors that need to be considered in light of the many complexities and sensitivities of working with this group.

Barriers to Accessing Prevention Work

Research has demonstrated that individuals who have been convicted of sexual crime would have accessed support or intervention services, had they existed, prior to their offending (Elliott et al., 2016; Lievesley, Elliott, Barnes, & Rodgers, 2018; Piché, Mathesius, Lussier, & Schweighofer, 2016). In addition, many non-offending individuals also report a desire to seek support for their sexual interests (B4U-ACT, 2011; Lievesley, Elliott, Mclocklin, Norman, & Harper, 2018). However, despite this apparent want or need for treatment, help-seeking, particularly among those with a sexual attraction to children, is much lower than in other populations (Cantor & McPhail, 2016). This is often attributed to the multiplicity of barriers and challenges that exist for these individuals, which prevent them from disclosing their attraction and seeking or accessing support.

A primary barrier is the underdeveloped and often complete lack of services available that provide appropriate support and treatment for non-offending populations (Cantor & McPhail, 2016). For example, research has indicated that convicted individuals had a desire and need for preventative support prior to committing any offence, but no such support existed (Lievesley et al., 2018; Piché et al., 2016). More recently, the field has developed, with the emergence of online support networks (e.g. Virtuous Pedophiles and B4U-ACT) and programmes such as those ran by the Lucy Faithful Foundation and Mersey Forensic Psychology Services (outlined within Chaps. 2, 3, 4, and 5 of this book). However, despite this, the availability of such services is still limited, or not publicised, meaning that those in need do not know where to go or are not aware that any such services exist.

Where potential support services do exist, there still remains a number of barriers which can prevent an individual engaging with them. Help-seeking is often viewed as unsafe by potential service users, and a fear of persecution, stigma or rejection can hinder the likelihood of engagement with services (Cacciatori, 2017; Jahnke, Imhoff, & Hoyer, 2015; Jahnke, Schmidt, Geradt, & Hoyer, 2015; Levenson, Willis, & Vicencio, 2017). Unfortunately, these fears are not unfounded, with research indicating the negative experiences of those who have tried to seek help, including rejection and minimisation of the issue (Lievesley, Elliott, Stevenson, Halliday, & Black, 2018). In addition, research indicates that only 4.7% of psychotherapists would be willing to provide support for individuals with a sexual attraction to children (Stiels-Glenn, 2010). This rejection or lack of help and support can leave individuals feeling like help is futile, resulting in them giving up or simply adding to the stigmatisation already present which discourages individuals from seeking help (Imhoff, 2015).

Furthermore, a lack of trust and fear of detection whilst searching for or accessing services has been identified as a barrier, preventing individuals coming forward until their risk is much greater, and in the worst case, not until they have committed an offence (Goodier & Lievesley, 2018). Similar to the points raised above, this fear is not unfounded, depending on the reporting laws and obligations of professionals to report concerns about child safety and offending behaviour. Whilst the need for professionals to report an admitted offence may be quite clear in most countries, the need to report concerns of potential risks to child safety can be subjective to each professional or organisation. This can elicit further fears in seeking help, particularly for those individuals who have children, or work with children, preventing them from accessing support for their mental health concerns surrounding their attraction, even if they feel they pose no risk of offending. In such cases, the risk of being 'outed' and losing loved ones or careers outweighs the need to seek support, meaning that instead people continue to suffer in silence. As such, some individuals discuss a desire to access anonymous treatment to reduce the risk of mandatory reporting. While this might be possible, it limits any support or treatment to phone conversations, closing off the opportunity for more beneficial interventions that can be experienced through, for example, group or one-to-one work (Goodier & Lievesley, 2018). The potential impact of mandatory reporting is outlined below by one of the two founders of Virtuous Pedophiles, an organisation established to support people in managing their sexual attraction and in leading offence-free lives.

> **An Inside Perspective: Issues of Mandatory Reporting**
>
> Well over 2000 pedophiles have written to us at Virtuous Pedophiles in the past six years. Most are deeply distressed, many are worried about child pornography viewing, and a few worry about making sure they never offend hands-on. We would like to be able to suggest they see a therapist; psychotherapists are trained to empathize with a patient, to be on their side, and to help them process shameful feelings in confidence. Except this isn't true after the word 'pedophilia' is spoken, despite the fact that a great many pedophiles (half or more) will never offend against a child, and that we have a condition that was not chosen and cannot be changed. We are not so different from people suffering from any other unfortunate conditions and deserve the same compassion and respect. This in part relates to the issue of mandatory reporting.
>
> Very few of the people who write to us have committed an offense in the past, and so mandated reporting laws that require reporting of committed abuse would not keep them from seeing a therapist. But most mandated reporting laws require a therapist to make a report if they believe that a child might be at risk of abuse in the future—and that makes all the difference. It is entirely the therapist's call—once a pedophile admits his feelings and talks about them, it is entirely out of his (or her) hands. Many therapists believe that all pedophiles will offend sooner or later, so little more than the word 'pedophile' could trigger a report. Of course a report is not a conviction—a team will investigate, interview people close to the pedophile, and might decide that no action is warranted. But the investigation itself can be a devastating punishment; they stand to lose friends, family, jobs, housing, and social support networks.
>
> This situation leads us at Virtuous Pedophiles to caution our members not to see a therapist without careful thought and research. Ironically, the pedophiles who are most in need of help are in the greatest danger. If a pedophile works or lives with children, or actually feels strong temptation to offend, we cannot in good conscience urge them to see a therapist. The law of unintended consequences applies with full force—when pedophiles understand the law, which was enacted to protect children, they stay away from therapists and children are at greater risk.
>
> Mandated reporting laws that apply to teachers, law enforcement, and other professionals about admitted or ongoing offenses do not pose this

problem. But when psychotherapists are obliged to file a report if they think future abuse is likely, pedophiles will no longer seek help.

Today, for those pedophiles who do want to seek therapy, we urge them to start by asking questions before they admit anything. They should ask the circumstances under which a therapist would break confidentiality. If child abuse is not mentioned, we ask them to bring it up. If the answers do not make the person feel safe, they should leave. We also encourage them to leave if discussing the topic makes the therapist notably uncomfortable. But my fear is that a distressed person who has made the considerable effort to see a therapist might find it hard to walk away if the answers are not what they want to hear—being an empowered consumer is hard work.

Our number one priority at Virtuous Pedophiles is the safety of children. The number two priority is the well-being of pedophiles. Civil liberties dictate that a just society never punishes someone for a crime they might commit. Mandated reporting laws as currently written do not grant pedophiles that basic protection.

Ethan Edwards, Virtuous Pedophiles

Health Led Service Provision

Barriers to accessing services for individuals concerned about their sexual interest exist in part because of societal conflation of a sexual interest in children with sexual offending. This has created a political and social climate in which non-offending paedophiles are vilified and construed as offenders or potential offenders (see Chap. 7 for more discussion of this). The result is a failure to recognise the mental health needs of this client group and instead frame their needs criminally, meaning societal response is motivated by a crime prevention, not a health-based agenda. The fallout of this is a system in which mental health professionals are not equipped to respond to the problem, putting those who need help at a significant health disadvantage. It is therefore imperative that the needs of this client group are recognised as a mental health problem and services are provided through a health-based not forensic-based care system. Paedophilia is listed in the Diagnostic and Statistical Manual 5 (DSM 5; APA, 2013), and the services offered to those with paedophilia should have parity with those for other mental health conditions. A key feature of health led provision should involve specialist training for mental health professionals, so they are able to respond compassionately and meaningfully to each individual.

Learning Lessons from Interventions for Convicted Populations

Many of the prevention treatment interventions in existence are based on models designed for people who have been convicted of sexual offences (PCSOs), for example, the Prevention Project Dunkelfeld (PPD; Beier et al., 2015—outlined in Chap. 2 of this book). The reasoning for this choice appears pragmatic, based in part on the absence of any other available intervention and the assumption that the same underlying factors are likely relevant to non-offending and offending paedophiles (Langström et al., 2013). In the case of PPD, their service is open to those who have committed offences but remain undetected, and are therefore ostensibly the same population as those convicted of sexual offences.

The application of treatment interventions for PCSOs to a non-offending population, whilst pragmatic, could be misguided. The effectiveness of interventions for PCSOs in reducing recidivism (official reconviction) shows at best only small, inconsistent benefits for recidivism (Schmucker & Lösel, 2017). If the impetus is to reduce first-time sexual offending, then turning to interventions that have not shown significant capability to reduce reoffending seems unwise. In a comprehensive examination of the explanations for the poor outcomes of interventions for PCSOs, Hoberman (2016) proposes several plausible and resonant arguments, which if go unheeded by those developing prevention interventions, may cause these interventions to fall foul of the same mistakes. Hoberman's key points and the lessons for prevention interventions are reviewed here.

Poor Quality Evaluation

The evaluation designs of interventions for PCSOs have long been criticised (e.g. Rice & Harris, 2003); they are characterised by weak methodologies that very often do not use an adequate control group, rarely use random assignment, are retrospective, and provide little information about intervention integrity. This radically limits the causal inferences that can be made about the effect of the experimental treatment, due to the presence of confounding variables that are present in observational, non-random assignment designs. The lack of random assignment means that evaluations of interventions for PCSOs have never attained high-quality status and the need for random assignment in order to realistically progress the field is outlined convincingly by Walton (2018).

Intervention for PCSOs is one of the rare fields in psychotherapy that has failed to implement as standard, random assignment methodology. Prominent objections cite the harm and moral outrage that would occur if someone was denied treatment and subsequently went on to offend, as well as the infringements on the human rights of the convicted individual if they are unable to gain sentence progression due to a lack of access to interventions (see Hollin, 2008; Marshall & Marshall, 2007). Those who support the use of random assignment methodology (Duggan & Dennis, 2014; Walton, 2018) argue that until an intervention has been proven to reduce recidivism, there is not good reason to suppose that it would indeed prevent someone from reoffending, thus making the likelihood of reoffending no different to those who do not receive the intervention. In the arena of first-time sexual offence prevention, the human rights objection is somewhat redundant, since participants would not be under the auspices of the criminal justice system, and to all intents and purposes are regular members of the community. Adopting a design that randomly allocates individuals into different experimental conditions, including the primary treatment being tested and alternatives such as self-help, or support groups, would ensure those in need are receiving some support, and avoid the possibility of pushing them closer to an offence due to feelings of rejection that a 'no intervention' design might render (Marshall & Marshall, 2007). It is therefore recommended that all emerging prevention interventions should embed within them a robust evaluation design that uses at the least a strong matching methodology and ideally a randomised control trial (RCT).

Appropriate Aims and Outcomes

Although it appears unequivocal, the aims of an intervention to prevent sexual offending need to be carefully defined. The core agenda for the provision of these services is implied in the term 'prevention'; however, this narrative may in itself lead to flawed intervention designs, focused entirely on a prevention agenda, which by definition is 'other' rather than 'client' facing. The consequences of an 'other' orientation to intervention are evident within those designed for PCSOs, where the prevailing agenda has been about reducing further victimisation. This saw interventions for PCSOs become adrift from their general psychotherapy counter parts, relying on confrontational, confessional approaches, placing emphasis on understanding victims' experiences and actively discouraging the exploration of one's own trauma experiences (Walton & Hocken, in press). Where an intervention agenda is driven by an 'other' orientation, this inevitably leads to a misplaced focus within the intervention design, delivery, and outcome testing. It is only in the last 20 years, led by the emergence of the Good Lives Model (GLM; Ward, 2002), that the orientation has shifted towards a strength-based, client-centred approach. However, corresponding outcome measures have not gained a foothold in the empirical literature. For example, the gold standard outcome for interventions for PCSOs remains as recidivism. This blunt measure discounts any client centred benefits such as mental well-being.

It is imperative then that the aims for interventions to prevent first-time sexual offending are client focused. This is especially true against the backdrop of emerging research that highlights some self-identified non-offending paedophiles strongly believe they would never commit a sexual offence and have instead sought help to assist them in living successfully with a stigmatised sexual interest that blocks their attempts to achieve sexual connection and emotional intimacy with another human being (Levenson & Grady, 2017). Consequently, services must be designed around the needs of those asking for help and primary outcome measures should reflect the intervention aims.

A Theoretical Basis

The development of interventions for PCSOs was formed out of a need to 'do something' about the social problem of sexual offending when relatively little was understood about the psychological facets of the crime. This led to interventions based on one or two prominent theories, and PCSOs were treated as a homogenous group (e.g. the behavioural conditioning approaches). These became accepted wisdom and consequently slowed progress in developing and testing other theories. The lack of established knowledge about 'need' is particularly relevant to first-time sexual offence prevention: '*There are no prospective studies of initiating etiological factors…consequently, little, if nothing, is known about risk factors for initiating sexual offending*' (Hoberman, 2016, p. 678).

As with recidivism, first-time sexual offending is likely to have diverse entry pathways, which rely on a constellation of contextual and internal variables, thus indicating that successful intervention approaches should adopt a therapeutic approach which recognises this heterogeneity. Advances in clinical science have seen a move towards new therapeutic approaches that acknowledge this need. For example, 'third wave' or 'process based' CBT (Hayes & Hofmann, 2017) focuses on an individual's relationship to their thoughts and feelings rather than the content of thoughts and feelings. This alleviates the requirement for thoughts to be restructured, or for feelings to be managed, and instead teaches individuals to accept their internal experiences and to metaphorically 'stand back' from them so that they can be free to take valued action to lead a rich, full, and meaningful life. Process-based CBT is heralding a move away from specific protocols for syndromes in favour of methods that are based on change processes themselves. These approaches place greater emphasis on human thriving, the aim being to build health, rather than simply reduce disorder. It is exactly these types of therapeutic paradigms that hold promise for prevention interventions, because they do not promote a change agenda but an acceptance agenda. As Hoberman (2016) concludes, a possible failure of interventions for PCSOs is that they attempt to change psychological factors that are not amendable to long-term change such as sexual interests; therefore, testing interventions which use acceptance-based methods seems plausible.

In order to prevent the 'accepted wisdom' trap, diverse intervention approaches need to be designed and appropriately tested, these should be used to feed back into the empirical literature on the initiation of sexual offending.

Treatment Methods and Components

Most interventions for PCSOs use 'second wave' Cognitive Behavioural Therapy (CBT) as their therapeutic method (Schmucker & Lösel, 2017), largely operationalised in standard manualised protocols. The assumption that CBT is helpful for PCSOs remains largely unchallenged; however, as Hoberman (2016) summarises, the specific components of CBT for PCSOs have not been explored, so it is unclear if CBT as a whole is helpful, or specific elements of it are most effective. It is likely that whilst helpful for some clients, it will not be helpful for all. For example, a meta-analysis by Beutler, Harwood, Michelson, Song, and Holman (2011) reports that clients who are prone to interpreting external direction as threatening did not do well in CBT. This type of threat-based interpretation of other's behaviour can be an indicator of shame in the client (Taylor, 2017) and shame is a common experience for PCSOs (Proeve & Howells, 2006). This is something also indicated for non-offending paedophiles (Cantor & McPhail, 2016), suggesting therapy methods that work with shame- and threat-based defensive responses might be a helpful avenue to test. Therefore, emerging interventions for the prevention of first-time sexual offending should go beyond second wave CBT towards a diverse range of treatment methods and select those that best meet the needs of the clients.

Mandated or Coerced Interventions

A key feature of many interventions for PCSOs is that they are mandated or at least contingent on consequences such as sentence progression and conditions. Consequently, it becomes almost impossible to empirically control for the effect this has on intervention evaluation since genuine motivation for therapy cannot be ascertained. Certainly, the research data suggests that where interventions are voluntary, they perform better than those that are mandated or coerced (Parhar, Wormith, Derkzen, & Beauregard, 2008). If prevention interventions are to have the best chance at success, they will need to be entirely voluntary. Ideally, they should be delivered by therapists not connected to criminal justice, in order to avoid the correctional agenda taking precedent over the therapeutic one (Gannon & Ward, 2014).

What Are We Treating?

Many of the prevention projects in existence around the world today (see Chap. 2 of this book for a review of the projects) market themselves as working exclusively with people who identity as minor attracted. This focus on preventing child sexual abuse is reflected in the general prevention narrative within the literature and conveys a message that prevention projects are not aiming to offer services to individuals who report concerning sexual thoughts and feelings that are not aimed at minors. However, sexual offences against adults are as much a social problem as those against children, for example, the 2017 Crime Survey for England and Wales found that 20,974 adults aged 16–59 reported being the victim of a sexual offence in a 12-month period (2016–2017). If prevention projects hope to meaningfully reduce sexual crime, it is imperative that prevention efforts ensure services are accessible to all clients who may potentially commit any type of sexual offence.

In summary, there are several important lessons to be learnt from the history of treatment interventions for PCSOs, in the design, delivery, and evaluation of prevention interventions. Broadly, these centre on the need to be evidence-led and responsive to the needs of the client population, not led by the needs of others. There are several recent advances in non-treatment interventions for PCSOs which, with adaptions, might have some utility for meeting the needs of non-offending populations. One of these is Circles of Support and Accountability (CoSA), which will now be explored.

Adapting Interventions for Prevention: Adopting a CoSA Model as a Secondary Prevention Approach

A tertiary sexual crime prevention approach which is growing in popularity worldwide is CoSA. There is increasing evidence to support its effectiveness, not only in reducing risk of reoffending in groups of convicted individuals but also in improving well-being and social and emotional loneliness (Wilson, Picheca, & Prinzo, 2005, 2007). What has not had much if any academic consideration is the idea of CoSA as a support initiative for individuals in the community who have concerns about their sexual interests, and possibly about their risk of offending, but who have not offended. Essentially, the use of CoSA is a secondary rather than tertiary prevention approach.

> **What Is Circles of Support and Accountability?**
>
> Circles of Support and Accountability (CoSA) is an initiative originally created to support those who have been convicted of a crime, helping them to reintegrate into society and lead successful, offence-free lives. The initiative works through a volunteer-led service, whereby members of the community (the volunteers) provide both emotional and practical support to the individual who has previously been convicted of a sexual offence, known as the Core Member.
>
> Originating in Canada, CoSA was set up following the release of a repeat offender called Charlie Taylor. Charlie had been convicted of child sexual offences and was a lifelong recidivist who had been institutionalised most of his life. He was at high risk of recidivism, having never been able to remain offence-free in the community. The local community responded to his release, and came together to support and protect him. Through this support, Charlie was able to remain offence-free until his death in 2011 (Wilson, Cortoni, & McWhinnie, 2009). The initiative has grown significantly since this first case, and has spread to the United Kingdom, United States, France, and Spain to name a few.

CoSA for Non-offending Groups: A Cautious but Hopeful Prospect

CoSA is a restorative community approach, which aims to provide support to an ostracised group who are often in desperate need of support to resettle into society. This focus on supportive community integration appears relevant when considering the literature which indicates that loneliness, stigma, isolation, and poor self-esteem are significant struggles for non-offending groups, which can in turn reduce mental well-being (Cash, 2016; Jahnke, Schmidt, et al., 2015; Mclocklin, Norman, Lievesley, & Elliott, 2018). The misconception that all child molesters are paedophiles and the media reinforcement of this does not help with these issues and instead contributes to a punitive, prejudiced societal attitude (Imhoff, 2015; Jahnke, Imhoff, & Hoyer, 2015; McCartan, 2010). Non-offending individuals who are attracted to children have significantly worse mental well-being than the population at large, with anxiety, depression, and suicidal thoughts not being uncommon (Cash, 2016; Mclocklin et al., 2018). Thus, an initiative which acts to support individuals with these issues appears appropriate; however, there are a number of potential barriers that must be considered before adopting this approach.

Accountability: Helpful or Counter-Productive?

Research has suggested that the 'accountability' element of CoSA holds limitations, and may not contribute to the success of the initiative to the same (if at all) extent that the supportive, relational aspects of CoSA do. The accountability element of CoSA has been cited as a reason for Core Member dropout, and those CoSA that are most successful are those which place more emphasis on support (Fox, 2015). It may therefore be that the accountability element of CoSA is much more for the benefit of the community and authorities than it is for the Core Member themselves.

Issues related to accountability are anticipated to be heightened when considering applying this to a group who have not committed an offence.

How will they feel about having to be 'accountable' for their behaviour, when until this point they have been managing this on their own? Reporting on so-called risky behaviours to a group of strangers may understandably produce concern. This raises questions over how the risk management element of CoSA would apply to a group who may not actually identify as risky, but may need the social support elements that CoSA can provide. This is a particular issue in the United Kingdom where due to the close alignment of CoSA and the Criminal Justice System, a clear balance between support and accountability has been deemed necessary. Alternatively, models, for example, in Canada have a much heavier focus on support as the most crucial element of a CoSA (McCartan, 2016).

It is therefore necessary to approach such an intervention with great caution and sensitivity, when considering applying it to non-offending groups. It is recommended that a much heavier focus on support is adopted, and consideration of whether the accountability element is needed at all may be necessary. This will largely depend on the presenting issues of a 'Core Member'. Do they, for example, consider themselves at imminent risk of offending and therefore require not just emotional and practical support, but an element of help managing risk? Or are their issues embedded within more general mental well-being, in which case more support and less focus on risk is required. Even with the former, the literature is beginning to shed light on the fact that accountability is still not the main contributing factor in reducing risk with groups of convicted individuals. Perhaps it is time to start considering that accountability relates much more to society's need, rather than the individual it aims to help, and in fact, applying stringent risk management to this population could simply act to add additional shame and stigma to an already marginalised group.

Issues with Terminology

A final point for consideration is the issue of terminology. Being a 'Core Member' is currently a description assigned to an individual who has committed a sexual offence. This is likely to cause tension and concern for someone who does not want to be associated with this label (for more on the issue of the label 'sex offender', see Chap. 7). This relates to an overarching issue that CoSA is associated with being convicted of a sexual crime, causing confusion for the public and creating a barrier for potential service users.

Based on this and the discussions above, it is suggested that a volunteer-led approach which adopts aspects of CoSA could be invaluable for a non-offending population, however, with a strong focus on the supportive elements and a movement away from accountability and the terminology associated with CoSA.

Conclusions and Recommendations

This chapter has considered some of the main issues that are faced by individuals who are concerned about their sexual interest trying to access and receive support. An obvious but crucial barrier discussed is the lack of support services available. Although prevention initiatives are becoming increasingly available worldwide, it is still an underdeveloped area. Moreover, a lack of awareness of the current initiatives available also means that those in need are not accessing possible help. However, once this is overcome there are still a multitude of barriers that have been discussed within this chapter when considering providing a suitable and helpful service to this population. These include issues around fear of judgement and stigmatisation, and of persecution due to rules around mandatory reporting—an issue which has been highlighted here through the perspective of one of the founders of Virtuous Pedophiles.

The chapter has also considered the issue of applying interventions originally designed for convicted individuals, to non-offending groups. In an attempt to consider ways to overcome this potentially misguided approach, this chapter discusses some of the main issues and recommendations based on this. These include robust evaluation, and possibly an RCT design, clear and appropriate aims and outcomes which align with the needs of the service users, an emphasis on avoiding falling into the 'trap' of following potentially inappropriate theoretical models about sexual interests, and a need to focus on a range of sexual interests, not just those towards children.

Finally, and despite the cautions discussed around applying tertiary crime interventions to non-offending groups, the chapter considers the possibility of applying CoSA to this population, deemed appropriate due to being community-based and focusing on emotional and practical support, something which the literature indicates is lacking for this population. However, barriers which must be considered were discussed and included the issue of 'accountability' and of terminology including 'Core Members'. Recommendations regarding these issues are highlighted below.

In summary, this chapter has explored the challenges and issues faced when providing and accessing support for non-offending individuals who are concerned about their sexual interests. Future directions for prevention efforts have been considered, and in light of all of this, a list of the recommendations put forward are summarised below.

> **Summary of Recommendations**
>
> - Increase awareness of support services currently available
> - Increase the accessibility of current services and continue to develop new services from a health-based agenda
> - Increase specialist training for mental health professionals so they are able to respond compassionately and meaningfully to each individual in accordance with a health-based agenda
> - Ensure all staff associated with any project specific to this field are appropriately screened and suited to the role in relation to their understanding of this groups needs and are sensitive to issues around stigmatisation and shame
> - Increase awareness and education about the needs of this group and issues regarding stigmatisation, shame, and well-being and the importance of not contributing to these issues
> - Prevention interventions and support services should be clear and transparent about limits to confidentiality and mandatory reporting obligations, and acknowledge the impact of these
> - Prevention interventions should embed robust evaluations, using at minimum a strong matching methodology and ideally a randomised control trial
> - Prevention service aims and outcomes must be designed around the needs of those asking for help (and clearly included in the evaluation), with caution being made when adopting theoretical models attempting to explain the initiation of sexual offending

- Prevention interventions should go beyond second wave CBT, and consider a more diverse range of treatment methods and select those that best meet the needs of the clients including working with shame and threat-based defences
- Any intervention aimed at supporting non-offending groups should be entirely voluntary, and ideally delivered by therapists not connected to the criminal justice system
- Prevention interventions should consider offering services to all clients who may potentially commit any type of sexual offence, not just those towards children
- Consideration of a volunteer-led community approach similar to that of a CoSA model, but with a focus on support and integration rather than accountability, and in particular considering the needs of this group in relation to stigmatisation and emotional well-being

References

American Psychiatric Association. (2013). *Diagnostic and statistical manual of mental disorders* (5th ed.). Washington, DC: American Psychiatric Association.

B4U-ACT. (2011). *Mental health care and professional literature survey results.* Retrieved from http://www.b4uact.org/research/survey-results/spring-2011-survey/

Beier, K. M., Grundmann, D., Kuhle, L. F., Scherner, G., Konrad, A., & Amelung, T. (2015). The German Dunkelfeld project: A pilot study to prevent child sexual abuse and the use of child abusive images. *Journal of Sexual Medicine, 12*(2), 529–542.

Beutler, L. E., Harwood, T. M., Michelson, A., Song, X., & Holman, J. (2011). Reactance/resistance level. In J. C. Norcross (Ed.), *Psychotherapy relationships that work: Evidence-based responsiveness* (2nd ed.). New York: Oxford University Press.

Cacciatori, H. (2017). *The lived experiences of men attracted to minors and their therapy-seeking behaviors.* Unpublished master's thesis, Walden University, Minneapolis, MN.

Cantor, J., & McPhail, I. (2016). Non-offending pedophiles. *Current Sexual Health Reports.* Online first. https://doi.org/10.1007/s11930-016-0076-z.

Cash, B. (2016). *Self-identifications, sexual development, and wellbeing in minor-attracted people: An exploratory study.* Unpublished master's thesis, Cornell University, Ithaca, NY.

Crime Survey for England and Wales. (2017). *Sexual offences in England and Wales: Year ending March 2017.* Office for National Statistics. Accessed 29 June 2018.

Duggan, C., & Dennis, J. (2014). The place of evidence in the treatment of sex offenders, *Criminal Behaviour and Mental Health, 24*, 153–162. https://doi.org/10.1002/cbm.1904.

Elliott, H., Lievesley, R., Blagden, N., & Winder, B., Briscoe, H., & Faulkner, J. (2016, September). *Resist not desist: A retrospective exploration of viable prevention strategies helping individuals to avoid committing their first sexual offence against a child*. Presented at the International Association for the Treatment of Sexual Offenders (IATSO), Copenhagen, Denmark.

Fox, K. J. (2015). Theorizing community integration as desistance-promotion. *Criminal Justice and Behavior, 42*(1), 82–94.

Gannon, T., & Ward, T. (2014). Where has all the psychology gone? A critical review of evidence-based psychological practice in correctional settings. *Aggression and Violent Behavior, 19*, 435–446. https://doi.org/10.1016/j.avb.2014.06.006.

Goodier, S., & Lievesley, R. (2018). Understanding the needs of individuals at risk of perpetrating child sexual abuse: A practitioner perspective. *Journal of Forensic Psychology Research and Practice, 18*(1), 77–98.

Hayes, S. C., & Hofmann, S. G. (2017). The third wave of cognitive behavioral therapy and the rise of process-based care. *World Psychiatry, 16*(3), 245–246.

Hoberman, H. M. (2016). Forensic psychotherapy for sexual offenders: Likely factors contributing to its apparent ineffectiveness. In A. Phenix & H. Hoberman (Eds.), *Sexual offending*. New York: Springer.

Hollin, C. (2008). Evaluating offending behaviour programmes: Does only randomization glister? *Criminology & Criminal Justice, 8*(1), 89–106.

Imhoff, R. (2015). Punitive attitudes against pedophiles or persons with sexual interest in children: Does the label matter? *Archives of Sexual Behavior, 44*(1), 35–44. https://doi.org/10.1007/s10508-014-0439-3.

Jahnke, S., Imhoff, R., & Hoyer, J. (2015). Stigmatization of people with pedophilia: Two comparative surveys. *Archives of Sexual Behavior, 44*(1), 21–34. https://doi.org/10.1007/s10508-014-0312-4.

Jahnke, S., Schmidt, A. F., Geradt, M., & Hoyer, J. (2015). Stigma-related stress and its correlates among men with pedophilic sexual interests. *Archives of Sexual Behavior, 44*(8), 2173–2187. https://doi.org/10.1007/s10508-015-0503-7.

Langström, N., Enebrink, P., Laurén, E. M., Lindblom, J., Werkö, S., & Hanson, R. K. (2013). Preventing sexual abusers of children from reoffending: Systematic review of medical and psychological interventions. *British Medical Journal, 347*, f4630.

Levenson, J. S., & Grady, M. (2017, October 18). *Obstacles to help-seeking for minor-attracted persons*. Presented at the Association for Treatment of Sexual Abusers (ATSA) conference, Lawrence, KS.

Levenson, J. S., Willis, G. M., & Vicencio, C. P. (2017). Obstacles to help-seeking for sexual offenders: Implications for prevention of sexual abuse. *Journal of Child Sexual Abuse, 26*(2), 99–120.

Lievesley, R., Elliott, H., Barnes, O., & Rodgers, C. (2018). *Resist not desist: An exploration of help seeking behaviour in individuals with sexual convictions*. Manuscript in preparation.

Lievesley, R., Elliott, H., Mclocklin, G., Norman, C., & Harper, C. A. (2018). *Understanding help seeking in non offending individuals who self-identify as attracted to children*. Manuscript in preparation.

Lievesley, R., Elliott, H., Stevenson, J., Halliday, M., & Black, P. (2018). *Living with a sexual attraction to children*. Manuscript in preparation.

Marshall, W. L., & Marshall, L. E. (2007). The utility of the random controlled trial for evaluating sexual offender treatment: The gold standard or an appropriate strategy? *Sexual Abuse: A Journal of Research and Treatment, 19*, 175–191.

McCartan, K. (2010). Media constructions of, and reactions to, paedophilia in society. In K. Harrison (Ed.), *Managing high risk sex offenders in the community: Risk management, treatment and social responsibility* (pp. 248–268). Cullompton, UK: Willan Publishing.

McCartan, K. F. (2016). *Circles of support and accountability: Cabinet Office – Social Action Fund evaluation*. Available at: http://eprints.uwe.ac.uk/28279/7/CoSA%20Social%20Action%20Fund%20-%20Full%20version%20final.pdf. Accessed 3 July 2018.

Mclocklin, G., Norman, C., Lievesley, R., & Elliott, H. (2018). *The mental health and wellbeing of self-identified paedophiles*. Manuscript in preparation.

Parhar, K. K., Wormith, S. T., Derkzen, D. M., & Beauregard, A. M. (2008). Offender coercion in treatment: A meta-analysis of effectiveness. *Criminal Justice and Behavior, 35*, 1109–1135.

Piché, L., Mathesius, J., Lussier, P., & Schweighofer, A. (2016). Preventative services for sexual offenders. *Sexual Abuse: A Journal of Research and Treatment*. https://doi.org/10.1177/1079063216630749.

Proeve, M., & Howells, K. (2006). Shame and guilt in child molesters. In W. Marshall, Y. Fernandez, L. Marshall, & G. Serran (Eds.), *Sexual offender treatment* (pp. 125–139). Hoboken, NJ: Wiley.

Rice, M. E., & Harris, G. T. (2003). The size and sign of treatment effects in therapy for sex offenders. In R. A. Prentky, E. Janus, & M. C. Seto (Eds.), *Understanding and managing sexually coercive behavior* (pp. 428–440). New York: New York Academy of Sciences.

Schmucker, M., & Lösel, F. (2017). Sexual offender treatment for reducing recidivism among convicted sex offenders: A systematic review and meta-analysis. *Campbell Systematic Reviews, 8*, 76.

Stiels-Glenn, M. (2010). The availability of outpatient psychotherapy for paedophiles in Germany. *Recht & Psychiatrie, 28*, 74–80.

Taylor, J. (2017). Compassion focused working in secure forensic care. *Journal of Criminological Research, Policy and Practice, 3*(4), 287–293.

Walton, J. S. (2018). Random assignment in sexual offending programme evaluation: The missing method. *Journal of Forensic Practice.* https://doi.org/10.1108/JFP-08-2017-0032.

Walton, J. S., & Hocken, K. (in press). *Compassion and acceptance as interventions for paraphilic disorders and sexual offending behaviour.* Available from: https://www.researchgate.net/profile/Kerensa_Hocken2.

Ward, T. (2002). Good lives and the rehabilitation of sexual offenders: Promises and problems. *Aggression and Violent Behavior, 7*, 513–528.

Wilson, R. J., Cortoni, F., & McWhinnie, A. W. (2009). Circles of support & accountability: A Canadian national replication of outcome findings. *Sexual Abuse: A Journal of Research and Treatment, 21*, 412–430.

Wilson, R. J., Picheca, J. E., & Prinzo, M. (2005). *Circles of support and accountability: An evaluation of the pilot project in south-central Ontario.* Ottawa, Canada: Correctional Service of Canada.

Wilson, R. J., Picheca, J. E., & Prinzo, M. (2007). Evaluating the effectiveness of professionally-facilitated volunteerism in the community-based management of high-risk sexual offenders: Part Two-A Comparison of the recidivism rates. *The Howard Journal of Criminal Justice, 46*(4), 327–337. https://doi.org/10.1111/j.1468-2311.2007.00480.x.

Glossary

Abreaction The release of emotion that is linked to previous, unresolved traumatic events, typically as a result of some form of intervention. In some circumstances, this can be experienced as reliving the emotions of the experience.

Adaptive Information Processing (AIP) A process that underlies Eye Movement and Desensitization and Reprocessing (EMDR). Considered to be a system that allows new information to become integrated with other experiences in memory, allowing people to adapt to new situations. When it does not function correctly, it is considered to be the basis of pathology.

All Party Parliamentary Group for Children A group comprising of members of parliament and members of the House of Lords who aim to improve policy affecting children and young people. The group is also informed by the views and experiences of children and young people invited to speak in Parliament alongside ministers, parliamentarians and the children's voluntary sector.

Chair Work A method used in Schema Therapy to communicate with the different parts (or modes) of the individual, separating the various modes onto different chairs.

Child Sexual Abuse The act of committing a sexual offence against a child.

Child Sexual Exploitation A form of child sexual abuse. It occurs where an individual or group takes advantage of an imbalance of power to coerce, manipulate or deceive a child or young person under the age of 18 into sexual activity (a) in exchange for something the victim needs or wants, and/or (b) for the financial advantage or increased status of the perpetrator or facilitator. The victim may have been sexually exploited even if the sexual activity appears consensual. Child sexual exploitation does not always involve physical contact; it can also occur through the use of technology (Department for Education, 2017).

Children Act of 1989 The act apportions duties to local authorities, courts, parents and other agencies in the United Kingdom, to ensure children are safeguarded. It centres on the idea that children are best cared for within their own families. However, it also makes specifications for instances when parents and families fail to co-operate with statutory bodies.

Cognitive Behavioural Therapy (CBT) A psychosocial intervention that aims to help people alter thoughts, beliefs and attitudes that are causing emotional distress and problematic behaviours.

Coolidge Effect Suggests that when sexual interest begins to diminish, it can be increased by the novelty of a new sexual partner.

Dehumanisation The process by which an individual is linguistically and/or metaphorically stripped of their personhood in order to justify and encourage stigmatisation.

Disclosure Scheme A procedure designed for the public to ask the Police for information on child protection issues regarding an individual they are concerned about who has contact with children.

Ephebophilia A sexual interest towards adolescents (post-pubescent).

Eye Movement and Desensitization and Reprocessing (EMDR) A psychological therapy used to change the impact of past traumatic events on current functioning.

Habituation The diminishing of an innate response to a frequently repeated stimulus.

Healthy Adult Mode Used in Schema Therapy to describe the mode of an individual that can experience and express emotions and get needs met in a non-problematic way.

Hebephilia A sexual interest towards pubescent children, typically those entering puberty.

High Deviance Refers to offenders with high levels of offence-supportive beliefs and socioaffective difficulties as identified by psychometric tests.

Imagery Re-scripting An experiential method used in Schema Therapy to change the maladaptive feelings, beliefs and expectations that have originated in childhood needs being left unmet.

Implicit Theories Core beliefs about the nature of a particular trait or behaviour, typically broken down as 'entity' (behaviour cannot change) or 'incremental' (behaviour can change) in nature.

Modes Emotional and cognitive states of an individual that dominate functioning. Maladaptive modes of functioning are an attempt to deal with the activation of schemas and have developed from childhood coping response to the unmet childhood needs.

Multi Agency Public Protection Arrangements (MAPPA) The process through which the Police, Probation and Prison Services work together with other agencies to manage the risks posed by violent and sexual offenders living in the community in order to protect the public.

Narrative Humanisation The process of overcoming dehumanised stereotypes by humanising a target group through the presentation of personal life stories.

Offending Trajectory The idea that for some people and/or some kinds of offences there is an identifiable pattern of escalation, stability or de-escalation.

Paedophilia A sexual interest towards prepubescent children.

Pesso Boyden System Psychomotor Therapy A therapeutic intervention utilised specifically for education around emotions and emotional regulation. It employs many techniques founded in neuroscience surrounding mirror neurons, empathy and the impact of language on theory of mind.

Primary Prevention Broad-scale societal initiatives designed to reduce the incidence of a particular problem behaviour (e.g., sexual abuse).

Reprocessing To change the perspective, understanding and meaning of stored memories, ideally to be more adaptive.

Schema Therapy A psychological therapy used to alter chronic and deeply entrenched maladaptive feelings, cognitions and behaviours. Designed for personality disorders and other complex or difficult to change problems.

Schemas A combination of feelings, physical sensations, memories, beliefs, expectations and attitudes that have developed from unmet childhood emotional needs and that continue to influence adult functioning.

Secondary Prevention Targeted initiatives designed to attract engagement from those who are at risk of engaging in sexual abuse before a crime is committed.

Sex Industry Describes any area of sexual behaviour that has been commodified, such as prostitution, pornography, live video-sex and stripping.

Sex Offender Treatment Programmes (SOTP) Typically refers to manualised prison programmes aimed at reducing the recidivism of sex offenders but is an umbrella term for a wide range of approaches seeing this outcome.

Stigmatisation The process of negative evaluation and discrimination based on some arbitrary personal characteristic.

Tertiary Prevention Focused initiatives that work with those who have engaged in a particular behaviour (e.g., sexual abuse) to prevent the repetition of this behaviour.

Victim Empathy The capacity to recognise the possible thoughts, feelings and experiences of one's victims or potential victims.

Index

A

Acceptance, 88, 94–96, 98–100, 115, 144, 189
Acceptance and Commitment Therapy (ACT), 87, 96, 98–102, 145
Accountability, 193–197
Adaptive information processing (AIP), 119
Anonymous, 31, 34, 48, 52, 61, 73, 75, 145, 158, 167, 183
Anti-contact, 28, 29, 42, 43, 46, 48, 49, 52
Assessment, 31, 33, 37–40, 58–60, 70, 91, 104, 122, 124, 126
Attitudes, x, 15, 16, 64, 86–88, 92, 117, 150–153, 157–174, 193

B

Barriers, vi, 36, 85, 114, 161–167, 173, 182–186, 193, 195, 196
Bystander interventions, 15

C

CBT, *see* Cognitive behavioural therapy
Challenges, vi, 8, 19, 34, 37, 122, 128, 138, 147, 182, 196
Child protection, v, 38, 46, 57–79
Child sexual abuse (CSA), v, 8–11, 13, 17, 18, 30–35, 38–41, 43–46, 50, 53, 57–79, 91, 118, 120, 125, 161–165, 167, 168, 170–173, 191

Index

Circles of Support and Accountability (CoSA), 83, 84, 152, 160, 161, 173, 192–197
Clinical, 9, 19, 28–32, 47, 60, 85, 94, 103, 163, 189
Cognitive behavioural therapy (CBT), 87, 94–97, 112, 113, 120, 189, 190, 197
Community based crime prevention, 12
Compassion, 97, 104, 184
Compassion-Focussed Therapy (CFT), 96–98, 102, 142, 144–145
Confidential/confidentiality, 30, 31, 34–36, 51, 61, 64, 65, 88, 185, 196
Control group, 31, 120, 171, 187
Core member, 84, 160, 192–194, 196
CoSA, *see* Circles of Support and Accountability
Counselling, 37, 122
Crime, v, vi, ix, x, 1–19, 121, 146, 159, 171–173, 181–197
Crisis, 8–10
CROGA, 75, 76

D

Dehumanisation, 92, 165, 172, 173
Deterrence, 71, 73–75, 78, 79
  campaign, 73–76
Developmental crime prevention, 12
Disclosure, 11, 88, 102

E

Education, 15, 35, 38, 43, 44, 49, 70, 71, 73, 78, 79, 117, 134, 136, 142, 152, 153, 196
Evaluation, ix, 34, 39, 59, 64–66, 68, 69, 77, 104, 112, 160, 186–187, 191, 195, 196
Eye movement desensitisation/desensitization and reprocessing (EMDR), 105, 119, 120, 127

F

Fear, 4, 32, 36, 52, 85, 114, 122, 134, 135, 139–142, 145, 148, 164–166, 170, 183, 185, 195
Female sexual offenders, 60
Formulation, 60, 88, 94, 104, 113, 114, 116, 118, 119, 124, 126, 128
Functional Analytic Psychotherapy (FAP), 96, 101–102

G

Gender, 2, 13, 18, 48, 60, 102
Get Help, 64, 73–77, 141
Get Support, 64, 76–77
Good Lives Model (GLM), 75, 147–148, 188

H

Hate crime, 168
Helpline, 35, 61–65, 67, 69–71, 73–75, 79

Help-seeking, 31, 84, 88, 171, 182, 183
Human rights, 173, 187

Impact of sexual abuse, 2, 9, 11
Implicit theories, 159
Indecent images of children, 63, 66, 158
Inform, 4, 18, 19, 47, 52, 67, 69–70, 113
Inform Plus, 67–70
Inform Young People (YP), 67, 70–71
Initiatives, vi, x, 8, 11, 27–53, 58, 61–79, 157, 158, 160, 161, 164–167, 170, 174, 181, 192, 193, 195
Internet-based, 90, 150
Intervention, 4, 10–12, 14–17, 30–33, 39–42, 44, 45, 51, 52, 58–60, 66, 69–71, 84–88, 90, 93, 95, 96, 99, 102–105, 111–115, 117, 118, 120, 121, 123, 125, 126, 128, 151, 166, 171, 181, 182, 184, 186–197

Judgement, 172, 195

The Lucy Faithfull Foundation, vi, 17, 57–79

Mandatory reporting, 34, 41, 183–185, 195, 196
MAP, *see* Minor Attracted Person
Media, vi, x, 2, 3, 7, 30, 33, 45, 49, 74, 75, 77, 92, 113, 148, 153, 161, 163–165, 169, 172, 173, 193
  reporting, 7
Minor Attracted Person (MAP), 29, 33, 36, 37, 42–43, 45–52, 85–89, 92, 93
Minor attraction, 35, 47, 51, 89
Modes, 115–118

Narrative humanisation, 173
Newspaper coverage of paedophilia, 164
Non-offending, 28–29, 40, 42, 43, 46, 48–50, 52, 58, 69, 79, 84–94, 160, 163–166, 171, 173, 182, 185, 186, 188, 191, 193–197

Online forums, 36, 46–52, 79
Organisational settings, 6, 15

Paedophilia/paedophile/paedophilic, vi, 28–31, 40, 46–52, 85, 89, 91, 92, 98, 99, 158, 159, 161–174, 185, 186, 188, 190, 193

Parenting programmes, 16, 171
Parents Protect, 65–66
Peer support, 36–37, 49–50, 145–146
Police, 3, 7, 10–12, 16, 65–67, 70, 71, 78–79, 83, 84, 120–122, 124, 137
Pornography, 29, 37, 41, 63, 64, 66, 68, 70, 95, 103, 104, 117, 142, 184
Practices, vi, 4, 16, 17, 19, 27–53, 98, 105, 112, 128, 163, 166
Prevention, v, vi, x, 1–19, 27–53, 58, 61–78, 84–95, 111–128, 133–154, 157–174, 181–197
    framework, 14, 61, 77, 78
    project, vi, 29, 30, 38, 41–43, 45, 49, 53, 67, 133, 191
    schemes, 158
Prevention Project Dunkelfeld (PPD), 30–34, 42, 46, 87, 186
Primary prevention, 11, 32, 39, 50, 61, 62, 157, 158, 161, 162, 168–173
Psycho-education, 42, 67, 68
Psychologists, ix, 40, 103, 124

R

Randomised control trial (RCT), 95, 187, 195, 196
Recommendations, 14, 173, 174, 195–197
Rejection, 6, 88, 92, 183, 187
Reprocessing, 116, 125, 126
Residential treatment, 58
Restorative, 193
Risk, 6, 9–12, 14–16, 18, 29, 35, 37–40, 42, 51, 52, 58, 60–62, 67, 70, 71, 85–89, 91, 92, 95, 103, 111–120, 122–128, 145, 150, 152, 157, 158, 160, 162, 166, 168, 172, 181, 183, 184, 189, 192, 194
    management, 59, 60, 113, 116–118, 125, 127, 194

S

Safeguarding, 6, 62, 121–125
Safer Living Foundation (SLF), vi, 43, 83–105, 133
Schemas, 101, 115–118
Schema Therapy, 115, 116, 118, 127
Schools-based programmes, 11, 13
Secondary prevention, 11, 12, 18, 19, 27, 61, 65, 74, 158, 161–167, 174, 192–195
Self-help, 75, 76, 187
Self-management, 33, 34
Self-seeking, 52, 53, 166
Service user, vi, ix, x, 76, 85, 94, 102, 112–114, 122–125, 133–154, 183, 195
Sexual
    abuse, 1–3, 5, 6, 9, 10, 12, 13, 27, 29, 34, 50–52, 58, 62, 86, 87, 113, 117, 120, 148, 157–174
    feelings, 33, 84, 101, 120
    harmful behaviour, vi, 84
    interest, v, 28, 31, 34, 37, 84–87, 89–91, 93–95, 99, 100, 102–105, 158, 159, 162–174, 181, 182, 185, 188, 190, 192, 195, 196
    offending, vi, 7, 17–19, 29, 34, 38–40, 53, 66, 83–91, 94, 95,

105, 113, 121, 142, 153, 159, 160, 165, 166, 172, 173, 185, 186, 188–190, 196
orientation, vi, 43, 89, 138, 151, 153, 163, 167–171, 173, 174
thoughts, vi, 10, 11, 41, 63, 64, 76, 84, 90, 91, 94, 98, 100, 101, 103, 105, 121, 133, 134, 137, 142, 143, 145–146, 148, 152, 154, 191

Shame, 4, 45, 89, 92–93, 95, 97, 100, 101, 104, 114, 116, 123, 125, 128, 140–141, 150, 154, 190, 194, 196, 197

Situational crime prevention, 12, 14, 15

Splash Pages, 72–74

Stigma, 36, 37, 43, 48, 49, 85, 89, 92–93, 99, 151, 163, 166, 172, 183, 193, 194

Stigmatisation, 93, 158, 160, 163–168, 173, 174, 183, 195–197

Stop it Now!, 10, 30, 34–35, 61–67, 73–75, 79, 158, 167

Support, v, 13, 27, 59, 83, 121, 133, 160, 182
 group, 30, 49, 52, 113, 166, 181, 187

T

Tertiary prevention, 11, 12, 27, 45, 61, 62, 72, 75, 158–161, 170, 173, 192

Theories of sex offending, 17–19

Therapy, 31, 84, 113, 144, 158, 185

Trauma, 86, 87, 104, 118–120, 125–127, 188

Treatment, v, 28, 58, 112, 133, 158, 182

Trust, 102, 111, 117, 122, 183

V

Virtuous pedophiles, 49–50, 182, 184, 185, 195

W

Well-being, 36, 43, 44, 47, 48, 68, 93, 105, 128, 133, 148, 167, 185, 188, 192–194

Wolvercote clinic, 58–59

Y

Young people (YP), v, 12, 16, 58, 59, 71, 84, 149, 153

Printed by Printforce, the Netherlands